Women*Prints*

A Detailed Plan of Action for the New Millenium

Ann Smith

Lucy Germany

Sister Heléna Marie

Nancy Grandfield

MOREHOUSE PUBLISHING

Morehouse Publishing
P.O. Box 1321
Harrisburg, PA 17105

A catalog record for this book is available from the Library of Congress.

Printed in the United States of America

Photos: Robin Dru Germany

Contents

Dedicated to the thousands
of women and men
who created the
United Nations Platform for Action

And

to the women whose stories have made
the *Platform* a living document

Preface

■ ■ ■ ■ ■ ■ ■ ■ ■ ■ ■ ■

*"Writing this book made me see wisdom in myself I didn't know I had.
It was a humbling and at the same time an affirming experience..."*
　　　　　　　　　　　　　　　　　　　　　　　　—Nancy

We are not writing another report on the Beijing conference. That
has been done and quite ably by many writers. Why this work is different is because it is a personal collective, it is our individual processes moving into the process of the group; as in the manner of several
small streams which meet at a river and become part of its complete
nature. We are not writing a series of personal journals; this also has
been done and by experts. We are collectors of stories that reflect the
condition of women all over today's world; beyond that we are carri-
ers of hope in our small water bottles as we strive up the steep and
often hazardous way of learning each other, careful always to preserve
one another's integrity. From the beginning at Beijing, we have taken
seriously the calls for action in the UN platform. These issues have
affected each of us differently and we have plunged deeply into those
differences, maintaining their validity while allowing them to be
accepted as part of our common experience.

We have written out of no great expertise, nor vested interest in
any particular issue. Our entry was rather more naive than Jesus's
entering the city on a donkey! We were deeply concerned that all
which had been entered into at Beijing with such high hopes, might
well die if no continuing attention was paid to it. The book is our
small way of providing some of that attention.

We met numerous times to talk about this book, whether we
could do it and what kind of book it might be. We met in New York,

in Connecticut, at Martin's Beach south of San Francisco. Our final meeting, just before saying—yes we can submit this to our publisher—took place at Martin's Beach in Nancy Grandfield's small jewel of a cottage perched above the Pacific looking down on slopes of wild blackberries and carpets of dusky orange nasturtiums. As we talked, the sound of the sea played percussion to our strings and woodwinds. In our conversations we spent time defining ourselves to one another, testing the waters to see how deeply we could trust. Surprising, perhaps, that four women of such widely varied backgrounds and experience, could do that so nimbly and by doing it achieve such heights of confidence in the rightness of our project. We gave thanks for the process many times. Occasionally we were so awed by the quality of our friendship that it was as if a bright light had entered our four pairs of eyes giving us the capability of seeing beyond the predictable and mechanical parts of us.

Ann follows a career that has to do with the furthering of women's identity, the erasure of gender discrimination through the opening of women's eyes to their potential. She does this through the generous facilities and resources of the Episcopal Church which she serves as director of the Office of Women in Mission and Ministry. Ann describes her coming to the writing project:

> "I had a dream to bring a spiritual presence to the Fourth World Conference on Women, a dream fueled by the potential for women's empowerment and what we could do to make a difference in a world that is crying out for healing.
>
> "Spirituality instills into the hearts of those ready to receive it, knowledge of something much greater than our present reality. It comes no matter where women are in the world, regardless of the conditions of that world. Once it has pierced our illusions, it lodges in our deepest selves and will not be subjugated by any of humanity's outrages—sexism, racism, classism or any other prejudice that defines us as anything less than whole. A woman's spiritual global movement is being born. Women are being interconnected around the world, empowered to embark on an unknown journey that will awaken us to the world's injustice and to our own complicity in it by helping maintain systems that limit human potential."

When Ann was first approached by Morehouse Publishing's Allen

Kelley about the possibility of writing a book on the Beijing Conference, she said it took her two seconds to say "yes," but with the proviso that she not do it alone. She knew it was not a task to be undertaken solitarily. It was obvious to her that it required shared perceptions, a variety of observations, the synergy of different but similarly motivated minds. Ann's "people" began to present themselves. Sr. Heléna Marie was an easy choice. She worked next door in the New York Office of Women in Mission and Ministry. She and Ann had worked closely on numerous projects and always with ease and an unqualified joy. Sr. Heléna Marie had been on the Peace Train (233 women and eight men rode the Peace Train, sponsored by the Women's International League for Peace and Freedom, from Helsinki to Beijing, over a period of three weeks, with stops in nine countries) and could bring to the book reflections from that long and fascinating journey. She was, furthermore, a published author, whose book had received enthusiastic reviews in numerous publications. Sr. Heléna Marie also had the singular perspective of having lived for 19 years as a member of the Community of the Holy Spirit, in the heart of New York City. An avowed environmentalist, she is constantly sensitive to that interest but also charges with enthusiasm into any issue of substance that affects the lives of people, particularly the marginalized and oppressed.

Ann defined Nancy as "the woman I do everything with. Well at least it seems that way."

Nancy, who studied advertising as an undergraduate student, went on to a long career as a copywriter and than a travel agent, had somewhere along the line become Ann's "Elder." Though she'd never been referred to as an "elder" before, she liked its reference to Native American women whom she had long admired and she realized it implied a respect for a lifetime of experience. Nancy is always in charge of the complicated arrangements for the annual Council of Women's Ministries conferences which are held in many kinds of facilities all over the western hemisphere.

"Nancy always gets us beautiful, comfortable places to meet," said Ann.

Lucy had been writing and assisting with the editing of the *Journal of Women's Ministries* published out of Ann's Office. Lucy's book, *Those Remarkable Village People*, describing incidents in the lives of the people of Malawi in Central Africa, was published by Friendship Press in 1995. Ann recalled going to Dallas for a meeting and asking Lucy to join her for talk about how best to report the

Beijing results. "We didn't know each other well before that time, but it was obvious that we shared something important—a vision of a world where women would bring their unique gifts to bear on the world's non-working structures and in so doing envision a new millennium to benefit all people."

They were gathered. Ann and Nancy, Sr. Heléna Marie and Lucy. In the center of their circle was the hearth fire. Their passion. Their energy. Their gifts. The fire went from coals to a leaping flame. *WomenPrints* is the product of the process.

A lot of women who went to Beijing wanted to keep it going. We didn't want women to say —"Yes, I've seen your slides, that's enough." This book is not for people who went to Beijing. It's to carry forward the work of all women. It's not just to chronicle the many disasters that militate against women. It's about hope. It's about how all sorts and conditions of women have helped themselves. It's about how a village can do what one woman is unable to do alone. It's about spirituality, the power of God and being co-creator with God in the universe.

As in every enterprise from surgery to writing a poem, there are side effects. In this case it was our growth, our changing perceptions about much that we had only dimly recognized in the past. We were suddenly opened up, acutely aware of issues when we read our magazines and newspapers. Nancy described the process: "I said... yes... that relates to Beijing. I remember the workshop where we all discussed it... the book, you might say, was always with us..." And Sr. Heléna Marie noted that from this time forward, places like Rwanda will be to her the image of people responding to their pain with courage. "I kept foremost in my mind the thought of how women will change the church," said Ann. "We need to be trouble makers in a troubled world. The church has been great about rallying its resources to help with disaster but it isn't sufficiently involved in the ordinary lives of people. If people come to it, they get what the church offers but the church doesn't often step out of its own rhythms to attend to the ills that exist in all our lives. There was nothing complacent about Jesus. He stirred things up. If you look for the twelve Beijing issues in the Gospel, you will find them... every one of them."

Sr. Heléna Marie likened the writing of a book with other women to the difference between playing a solo recital and playing in a string quartet. Sr. Heléna Marie, herself an accomplished pianist, said, "As a soloist, it's just you. In a quartet you have to listen to others, you are part of an ensemble. Writing this book together has required listening, interacting, compromising."

"As a poet who read aloud her new-born poem before 45 women at the Council of Women's Ministries meeting in Arkansas last year, I am aware of just how risky it is to let your lone voice be heard. Here, the risk is muted, but the voice is still clear and recognizable," said Lucy.

Individual words have different meanings now for these writers. For example—economics. It will never have the same abstract quality—never again will it be detached from human life—for Sr. Heléna Marie. For Lucy the word "environment" now takes her bodily into the rain forest, puts her at the edge of a foam-crusted lake, brings her into contact with rows of dead, silvery fish washed up on the shore, with newly cut trees. Those words that repeated themselves so many times during the Beijing experience and the writing afterwards, now represent sense experiences bringing to the receptors of mind and body, the elements of human suffering.

"We want to be sure to say," said Ann, "in response to anyone who hears about this book, that we are affirming people and relationships. We are not bashing men, we are not placing responsibility on any one group. We have all been implicit in the troubles of the world and we all have to change it. It's that women are late coming to their sense of power and strength and the world needs women so very much."

"We are writing about community—our community with women around the world," said Ann. "So many women I have talked to have said, 'Thank you for being my voice,'" said Nancy. "What we have said in this book was not said with our voices alone but those of the hundreds and hundreds of women who—in one way or another—have been with us."

This book takes us beyond Beijing. We stand on the sand where the footprints of women continue to be the indelible marks of hope for the world. The sea is in our ears. It is the everlasting voice of drowning women, of strong women who swim. We leave the sand and plunge into the ocean where fearsome creatures live of whom we are not afraid.

Prayer for the Millennium

Ann Smith

■ ■ ■ ■ ■ ■ ■ ■ ■ ■ ■ ■

Prayer opens our ears to the cries of a suffering world and the healing melodies of peace, empowering us to be instruments in bringing about God's justice and equality everywhere. I had a dream to help bring a spiritual presence to the United Nation's Fourth World Conference on Women. Spirituality instills, in the hearts of those ready to receive it, knowledge of something much greater than our present reality. It comes no matter where women are in the world, and no matter the conditions. Once it has pierced our illusions, it lodges in our hearts, minds, and souls and will not be subjugated by racism, sexism, classism, or any other prejudice that defines us or any woman, man, or child as anything less than whole. A spiritual movement is connecting people around the world on a journey that awakens us to injustice and oppression; and shows us our own complicity in maintaining systems that limit the human potential.

Spirituality empowers women to be on a journey of self-discovery not limited by gender biases but liberating us to become scientists, poets, politicians, visionaries, theologians, community organizers, stateswomen, writers, actors, prophets, diplomats, producers, teachers, sages, and healers. We are beginning to believe that we are created equal in the image of God. It is from this awakening that we are healed from sexism and racism.

Spirituality is the magical water that can revive a dehydrated world parched by greed and hatred. Spirituality was very present at the NGO Forum and the Fourth World Conference in Beijing. This event changed the lives of 60,000 women and men, and I know that my life and the lives of all people will never be the same.

*O God, Creator of the heavens and the earth, we pray for all who
gather in Beijing. Bless them. Help them and us to see one another
through eyes enlightened by understanding and compassion. Release
us from prejudice so we can receive the stories of our sisters with
respect and attention. Open our ears to the cries of a suffering world
and the healing melodies of peace. Empower us to be instruments in
bringing about Your justice and equality everywhere.*
—Noonday Prayer for Beijing

The dream for a noonday prayer written specifically for the Beijing
conference came to me in the middle of the night back in October
1994, in London. I was meeting with the leadership of the Worldwide
Mothers' Union, one of the largest women's organizations. We were
preparing to create an Anglican presence at the UN conference and
forum. In our Anglican tradition, noonday prayers are spoken around
the world. So why not create a Beijing prayer?

Everywhere I went and talked about this idea it grew in support
beyond the Anglican Church. It caught the imaginations of women
from all religions and became an interfaith project.

The prayer was written in my office by myself and three other
women who had brought ideas with them for an international, interfaith prayer: my colleague, Sr. Heléna Marie, Eileen King, the staff for
the World Day of Prayer Office, and Florence Kelley, from the Bahai
faith. Together we composed a draft that was sent to other women for
ideas.

The staff of Church Women United translated our English version into Chinese, Spanish, Arabic, and French, the five official UN
languages. They also created a logo and made it into a beautiful postcard. The prayer became a spiritual bond for women and men around
the world. Those who could not attend engaged in prayer vigils during the conference, and women who came brought the postcards with
them. This prayer reached every corner of the world when Hillary
Clinton, representing the United States government, finished her
speech to the UN forum by reading the Noonday Prayer for Beijing.

From Mexico City to Beyond Beijing

Ann Smith

I served as a grassroots volunteer in the preparation of the 1975 First World Conference on Women. Throughout the state of New York, community meetings were held at which women talked about issues that related to their community and concerns that we wanted taken to the state level. From the state of New York our concerns were incorporated into the U.S. document and taken to the first United Nations Conference on Women in Mexico City in 1975. Even though I was not actually going to go to Mexico, I felt involved every step of the way.

I first met Bella Abzug, one of the birthmothers of the 1960s women's movement, when she agreed to speak on a women's issues panel that I had organized for northern Westchester. On the panel with her was Jane Bryant Quinn, a well-known economist, and several other experts on women's issues. This was a first-ever women's issues event for this part of conservative Westchester County, known as the home of the "Stepford Wives."

On the evening of the panel, speakers and facilitators all met at Jane's house for dinner to discuss how they would interact. Bella, however, informed us by phone that she would meet us at the high school auditorium.

Fearful that only a few people would come to such an event, I thanked God when I saw that the parking lot was full. But there was no sign of Bella. When I phoned her husband, he said she had left two hours earlier, which was plenty of time for her to have been there for the start of the panel.

Bella was stuck on the West Side Highway because of a flash flood, and if it were not for her powerful, take charge manner, she would not have arrived until after the event was well over. But Bella, a powerful force in any setting, asked the police to direct her to an alternate route, through almost impenetrable traffic. Bella arrived just at the climatic point of the evening, when all had said their piece and questions were beginning. She flung open the doors to the auditorium, caught her breath and made her way to the stage. Bella filled the room with her voice and her spirit, captivating the audience with her message for women's equality and the importance of the First International Year for Women.

Bella attended the 1975 International Women's Year Tribune in Mexico City, serving as a congressional advisor to the U.S. delegation. This meeting was a first in several ways. It was the first UN meeting on women and the first parallel meeting to the official UN conference, a meeting of women and the non-governmental organizations (NGOs). Four thousand women attended.

At the "Feminist Majority, Expo 96" meeting, held in Washington, DC in January 1996, Bella, who now serves as co-chair to the Women's Educational and Development Organization (WEDO), spoke about her role in all four UN conferences on women:

> Although it was a woman's suggestion that brought about the first UN conference on women and then a decade for women, I always say that you gave us first a day, then a year, then they decided to give us a decade. Who knows? If we behave, they may let us into the whole thing. Well, women didn't behave and we got into the whole UN thing by using our joint force and our multicultural international organizational efforts to change the nature of power and to change the voice. So although women were not represented in the government delegations, they were represented in a caucus.
>
> Now this is crucial. If you sat in Mexico City, you were lucky to be among 4,000 people. It was an enormous event because we got to know each other, from every walk of life, from every background, every religion. We broke the boundaries. That was the beginning of the global feminist movement. It was the beginning of a global women's network.
>
> We had political problems, a lot of differences. Third World women had never met First World women. First World, Third World is what they called us, and we were fighting one another. I said I know about this Third World, this other world: we have a Third World in our own midst and therefore we have to connect it.

It was from this first international experience that I really began to grow in a different way.

In 1980 there were more than 10,000 women in the parallel forum, the Second Conference on Women, Mid-Decade on Women, in Copenhagen, Denmark. The Decade on Women provided a process for gathering information on the real situation of women in various societies, and this process led, among other things, to a strengthening of the women's movement in many countries and to the increase in research primarily by women within governmental bodies and universities.

Bella served as a CNN reporter to the forum and UN conference. "We still had many problems and our differences kept getting in the way."

In 1985, Bella attended as an NGO representative to the Third World Conference on Women, the End of the Decade, in Nairobi, Kenya. "Fourteen thousand women attended in Nairobi; Nairobi was the greatest excitement of that decade. That was when we began to come from our strength in our diversity, our multiculturalism in our approach. We found that North, South, East, and West had much in common because what we had together is that we were all discriminated against. Oh yes, in many different ways, but what we had in common bonds us and we can come to consensus quickly."

Women in Mission and Ministry sent a delegation of ten women to that NGO Forum. With the Anglican women of Kenya we also made up the first Anglican delegation to attend a UN meeting. Three weeks before the UN meeting the Anglican Church received their UN status as a non-governmental organization (NGO).

It was here that I first witnessed the global women's movement. I was truly amazed by how many African women came to the End of the Decade Conference, some walking for days, others coming in jam-packed buses on which they rode for a week. I had met many Anglican women from Kenya at a women's leadership training program that we had sponsored with the Anglican Church of Kenya three months before. Before parting, the Anglican NGO delegation discussed the formation of an official Anglican Women's Network, and we submitted our request to church officials.

We came home from the Third World Conference on Women in Kenya full of enthusiasm that I wanted very much to share with the people in the United States, but I soon found out that it was not going to be easy. People had either not heard about the conference or did not feel connected to it. We produced a book, *Out of Nairobi*, and a slide program. The Episcopal delegation offered to speak to groups and at events but received very few requests. The church and secular press gave the event minimal coverage and no where could be found any traces of the excitement felt by the 14,000 women who had been to the Kenya conference.

In 1987, the World Council of Churches declared 1988-1998 a decade for women: to be called Churches in Solidarity with Women. It was the answer to a painful and frustrating time for women who were associated with national and international church structures and who continued to experience gender discrimination. Most of us mourned the end of the UN Decade on Women which had passed with little note. We were frustrated to discover that The Forward Looking Strategies were virtually unheard of in most church circles.

At the 1988 Lambeth Conference, a gathering of Anglican bishops that takes place every ten years in Canterbury, England, women were the topic for two out of the three weeks of deliberations. Women's equality in the priesthood was a major concern, with most of that concern being negative as women were viewed as a threat rather than an asset. When I arrived home I asked the Presiding Bishop of the Episcopal Church to host a worldwide event that would be a positive statement by the church about women. The Rt. Rev. Edmond Browning said yes to this dream.

In March 1992, the Anglican Communion hosted 600 women, 40 men, 20 children, and two babies to a life-changing event—the Worldwide Anglican Encounter, in Salvador, Brazil. People came from 52 nations and 25 indigenous tribes. Women from Salvador increased attendance at the Encounter by 200 or more. Women from Rio Grande do Sul in south Brazil traveled more than 5,000 kilometers by bus to get to Salvador.

Three months before the event, the Planning Committee began to realize that we were in financial straits. Promised funds—in the form of diocesan contributions of $1,500 from each of 100 dioceses of the Episcopal Church—had not been forthcoming. We had given the dioceses three years to make this contribution; when it did not happen we felt as much discounted as disappointed. Pressure to cancel the meeting mounted. But it was hard to think of letting down the many women who had worked so hard and undergone such great personal sacrifices to make the Brazil meeting possible. We prayed for guidance and courage to continue.

The government of Salvador, Brazil, and the Roman Catholic Church assisted us greatly, eager for the event which they knew would benefit all who came. The Planning Committee, which represented the Anglican Church throughout the Americas, walked in faith and worked beyond exhaustion.

The women who came to Brazil from the North were struck by the devastating reality of poverty. Because the conference took place in a public conference center, rural and urban women from the South felt welcome and free to interact with women from around the world. This would not have happened if we had chosen a "First World" Brazilian hotel.

The conference center was obviously in need of repair. On the first day, when the air conditioning quit functioning we had our first real crisis—not enough drinking water for the crowds of people who were suddenly suffering from dehydration. The city responded quickly with a truckload of bottled cold water and we saw in that mini-crisis an opportunity for appreciating the things some of us take for granted—the things many people are forced to live without.

Women who visited the slum areas and talked with the street children were horrified. They grasped the connection between these poor and the constantly increasing number of poor in their own countries of Europe, the United States and Canada. Men, hearing stories of violence against women, were shocked. Bishop Frade from Honduras said, "It was like a great revelation to many of the male clergy present, including the bishops, to find out in such a powerful way the extent of violence perpetuated against women. The anguish and pain of our sisters was so great and so well described that we could not but suffer with them. We could not understand how we had allowed it for so long, how we could have permitted ourselves to be deaf and blind to it. The truth hurts when you are faced with it, but there was growth for us."

No longer was the cause being championed by a mere handful of women. Now hundreds went back to their homes and churches, clamoring to share stories.

Simultaneously with our planning of the Anglican Encounter, Bella Abzug was forming the Women's Environmental and Development Organization, a multinational, multicultural, institutional mechanism for women's equality:

WEDO "became" a major player as the women's caucus for the UN Environmental Conference in Rio, Brazil. We noticed that the draft document for the Environmental

Conference had only two references to women and this document was to determine the fate of the earth with only two
mentions of women and no involvement of women. WEDO
sponsored a women's international preconference to the UN
meeting, called Women for a Healthy Planet. At that meeting held in Miami, Florida which I attended, thousands of
women from around the world produced a consensus document called Women's Agenda 21 which was presented to the
UN Commissioner on the environment. It was a comprehensive document giving women's issues and women's sustainable development work full voice. We took our document to all UN planning meetings before and at the Rio conference. We were there with our document changing concepts and developing policies. We had the strength of an
international impact, and we have continued these caucuses
at all UN conferences.

   We begged in the decade, we are not begging now. We
demand a voice, the voice of spirit and of passion, of who we
are. We are now a partner. The *UN Platform for Action
Document* is a contract, a contract with the world's women. It
is politically binding because it represents a commitment
from every one of the 189 countries.

In preparation for the Fourth World Conference on Women, Christine
Eames, President of the Worldwide Mothers' Union, and I represented the Anglican Communion at the regional prepratory meeting for
North America and Europe held in Vienna in October 1994. It was the
first time we in North America had joined with Europe to represent a
region. I missed being with women in the South but gained much
understanding from the way women in a uniting Europe were facing
their issues. Christine, who is from Northern Ireland, focused on peace
issues and I focused on women of faith. We both asked: What do we
bring to UN meetings? What do we have to offer?

   In a workshop on women and faith, the issue of fundamentalism
became a subject for passionate discussion. In achieving consensus, we
said that fundamentalism of all religions is oppressive to women and
must be addressed by both the UN and women of the NGOs. We also
wanted spirituality to be shown as the real gift religion has to offer the
world, one that transforms women. In a small-group session I became
involved in both of these issues. A young French woman told how her
spirituality had sustained her during the dark time of her life when she

had lost her infant child. Having come to France from the Caribbean, she had never experienced racism before but here its impact, along with the tragedy of losing her child, would probably have destroyed her but for her spiritual strength. When she talked about her baby's death, two other women and I, who had also lost babies, talked with her and we wept together. In our small circle we had become united into a sisterhood that transcended region, race, and culture.

From this workshop we drafted two statements for the UN document: Spirituality is the gift for all creation that religion holds up and gives freely; it is the hope for the world. Fundamentalism, found in all religions, is oppressive to the human condition. A small committee set forth to include these statements in the UN document and with this intent, religion became a key player in the United Nations deliberations and at the NGO Forum.

What can we say that you have not already heard about the Fourth World Conference on women, except that it was the largest gathering of women in the world and that it has already profoundly changed the world? I was able to experience the global women's movement from its days of problems and struggles through its 20 years of adolescence to its maturity.

Betty Friedan, another birthmother of the U.S. women's movement, held a workshop in which secular and religious leaders spoke about spirituality and how the secular and sacred, the political, social and personal were interconnected. Thousands of workshops were given in which women shared information and gave of themselves. A critical mass of women leaders gathered in Beijing at the forum and the UN conference, making a profound difference in exposing the realities of the world and empowering women and men to bring about actions for change in their governments, communities, and homes.

The *Platform for Action* is organized into 12 issues that give us a blueprint ("Women*Print*") for the future. A "Beyond Beijing" movement is spreading. Books have been written about it; video and TV films have been made. All of these, plus the conversations that take place around those proverbial kitchen tables and in board rooms are continuing the impetus as women talk about the harsh realities of the issues that affect every person on this earth. Daily more and more people are expressing their commitment to carry out the actions that will make a difference.

The 12 issues give us a blueprint for the new millennium, a litany for justice and peace, a real chance to make the world a better place for all of God's creation.

Education

Lucy Germany

Close the gender gap in primary and secondary school education by the year 2005.

Eradicate illiteracy of women worldwide by the year 2000.

Improve women's access to and provide funding for vocational training, science, and technology.

Develop curricula, textbooks, and teaching aids free of gender stereotypes.

Platform for Action

As I began to write this section about education, I found myself pondering its boundaries. Where does education begin, and does it indeed have no ending? Many of us think of education as the key to what we like to call "success," achieving those things the ads convince us are necessary to human life. In many parts of the world that door opens to what we consider "basics": food on the table, clothes, medical care. But what education does for all of us is to give us a sense of identity and courage, the vision to see beyond the way things are. Because training is a facet of education, I have included in this chapter the story of Tee Garlington, her work of helping young women and men, and how she opened a door for "O" which led to her education and training and to her eventual independence. I have included a story on training in craft skills in Nepal, the forming of classes for and by women in England, stories that may seem only peripherally related to education as many of us know it. But if education is the apparatus that can help people rise above the defeating text of every-day life, to see further and further beyond boundaries, then all of these stories most definitely belong in this chapter. Though education defies specific definition, it can be most closely defined as a process for making life better than it is. What we are looking at is not one shape but many shapes.

Non-discriminatory education benefits both girls and boys and thus ultimately contributes to more equal relationships between women and men. Equality of access to and attainment of educational qualifications is necessary if women are to become agents of change. Literacy of women is an important key to improving health, nutrition and education in the family and to empowering women to participate in decision-making in society. Investing in formal and non-formal education and training for girls and women, with its exceptionally high social and economic return, has proved to be one of the best means of achieving sustainable development and economic growth that is both sustained and sustainable…

Thus reads the introduction to the education portion of the *Platform for Action* of the United Nations Fourth World Conference on Women.

It is obvious from both the language and the intent that education is considered to be the undergirding factor in all areas of development for women. The importance of education to improvement in status for women at all levels cannot be underestimated.

Education has been called "a chocolate bar wrapped in a cactus." It is difficult and painful to get into, but the rewards within are rich and infinite.

Education: why not?

It is difficult to think of reasons why anyone should not be educated. But in many parts of the world there are as many of these reasons as there are varieties of the human condition. A girl child in Nepal is needed at home to give care to her young siblings. An eleven-year-old girl in India is already married and faces a life of household chores. A teenage girl in the United States sees no life outside her neighborhood gang. Another cannot finish school because she is pregnant. A girl in Mexico must join her family in the fields if there is to be food on the table. In many countries no vision for an educated woman exists. "What happens after school?" "Will I be better off?" Life is a composite of harsh, persistent practicalities. They are the engines that drive life in much of the world. It is hard to think of working and sacrificing for an education in order one day to have a job at a fast-food restaurant. The opportunities for education for women must be accompanied by dreams and visions. These must become part of the driving engines.

The UN draft platform called attention to the prevalence of unequal access to and inadequate educational opportunities for women in every part of the world. Among the recommended changes are:

1. Equality of access. This brings to mind a variety of questions. What does such equality mean? What level of education does it imply for everyone? College? Technical training? Survival skills? Education must begin at the beginning with certain basics of information and method. Where do women stand in "X" country in terms of educational access? Is such education mandatory? Do women, i.e., girl children, attend, in any numbers, elementary, middle, and high schools and are they offered education and training at the same levels as boy children? Does their education fit them to function at improved levels in the world of today and tomorrow? Education must exceed training and skill development for today; it must take a giant step beyond present levels of occupation to those things that will be significant in the future. Education must be more than learning; it must enfold within its processes and rote methods a clear and certain vision for all people.

2. Basic literacy. Is basic literacy, the ability to read and understand language, an acute problem for persons of one gender, one age group, or all? Is literacy a matter of learning a local language, several languages, a local language and English (which has become in many countries, at least the second language taught in public schools)? Is literacy seen as a means to move beyond the association of sounds and things to concepts and lore? The demand for literacy must be met with the teaching of practical skills as well as the formation of a matrix for both creative and investigative learning. Literacy teaching must be both short- and long-term, with the goals of teaching culture and providing an asset for immediate employment.

3. Gender-sensitive curricula. Within "book learning" are all the subliminal messages: how people respond to one another, what they respect, how they show that respect, how they can live within differences, how they can recognize and understand the strengths of people of other genders, races, and cultures. Gender sensitivity is essential if humans are to move toward greater understanding of one another.

4. Mass media. How can its possibilities as an educational tool be fully realized? How might opposition be expressed, subterfuge detected? How can the public determine what the message is and distinguish it from the messenger? How can the impact of the message on gender equality be evaluated? These critical abilities are important for all people but particularly for women who are regularly exploited, ignored, or caricatured by the major media. Beyond all of these, it is also essential to know how to monitor, contribute to, and otherwise use the media to assure the promulgation of public truth.

Changes in education cannot be made without changes in governmental policies and development of implementation processes. Inherent requirements in such a change process include an understanding of public funding and private sector resources, awareness of how funds for education are used and to what sector or sectors of society they are targeted. Furthermore, understanding of progress calls for cognizance of the existing gap between education for men and women and the occurrence of any changes in it. We must constantly raise benchmark questions: Are pregnant girls and young mothers barred from schooling?… Do religious or cultural practices mitigate against educating women?… Is sexual and reproductive health education included in publicly funded training programs?… Does education emphasize the status, role and respective contributions of both men and women in the family and in society?… Is education seen as a lifelong process and are efforts being made to assure that this is a function of both the government and the private sector?

They started a magazine

"The women I met in Beijing are practical and pragmatic. They are setting up hot lines and family counseling centers, organizing women's studies programs and carefully analyzing (China's) economic reforms, family planning, rural women's status and the legal system. They have started a magazine, *Rural Women Knowing All*, geared to the literacy level of Chinese women in the countryside, with simple articles on hygiene, health, business and agriculture, how to get a divorce, build networks."

Cynthia McLean, Canada China Programme

Differentiated learning: keep the girls in the kitchen

"A recent review of gender and curriculum [in Namibia] highlighted the extent to which differentiated learning pervaded the curriculum and its built-in assumption that practical subjects for girls should relate to their future roles as mothers and homemakers, while boys need more specific and in-depth learning to prepare them for the more likely eventuality of entering formal employment. Linked to this is [the fact] that primary and secondary education serve to promote gender stereotyping in respect to future employment.

"Drop-out rates are strongly related to the demands placed on children to contribute to domestic and agricultural tasks in rural households. For girls, the major impediment appears to occur at secondary level, particularly for girls in female-headed households, when they must assume responsibility for a range of domestic duties including the care of younger children. It is also evident, as a consequence of a number of factors including the older age of girl students (due to starting late and repeating and lack of parental supervision), that a significant number of girls may also drop out of school due to pregnancy."

From Namibia's National Report to the Beijing Conference, prepared by the Department of Women Affairs

A woman's dream: Nepal

I am sitting on this bare ground
Peeling, chopping
I do not know that there are other arrangements
Though I dream
Last night I heard the thumping of wood
against wood and I felt my arms rise and fall

And I knew it was I, doing what I always do
It was no dream; I am pounding corn
Are my arms not fit for other things?
I dare not change the way I dress
Or where I go
Though I conjure myself
Away from this village with my children
Tucked at my side.
What I want for them hurts more
Than what I want for me.
My girl child must have a voice
Louder and clearer than mine
She must be able to move with certainty
Shoes on her feet, walking with dreams
at her side.
The present I have given her
Is not enough
Her arms are different
They will never pound corn or pound corn only
They will reach for the sky
Where freedom lives.

Today's Cinderellas

On the edge of puberty the girl child begins to replace childish dreams with the recognition of her future responsibilities. In industrialized countries she is still in school and dependent on her parents. But in many poor countries, even though schooling may be universal, girls aged ten or 12 are sent out to earn, not learn. They are placed as domestic servants cleaning, minding babies, running errands in return for a piece of floor to sleep on and leftovers to eat. These are the modern Cinderellas, only without a pumpkin coach and a glass slipper.

Those girls who are forced into the streets because of violent or abusive homes or sheer family poverty may trade in street sex as a matter of survival. Their work options are limited. There are hundreds of thousands of girl child prostitutes in Asia and Latin America.

"The women we had seen by the roadsides and in the streets were often bowed under heavy loads of up to 100 pounds, carried in six by four net string bags suspended from their foreheads and worn down their backs as far as their knees. I wondered about their lives. Mervyn stretched himself and cleared his throat, 'You know the answer: while they're women, they'll be slaves.'"

A glimpse of women in New Guinea from
Outback and Beyond by Cynthia Nolan

One way to keep girls from being pushed into early marriages or early work lives or onto the streets is to keep them in school. Some countries are taking this challenge seriously.

Separate washroom facilities in coeducational schools in Pakistan, for example, have encouraged many parents to keep their daughters in school.

The Bangladesh Rural Advancement Committee, a non-governmental organization, has set up over 8,000 simple village schools in which 70 percent of the pupils are girls. Ninety percent of them enter regular school when the time comes.

A story from an article in *World Woman* by Xiong Lei tells how one woman from rural Pakistan tackled the need for education. In a country where 75 percent of the women cannot read or write and only about five percent receive education beyond grade eight, it would have been easy to say, "That's how it's always been and that's how it will always be." But Zahida (Saddad Qazi) didn't see it that way. She helped launch an educational program 12 years ago called "Allama Iqbal Open University" in which those who could not go out for education had it brought in to them. The program allows women to study at home while continuing their work. The only requirement is that they go to a nearby study center twice a week for lessons and coaching via audio-cassettes. The school work is linked to their daily life and is conducted in their local languages. But the benefits do not stop with the women who enroll. They in turn sign up with a program to pass on their benefits to others in their villages. They also encourage their daughters to go to school and on to college. The subjects are health care, environmental protection, and other topics relating to the experience of the local women. The network of centers employs more than 100 people and thousands of volunteers.

It's the kind of job, says Zahida, that lets you see the results with your own eyes. Could this approach be usefully replicated? Yes, and all over the globe, wherever there is a need for education and a lack of educational facilities. This program can be likened to the bush schools in many parts of Africa where volunteers teach and the educationally needy are reached.

Hear Rigoberta Menchu of Guatemala on the subject:

One of the most important things I've learned is that one must remain humble before knowledge. I'm still a student, a student of time, of life, and I hope to keep on learning until my dying breath. People should constantly renew themselves, their ideas and their feelings. Every question teaches me something.

From an article, "We Have Come A Long Way," in the *UNESCO Courier,* March 1995

My mother used to tell me that if I swallowed a watermelon seed a watermelon plant would grow inside me and would take up all of my stomach space. Education is like that seed. When swallowed it becomes enormous.

Why is schooling for girl children important? What if Cinderella had never gotten to the ball? With education the girl child learns to think for herself and gains confidence in her own judgment and her ability to earn and manage money. As a woman she will understand the benefits of having fewer and healthier children and how to achieve both. She will be more inclined to pave the way for her children's education and will in that way make a contribution to a better, healthier society.

The good news worldwide is that girls' school enrollment is climbing. For girls, education is a giant step toward a better world for all women.

Education: training

These are two heads of the same animal. In Quebec, Canada, the government acted recently to reserve for women five places in every 15 in non-traditional trades training courses. Two of these will be for women without welfare benefits. The action is a result of a demand by the Women's March Against Poverty for access and support for job training. Additionally the Quebec government froze student fees and increased scholarship support for students in universities.

"There are many interventions that could help raise the status of women but Girls' Education remains the single most important intervention that can achieve all these…"

Bernadette Cole writing in *Forum '95*

Women who are making changes

Gennet Zewdie is president of Forum for African Women Educationalists and Minister of Education in Ethiopia. FAWE is established in 25 African countries where it has built a broad base of support for female education.

Alice Tiendrebeogo, former Minister of Education in Burkina Faso and founding member of FAWE, pushes for mass mobilization of people at grassroots.

Education at ground level

The eyes of Huang Qizao light up when she talks about her home province (in China) and the art of Sichuan cooking. Like most married women in the world she carries a double load, including her day work for the development of women and her housework with her family and two daughters.

While she was a girl, the Japanese still occupied the country. Huang fled with her family from province to province several times and many of her family members were killed.

When she graduated at 17 in 1951, the new China had come. The country badly needed teachers and the idealistic young girl decided to study physics and be a teacher. She studied and taught a literacy group for women at the same time. The women were especially enthusiastic about learning how to read and write. They practiced their writing on the soil and they carved the complicated Chinese characters into the wood of their agricultural tools. Each piece of furniture was carved with characters.

"We made the teaching close to their daily life and later (in her role as vice-president of the All-China Women's Federation) we used the same principle, a combination of learning and practical skills. The government granted one million Yuan to that campaign which went all over the country."

Birgit Wiig writing in *Forum '95*

Catalina's story: is it better to be illiterate?

Catalina is a Guatemalan Indian woman, the youngest in a family of six children. None of her siblings were educated beyond grade school. Her father, going counter to the prevailing male wisdom, urged Catalina to proceed with her studies, seeing it as a good business investment because she was bright and eager to learn. "He also did it as an expression of love," says Catalina. When she finished high school, her family made an extra effort to get the money to put her through a college preparatory institute so that she could go to university. She became troubled, however, at the magnitude of the sacrifice and by the fact that she had to leave her village and to accept money for fees that drained the resources of her family. At the institute she came up against racism when teachers and non-Indian students assured her that she was second-class. "My preparation was deficient since our village school teachers had been poorly prepared. It was hard for me to keep up," she recalls. After finally finishing the preparatory course, she discovered that her father did not have the money to pay for the remainder of her studies. On her own she signed up to study medicine at San Carlos University where she found herself in the lonely situation of being almost the only Indian enrolled. "It was as if," she said, "we Indians were trapped in a huge net, unable to get out." In order to support her studies, Catalina worked in a restaurant and opened a small business selling the hand-woven blouses made by the women of her village. Eventually the many demands on her time and intellect exhausted her. She dropped medical studies to take up secondary education, a curriculum that could be completed in two years instead of four.

After graduation, she taught in village schools where her pupils were forbidden to learn in their indigenous language and where, compared to schools in wealthier areas, supplies were scarce and teacher preparation was poor. Furthermore, teachers who explored beyond the simplest subjects with their pupils came under scrutiny by the Guatemalan government.

Catalina reflects that, while her father dreamed big dreams for her, he did not understand that knowledge also brings suffering. "When I am depressed," she admits, "I almost think it would be better to be illiterate. When I am optimistic, I dream that one day all of us will be educated beyond reading and writing."

From Ch'Abuj Ri Ixoc (The Voice of Women),
Guatemala news bulletin

Of course the U.S. is an exception!

"Nowhere is competition between girls more intense than it is in high school. After 12 years of learning that we don't matter, what else can you ******* expect? The education system has taught us little else but to hate ourselves."

Sinead O'Connor, in *Ms Magazine*

Remembering Nepal

One of many things I remember about Nepal was the uprush of energy from women intent on helping one another. Their connectedness, their durability, their enthusiasm was a bright lamp in an otherwise smoggy, crowded, noisy city (Kathmandu). At the Manushi Arts and Crafts Center I entered a world of working women, but not only were the women working for Manushi, they were also learning skills that would eventually enable them to support themselves. It was like plant division. Each small, separate plant is equipped with all the necessary ingredients for growth, eventual blooming and finally splitting off yet another plant. Manushi's philosophy is that sustainable livelihood for women is a prerequisite for Nepal's sound and sustainable development. At Manushi, women are trained in the principles of entrepreneurship awareness. They learn management techniques, how to locate market sources and outlets for their products, how to provide quality control, how to train and develop opportunities for others. Their target groups are female school dropouts, female members of an indigenous ethnic group, literate and semi-literate women. Currently, most women in Nepal are engaged in some aspect of agriculture. Most are not employed outside the home. Manushi recognizes that fact and that the currently installed "growth model" under which the government operates does not recognize its oppressive nature, nor does it take into consideration the rapid erosion of the country's natural resources. Women and children, Manushi believes, must be given a key role throughout their communities in environmental protection and management. Key words of Manushi's philosophy are: networking, community initiatives, partnerships, development of entrepreneurial skills.

Behind the beautiful textiles, the tie-dyed fabrics, the piles of sweaters, gloves and mufflers, stand the philosophy and the faith. Women can learn. Women can lead.

Whose concern is it?

The fact that people are dying unnecessarily in many parts of the world, that they have not enough to eat, that they have no opportunity to become educated is important for everyone to acknowledge. "How could it not be? Unless you believe that every human being's mind is quite separate from every other, separate from the common human mind. An unlikely thing, surely."

From Doris Lessing in her autobiography
Under My Skin (Harper Perennial)

Haven't we made progress?

Over the past 30 years an education avalanche has been sweeping across much of the world. Its characteristics include increases in general student enrollment, government spending for education, and above all, women discovering their own power, making demands for local learning programs, and organizing grassroots schools. The demand for education never stops. Unfortunately, the girl child who completes primary and secondary school and then stands at the door of higher education frequently finds it closed due to the tremendous gender inequalities in many parts of the world. Despite some progress for women in education, there remain high illiteracy rates among adult, especially rural, women in most developing countries. Because they are responsible for the health and welfare of family members and often must grow a good part of the country's food, women are often deprived of the basic means to perform these functions efficiently. They can neither read nor write. This condition perpetuates dependency and impoverishment. Lack of education impacts health, economic, and all general welfare areas.

From information contained in *Women: Looking Beyond 2000*, published by the United Nations

It's big... it's enormous!

Looking at the enormity of the problems facing women around the globe and surveying all the "in-place" mechanisms designed to perpetuate those problems gives ample reason for discouragement. It's a lot like standing on a beach with a small bucket hoping to bail out the ocean. But there are a lot of "bailers" out there.

Take Zhou Ping, a nine-year-old in the third grade in Gansu Province of western China. When her father died, her mother told her that she and her sister would have to give up schooling. Schooling is of no use, she said. "You don't even know how to plait the straw to make hats."

But Zhou Ping didn't quite give up. Every day when she heard the school bell she would put her books in her bag and carry them to where she worked on straw hats. She did not forget her love for learning. Later a teacher paid for her tuition so that she could go back to school.

Zhou's story stands out in a dreary record of illiteracy for girl children in China. In 1992, 2.11 million Chinese children dropped out of school. Education barriers have been particularly steep for girls because their mothers, 70 percent of whom are illiterate, forbid them to go to school. The reason is that they will live with other families after marriage, and therefore any investment in their education can reap no rewards. In some cases, religion stands between girls and school—the problem being shared male/female classrooms. In many rural regions there are not any schools.

In a survey made in Gansu and Qinghai provinces that covered 5,000 girl children, it was found that 30 percent of them had to walk an hour to get to school, often traversing mountains and rivers on their way. A pilot project launched in 1992 aims to teach parents and local governments about China's law of compulsory education. Training classes held for local people teach that the key to eliminating poverty is to improve the quality of the people through education.

From a story by Wandi Jiang in the Sept. 7, 1995
issue of *Forum '95*, published as a daily for the NGO Forum

The story of "O"

"O" lives in the most developed country in the world. She fits the picture of an average girl child from an average family, living in the suburbs of a large city. Her father has a job. Her mother works. She and her siblings are cared for.

"O" becomes involved with a young man from her area. He is attractive. He has promise. However, he is an alcoholic and a drug addict. "O" and he move in together. "O" drops out of school.

The difference between "O" and many another young woman in a similar predicament is the church, in this case an inner-city church whose congregation is largely African-American. The church has a staff of professional counselors and care givers skilled in helping young people who are temporarily off the path. One of them is a professional counselor named "Tee," a tall, eye-catching woman whose appearance and self-possession fit the American prototype of fashion model or actress, one of those who in America's media-scripted culture is entitled to be called a "successful woman." But Tee has dedicated herself to the church and to young people like "O." Tucking "O" under her wing has been hard but Tee believes in the potential of young women, regardless of how they have been treated by circumstance. "O" and her boyfriend, now lover, fight often and hard. "O" has a son. "O" has given up on going to college but now knows, thanks to Tee, that she has a future. She agrees, at Tee's urging, to enroll in training in cosmetology. She gets a job. Her "man" tries rehab. They come back together, drift apart, come back together in a classic pattern of death and resurrection. Because "O" believes in him and his promises, she marries him. She has two more sons, one after the other. He goes to jail. Now she is alone and responsible for four lives. She sees herself as a woman, life as a serious challenge, her sons as serious business. Under Tee's mentorship, she makes an assessment of her capabilities. She gets a loan, buys a beauty salon. Her business grows to the point where she is able to employ 15 operators. She is doing well. She can fly. She can soar. She can carry her sons with her, make better lives for them. She tells them about her dreams. A stable life. An owned home. College.

There are many different kinds of education, many life paths for the young women of this world. Education may not mean college. It may mean basic skills. It may mean training for a profession. But whatever it is, it means a better life. An opening door. "O" waited long at the doorstep. With human help, fueled by her faith, she finally entered.

The story of Tee

Every time I see Tee I think of blooming plants, of rich, deep singing, of wonderful cookery luxuriant with spices and redolent with aromas. She is tall with the kind of presence that surrounds you with confidence, that makes you feel at least a foot taller than you were before. "Tee" is Tee Garlington, Virginia-born professional organizer and trainer in the field of human relations, who for a number of years served as a public relations counselor for her church in Upper

Marlboro, Maryland. Tee has been a policewoman. She has been a TV producer and director, she has been involved in politics; she has been a sales analyst for a major oil company, she has been an office administrator. There is not much she has not done in the field of human relations. Her church work was with a coalition of churches of which her Evangel Church was the hub, educating congregations on political issues affecting families, acting as liaison to the public and the media concerning various outreach ministries. Her task was to get the word out to the community, to motivate and educate on the needs and status of their children. She believes in long-term solutions to the problems of cities. She believes that morality can be taught and "retrofitted" onto an individual who has taken a wrong path. She is committed to encouraging young people to recognize their life's purpose and to achieve a place in their communities. She believes in personal discipline. Youth must be taught how to respect themselves, says Tee, apart from that false sense of respect they acquire with gang membership. She believes in education which encompasses sports, social skills, sexual and personal hygiene, and training for specific careers. She believes in "believing." The church is a vital part of all that she does. Her faith undergirds her actions. Tee is a single parent who has successfully raised three children. It's not just what she says; it's what she does and how she lives that earn her widespread respect and love. She calls her children "the greatest blessing God has given me." She believes all children are blessings.

The story of "Y"

"Y" is an old woman I met in Africa when I was on a trip for my church. I asked about "Y," who seemed to spend a lot of time sitting in the doorway of her home and talking to everybody who passed by. I frequently heard her singing. "What is she singing about?" I asked. "About everything," I was told. "Y sings to learn." I was struck with the simplicity and beauty of that comment. That a woman can learn by singing is something new to me. It is not one of the revealed mysteries of the Western world. But "Y" was putting her thoughts in order as she sang. She sang of the village, of her life, of the seasons and the harvest. She sang about the lives of the people of her village. It was as if she were making a beautiful weaving. And as she sang, I noticed groups of children surrounding her, pausing to hear her, sitting sometimes at her feet, looking at her shyly, yet with obvious interest. "Y" is teaching, said my friend. "She is passing on some of the history of her people to the children." To learn by singing, to teach by singing. The church has been using the medium for years, I thought, feeling suddenly at home. The beautiful lyrics of the hymns we sing teach us about our faith. It is not only books or computers that can teach us. "Y," I learned, cannot read or write. Yet she is certainly not illiterate!

I recently ran across a quote from an Englishwoman written back in 1868 which offers yet another take on education. Josephine Butler allowed that the desire for education (widely felt among English women of her time) was not a matter of wishing to be clever or acquiring knowledge as "the only way to get bread," but more importantly, it stemmed from "the instinctive craving for light which in many is stronger than the craving for bread."

It is ironic, noted Ann Firor Scott writing in 1972 and quoted by Paula A. Triechler and Cheri Kramerae in their book *Amazons, Bluestockings and Crones,* that education, "an institution which women had a large hand in creating, and for the development of which women have been largely responsible throughout history, should be viewed as something that women don't really need." Triechler and Kramerae also quote French feminist Hellene Cixous, "Women must write through their bodies, they must invent the impregnable language that will wreck partitions, classes and rhetorics, regulations and codes; they must submerge, cut through." Isn't that what the new awareness for women is about? And isn't education as a means for enabling women to express themselves, at the heart of these changes?

And education is part of any solution to the world's looming overpopulation problem. One critical element of any solution to overpopulation, says Gretchen Daily in *Mother Jones* magazine, is "social and economic equity at just about every level. There's a lot of empirical evidence that sexual equity within the household is critical to lowering fertility rates. As it stands it's in poor families best interest to have a lot of children. One way to reverse that is to give women access to employment outside the home which also means access to education, health care and basic civil rights…"

From "Visions" by Ms Daily
in *Mother Jones*, Nov.-Dec. 1994

Speaking of bailing out the ocean with a cup

In the town of Castleford in the United Kingdom, five women braved the town council to request that they be allowed to use an abandoned building for which the town had other plans. The council wanted it for a halfway house for juvenile offenders on probation, which was vigorously opposed by local residents. The five woman organizers had a plan to help the wives of unemployed miners, women who included an employee of a butcher shop, a proprietor of a garment shop, an employee in a bingo parlor, and a lifelong homemaker. They had all come together at a soup kitchen where they formed the Castleford Women's Center in 1986. When the women of the town were asked what they most wanted they said almost with one voice: "Education!" The Center entered into a partnership with a local university to offer bachelor's degree courses in sociology, history, women's studies, and English literature. The once-abandoned building became a thriving educational center. The women emerged from their educational experience primed to take on other problems: open mines that blight the environment, and "Women Against Pit Closures," a protest against the elimination of thousands of the region's jobs.

One of the women who benefited from the learning center recently sat for examinations in English literature and has been appointed to the governing board of two local schools. Still, set off against these advances are the continuing indifference and occasional hostility to the idea of women and education. Britain's long history of class distinction mitigates particularly against improvement of status for underprivileged women.

From a Women's Feature Service story, Beijing Watch, Sept. 6, 1995

Bicycles and rubber boots

Bicycles, rubber boots and horses figure in the transportation scheme for school children in the remote Nicoya Peninsula of Costa Rica. Though 98 percent of the students in these elementary schools successfully completed their final exams according to 1994 statistics, up to 40 percent of them were unable to continue their education due to a lack of accessible high schools. Though Costa Rica has one of the lowest illiteracy rates in all of Latin America, 7.5 percent, and every child under government policy receives a free education up to the ninth grade, there remains the problem of sufficient schools to serve people in outlying areas. High schools are across the gulf from the children of the Nicoya Peninsula, so the only way to get there is by boat, too expensive for most of the inhabitants. Those who do come up with the fare often do so by buying less food for their families. Increased migration of people to cities only increases the plight of those who stay behind. Rural schools, with too few students, are forced to close. The problem in the Nicoya Peninsula area is currently under study by an NGO known as Integral Peninsular Rural Development.

"Until women enter all fields of endeavor, the world of humanity will not progress," says a recent statement made by the worldwide Baha'i Faith. Can they do this without education?

It's tough being a girl

In many societies, schooling for girls is a luxury and often it is second-class. In both industrialized and developing countries, girls receive less attention from their teachers than do boys.

Education watch:

Are girls, in fact, getting educational opportunities equivalent to those offered boys? Is anybody monitoring?

If there is no established school system or provision for learning, can local people be organized to provide education? If there are already organizations or structures in place, can their energies be solicited for this purpose?

Book check. Are the books being used written in a gender neutral form? Do they uphold antiquated social values, particularly those relating to gender stereotyping? Is anybody watching?

Is there adequate training for jobs being offered? Not everyone benefits from being offered a college education. Job skills of all types must be taught in order to provide a healthy infrastructure and to benefit individuals heading into adulthood.

Are there role models and are they called upon to exemplify values? Those who have made it through education should be "delivered" to aspiring young people, to help show them the way.

Is mentoring, both long- and short-term, being offered to children who need a boost? Is the community recruiting mentors?

The one from which all flow

It is interesting to note that although education is one of 12 issue areas identified in the United Nations Platform, it turns out to be, along with health, the undergirding structure from which all change must flow. All over the world, women leaders are taking the position that not only governments but all social structures must build and support viable, gender sensitive educational systems.

"Women need to think big, be firm and make their own decisions," says Zhu Lilan, executive vice-chair of China's State Science and Technology Commission. The three are inextricably interwoven and none can be accomplished without their common base of education. Education stimulates creativity, enabling "bigness of thinking." Education builds confidence, resulting in firmness of conviction, and education gives wings to the process of decision making. All women must cry out on behalf of this worldwide need. All women must remove the scales from their eyes to see and judge their own local educational systems. But the bottom line is that women must believe in the absolute necessity of an educational system that is solid and appropriate for all the people of today and which also builds toward the future. And then, to use a colloquial phrase, they must "go for it!"

Economic Disparity

Sister Heléna Marie

■ ■ ▩ ▩ ▩ ▩ ▩ ▩ ▩ ▩ ▩ ▩ ▩

Women still… perform the great majority of unremunerated domestic work and community work, such as caring for children and older persons, preparing food for the family, protecting the environment and providing voluntary assistance to vulnerable and disadvantaged individuals and groups. This work is often not measured in quantitative terms and is not valued in national accounts. Women's contribution to development is seriously underestimated, and thus its social recognition is limited. The full visibility of the type, extent and distribution of this unremunerated work will also contribute to a better sharing of responsibilities.

Platform for Action

At the outset of this chapter, I must admit that I am hardly an expert on economics; in fact, I am a novice. Yet I wanted specifically to write this section of the book.

The reason is that I was "bit by the bug" on the Peace Train; I took five workshops on the train on alternative economics, developed an intense interest, and have been pursuing it ever since. Prior to that I knew and cared little about economics, and figured I couldn't understand it, anyway. I cared about people, but didn't think the boring subject of economics had anything to do with them. When economics was put into plain English, however, and when I started connecting with women whose very quality of life was largely determined by economic systems over which they had little control, my conversion began.

I want to share my enthusiasm, especially with women who think they can't understand the subject. If I can understand it, just about anyone can! Economics *does* matter, especially for women. Let me begin with some personal examples.

When I was a little girl growing up in California, my father, a Lutheran pastor, worked six full days a week, and often attended church-related meetings at night. For this heavy work load, he received a monthly paycheck that put food on our table and kept our family clothed and healthy. His work was counted as "income."

As my two sisters and I grew older, our needs increased: braces, music lessons and other amenities. My mother, a talented pianist, began teaching piano lessons to supplement the income. Eventually she acquired 65 students, teaching more than 50 hours a week. Money was still tight, so she added a night job teaching adult piano students at a local junior college. The money she made from these efforts was counted as "income."

But in addition to all of this, my mother did the housework, cooked the meals, sewed our clothes, washed and ironed, maintained the family finances, and tended the gardens: in short, she performed the duties that every homemaker knows is a full day's work. She also helped my father with his church work, accompanying him on hospital calls, hosting church meetings in our home, and doing all that is (or was then) ordinarily expected of a clergyman's wife. For none of this work did she receive any pay—nor was it ever considered work of monetary value as were my father's and mother's paying jobs. It was unpaid women's work.

My parents have both retired from their paying jobs. Their only income is my father's pension; yet my mother continues to perform all the duties of a housewife—unpaid, of course.

I have a job working in women's ministries in the Episcopal Church, for which I am paid a salary. I come home after a long day's work, tired after meetings and phone calls and coping with the New York subway system. I come home to a community in which most of the Sisters have been working in the convent, doing the laundry, buying the food, creating brochures, fixing the plumbing, taking care of guests, giving spiritual direction, writing letters to seekers of God, walking the dogs, and cleaning our huge facility.

My stay-at-home Sisters have been working every bit as hard as I have, but much of their work is unpaid. Sometimes they have to put up with attitudes that say, "Those of us with outside jobs can't volunteer to help tonight; we've been working all day!" (And they haven't?) When the annual budget sheet is passed around, my work is represented by a five-digit figure; much of their work does not appear in the figures at all (although we are working to change this).

Some work is, in a word, invisible

Women's unpaid work. We all do it. We all know what it's like, and what it feels like to have that work discounted and devalued because it does not bring in money. On a personal level it may be frustrating and belittling, although many women accept it as inevitable. But on a national and global level, it becomes more complicated.

The Gross Domestic Product (GDP) of any country (sometimes referred to as GNP or Gross National Product) is the central measure of the modern global economy. It reflects the dollar value of all the goods and services produced within that nation. It is used to evaluate how well each nation is doing, and to compare nations with each other. In a word, it indicates a nation's "worth."

When a nation's GDP rises, this is called "economic growth;" a falling GDP indicates a declining economy. The nation with the highest GDP in the world is the United States.

In this system, the only goods and services that count are those in the public sector which make money. With few exceptions, no value is assigned to non-money-producing, non-public labor or products.

So, for example, an ancient forest has no value and is not counted in a nation's worth until it generates money. If a lumber company comes in and cuts down all the trees, then the forest is counted as having value. If a woman works all day keeping house and taking care of her family, her work is not given value because it does not make money. But if she does the same thing as a maid and a nanny in someone else's home, and puts her own small children in a daycare center, this is all considered to have value, because it generates money.

Barbara Brandt, in *Whole Life Economics: Revaluing Daily Life* (New Society Publishers, 1995), makes the same point as she tells of the strange case of the disappearing maid:

> If a woman cooks and cleans in a man's home as a paid domestic servant, she is counted as part of the economy because her paid work is included in society's key economic measure, the GDP. However, if a man marries his maid, she no longer gets paid for her housework in his home, and her contribution to the GDP is suddenly eliminated from the official statistics.

The woman may still be doing exactly the same work she was doing before her nuptial ceremony—in fact, she may now be doing even more—but because she is no longer being paid for that work, she has in essence disappeared from the economy.

And just wait until she starts having children! Her day-care providers, being paid for their specific and strictly limited services, will be included in measures of the economy. But the mother's 24-hour-a-day, seven-day-a-week commitment does not appear in the GDP.

So does the GDP really reflect the wealth of a nation: the work done and the value of its resources? No, because it counts neither services provided by homemakers nor those that people freely give to others in their communities. It does not count the value of women's unpaid work, nor of business done in the private sector, nor of a country's natural resources.These things are considered to be free for the taking, from rain forests and oceans to a woman's homemaking labor.

So, for example, while my father's work was always counted in the annual GDP, much of my mother's was not. The GDP did not take into account her volunteer work, or her housework, or her "reproductive work." Nor did any of my mother's work qualify her to receive benefits, vacations, or a pension.

Why does it matter? Why don't women quit worrying about whether or not their work is assigned value in the economy and just get on with it?

In some cases it probably does not. My Sisters and I live in a communal fashion, sharing everything from paper clips to five-digit salaries. Since we have a common purse and share our resources, no Sister's work is considered more or less valuable than any other's, whether paid or not.

When we operated a private school in Manhattan, however, we ran into difficulty by not recognizing the value of women's unpaid work. For 35 years the school depended on an army of Sisters who did everything from managing the cafeteria to programming the computers. The Sisters were given a minuscule stipend in return for their work (less than they would have gotten had they been on welfare). Decisions to expand and diversify were based in part on the assumption that this essentially unpaid staff of Sisters would remain stable. When the number of Sisters dwindled significantly at the same time that student enrollment dropped, the school was thrown into a financial crisis that has taken more than a decade to resolve.

Perhaps no one could have predicted the drop in numbers of students and the attrition of Sisters; but a financial crisis may have been averted if the Sisters' essentially unpaid work had been attributed its real monetary valuation. This process, called imputation, would have allowed the school's leaders to realize how heavily dependent they were on virtually free labor that could not be assured forever, and to take steps for a future without it.

Fortunately, the Sisters learned from that experience. When we began a new ministry of retreats and cultural events, we built the Sisters' salaries into the budget from the beginning. This has helped the Community financially and given a sense of dignity and value to the work that we do. It has meant that at least some of the Sisters' work at home is beginning to show up on the annual budget sheets.

New Zealand economist Marilyn Waring, in *If Women Counted: A New Feminist Economics* (Harper San Francisco, 1988), explains why it matters for women to be visible in the economy. The United Nations System of National Accounts (UNSNA) is an international system of economic measurement and uses the GDP as a standard national measure. The UNSNA is used frequently and broadly: the United Nations uses this system to assess annual contributions; the World Bank uses it to identify nations that most urgently need financial assistance; multinational corporations use it to locate new areas for overseas investment; and individual countries use it for everything from analyzing their own productivity to deciding who gets loans, resources, and benefits.

Now if women are virtually invisible in this system—if they do not even appear in the figures—how can they receive aid, resources, and benefits flowing from the system? If women do not appear in a system that is used to determine public policy, how will those policies affect them?

United States Senator Daniel P. Moynihan wrote, 25 years ago, "If American society recognized homemaking and child-rearing as productive work to be included in the national economic accounts, the receipt of welfare might not imply dependency. But we don't. It may be hoped that the women's movement of the present time will change this"
The Politics of a Guaranteed Income,
New York: Random House, 1973, p. 17

Unfortunately, the women's movement has not yet been able to accomplish this. In fact, as of the time of this writing, Congress has just passed a bill dramatically cutting welfare aid which many single mothers depend on to feed and clothe their children. How is it that we can define as "not working" a single mother struggling to raise several children? And how can those who cry for "family values" glibly castigate welfare mothers, while failing to recognize and financially support that most essential of all work, raising a family?

Marilyn Waring, in *If Women Counted*, shows that the GDP is a product of Western patriarchy, which throughout history has actually promoted exploitation of natural resources and developing countries. Not to mention exploitation of women! She calls the United Nations System of National Accounts "an essential tool of the male economic system." It encourages a massive, lucrative weapons industry and the destruction of our environment, and it keeps women on the bottom rung of the economic ladder by not recognizing their work as "productive."

In many African nations women grow most of the food that feeds their families. "Women today dominate Africa's agricultural industry, laboring in fields to produce about 75 percent of the continent's food despite laws and social customs in many countries that block them from owning lands and tools," comments a story in the August 7, 1996 *San Francisco Chronicle*. Because their work is not paid it does not show up in the GDP. Men, on the other hand, are paid for agricultural work (which is mainly crop exportation) and therefore have access to loans and subsidies. Only the work done by men shows up in the nation's GDP.

"The concept of working women is not new to Africa, where UN surveys show that a woman's average workday is nearly twice as long as a man's when child care, cooking and housekeeping are considered," says the same *Chronicle* article. Yet it is the men who own the land, collect the money, and make the rules.

Marilyn Waring gives the example of the Beti people from southern Cameroon. Beti men work about seven-and-a-half hours a day. They raise cocoa for export, make beer and palm-wine, build and repair houses, and produce simple commodities for market. Beti women work eleven hours a day, including five hours or more on daily food production, three to four hours in food processing and cooking, two or more for firewood and water collection, washing clothes, child care and care of the sick and elderly. The United Nations' International Labor Organization counts the Beti man as an "active laborer." But because none of the Beti woman's working day is spent "helping the head of the household in his occupation," and because work done in the home that directly meets family needs is not counted as part of the economy, the United Nations International Labor Organization concludes that she is not an active laborer!

The GDP is a flawed system of measurement

Heléna Norberg-Hodge, in her book *Ancient Futures: Learning From Ladakh*, gives examples of why the GDP (GNP) is flawed:

> There is clearly something wrong with a system of national accounting that sees GNP [GDP] as the prime indicator of social welfare. As things stand, the system is such that every time money changes hands—whether from the sale of tomatoes or a car accident—we add it to the GNP and count ourselves richer. Policies that cause GNP to rise are thus often pursued despite their negative impact on the environment or society. A nation's balance sheet looks better, for instance, if all its forests have just been cut to the ground, since felling trees makes money. And if crime is on the increase and people buy more stereos or video recorders to replace those stolen, if we put the sick and elderly into costly care institutions, if we seek help for emotional and stress-related problems, if we buy bottled water because drinking water has become so polluted, all these contribute to the GNP and are measured as economic growth.
>
> The situation has become quite absurd: rather than eating a potato grown in your own garden, it is better for the economy if you buy a potato grown on the other side of the country, which has been pulverized, freeze-dried, and reconstituted into brightly colored potato balls. Consuming in this way, of course, means more transportation, more use of fossil fuels, more pollution, more chemical additives and preservatives, and more separation between producer and consumer. But it also means an incremental increase in GNP, and is therefore encouraged.

Ancient Futures: Learning From Ladakh,
Sierra Club Books, 1991

Peace Train revelation

In 1995, the Women's International League for Peace and Freedom (WILPF) sponsored the Peace Train, an historic crossing of borders for peace, development and equality that took 233 women and eight men from Helsinki, Finland, through Eastern Europe, and across Asia to Beijing and the UN Fourth World Conference on Women. I was one of the 233 women riding the train through countries in economic and social transition, and through countries affected by conflicts and war.

During the long journey, I talked to Rose (from the Philippines), Manel (Sri Lanka), Sonia (Guatemala), and Tayba (Sudan). I gradually began to see the connection between "the people" and the global economy. I began to listen to their stories about how this system affects the poor, mostly women and children, in their countries.

As the scales fell from my eyes, I began to be angry, then indignant, then outraged. It sounds so noble: a global economy. It sounds like an element in the concept of global consciousness. It sounds like the best of all possible worlds where everybody is growing and producing, everybody is making money and consuming, everything is renewable!

But far from being a system that unites people around the world, the global economy actually separates us by making a few wildly rich, while keeping more than a billion people in dire poverty, and by hiding that poverty from both the wealthy and the middle classes. Here's what I learned on the Peace Train and in subsequent study.

Build-up to a crisis

In the early 1970s, the price of oil rose sharply. This placed oil-importing low-income countries in the critical position of needing to borrow money to obtain the oil they needed. At the same time, the commercial banks were awash with petro-dollars and were looking for places to loan them profitably. It seemed to be a perfect fit: the low-income countries needed to borrow; the banks needed to loan.

Low-income countries were encouraged to take out large loans to help with their development. Interest was low. Opportunities abounded.

The following decade, however, saw their slow slide into deep debt. The bottom dropped out of the markets for many of the low-income countries. The price of exports plummeted; the price of imports rose. Interest rates increased steeply. Suddenly the borrowing countries were paying more for their imports, receiving less for their exports, and accumulating huge debts from high interest.

Industrialized countries began protecting their markets by imposing duties and other import restrictions, tightening the noose around the economic necks of low-income countries. And while less was being spent on basic necessities, more was going toward military expenditure. The borrowing continued. The more the indebted countries borrowed, the more they owed. It was like a drug addiction.

Low-income countries now faced a crisis. They owed the banks huge amounts but were unable to repay the loans. They could neither earn enough money nor borrow any more because they were now deemed bad credit risks. Private lending dried up and development aid stagnated.

When the price of oil rose again and a major world recession hit in 1978-79, the low-income countries became so mired in debt that they faced defaulting on their loans. They were forced to go to the only institutions who would still lend to them: the World Bank and the International Monetary Fund (IMF).

These two global institutions took control, agreeing to lend to the indebted countries if they accepted certain proposals, called Structural Adjustment Programs (SAPs).

"SAP" is an appropriate acronym for these programs, because although they were profitable for those countries who controlled the World Bank and the IMF, they **sapped** the low-income countries of their resources, money, and social services. The SAPs sucked these countries dry, at the same time harnessing their economies to the world financial system so that they became even less productive in terms of meeting their local needs and more profitable for the global financial institutions.

The World Bank and the IMF, through the SAPs, imposed economic policies on these countries, devalued their currencies, and forced legislated cutbacks in social services to the poor. The result was that the poor lost what little they had in terms of health care, child care services, education, jobs, credit opportunities, and subsidies. They even lost basic necessities like clean water, sanitation and immunization against diseases. These austerities were suffered by as much as 70 percent of the total population of these countries.

After more than a decade of "structural adjustment," third-world countries have become poorer than ever. Millions live in extreme poverty. Jobs have been lost, wages have decreased. The cost of necessities has risen to a level that puts them out of reach for most of the poor. Malnutrition and starvation are claiming the lives of millions. Diseases that were once nearly eradicated have reappeared. Schools have closed. Crime has increased, as has violence, particularly violence against women.

And development?
It has come to a halt.

As always in an economic crisis, women and children suffer most. Women are the first to lose their jobs, the first to feel the effects of falling wages. Since women in most developing countries manage the households, cuts in basic services like primary health care and child care increase the work that women are forced to do. When food is scarce, girl children often are fed less than boy children. Mothers eat less so that their families will have more. When more hands are needed to help with domestic work, girl children are taken out of school first. Domestic violence increases when jobs are scarce and living conditions are intolerable. Women and children bear the brunt of such violence.

Although the World Bank and the IMF seek to create an image of serving the poor and their borrowing governments, they are primarily creatures of the transnational financial system. How do transnational corporations fit into the scheme? They are one of the Bank's most powerful political constituencies, and the Bank's projects usually involve large procurement contracts with these firms. It all fits together in a world financial system that has been created by the most powerful industrial countries. This is the global economy.

Who is ruling the world?

Transnational corporations have gradually gained control of the world's markets. Larger corporations have gradually eaten up smaller ones or merged with competitors so that they dominate entire markets. They have penetrated local economies the world over, burrowing their way into the minds and psyches of even the most remote villagers (see David Korten's book *When Corporations Rule the World*, Kumarian Press, Inc. and Bennett-Koehoer Publishers, Inc., 1995). So powerful are they that they "buy" governmental legislation concerning economic policy, in effect creating a world economic system of their own, maximizing their profits at the expense of millions of others.

Many of these corporations have devoured the resources of their own countries and moved on to colonize the resources of other countries. Like a voracious monster, the transnational corporation has invaded developing countries, mining out their earth treasures, fishing out their seas, taking away the land from their people, cutting down their rain forests, turning the world's bountiful fields into billions of square miles of polluted cropland for huge agribusiness. In the process, they have poisoned much of the air, the water, and the soil around the globe.

In this new form of colonization, free trade zones have been set up in developing countries, employing millions of people—mostly women and children—in maquilladoras (sweatshops) and other wretched factories. Here the wage average is a few dollars a day, and the working conditions are ghastly. Many transnational corporations relocate production facilities to these countries, which causes millions of local workers to lose jobs in the corporations' countries of origin. The new, cheaper production costs drive the market down so that competitors are forced out and even more jobs are lost.

Corporations have "downsized" and "outsourced" to such a degree that production and marketing and almost all other aspects of corporate life are now carried out in developing countries, and all that is left locally is a core group at the tip of the iceberg to collect the profits. This economic monster cannot long survive its own destructive practices.

It is a documented fact that a mere 1,000 top corporate players own a quarter of the world's wealth. Even in the United States, a swelling mass of people live in third-world conditions, and the gap between the rich and the poor widens every day. How is it that Wall Street speculators can sit in plush suites slinging literally billions of dollars around the globe at a single keystroke, while a quarter of the world's people live in squalor, go to bed hungry and suffer from curable diseases?

Have the men (almost invariably it is men) at the top paused to think about the world they are leaving to their grandchildren? A world whose lands and seas and skies have been savaged, poisoned, destroyed? The vast majority of whose people will live in destitution and poverty? Whose governments have to cut most social services to its people in order to buy the military equipment necessary to protect the ever-shrinking tiny upper class from the needy masses?

What's wrong with this picture?

Says James Gustave Speth, administrator of the United Nations Development Program (UNDP): "An emerging global elite, mostly urban-based and interconnected in a variety of ways, is amassing great wealth and power, while more than half of humanity is left out. We still have more than half the people on the planet with incomes of less than $2.00 a day—more than three billion people. For poor people in this two-class world, it is a breeding ground for hopelessness, for anger, for frustration" (*The New York Times*, Aug. 14, 1996).

The 1996 Human Development Report (published for the United Nations Development Programme by Oxford University Press) states that worldwide, 358 billionaires control assets greater than the combined annual incomes of countries with 45 percent of the world's people. That's 358 individuals—30 football teams not counting the reserves! It also reports that 89 countries are worse off economically than they were a decade or more ago. In 70 developing countries, incomes are lower than they were in the 1960s or 1970s. These figures underscore the growing gap between the rich and the poor, a gap that may be seen nationally as well as globally.

One of my favorite American thinkers, Wendell Berry, has this to say on the subject of the global economy and America's role in creating it:

> The Civil War made America safe for the moguls of the railroads and the mineral and timber industries who wanted to be free to exploit the countryside. The work of these industries and their successors is now almost complete. They have dispossessed, disinherited, and moved into the urban economy almost the entire citizenry; they have defaced and plundered the countryside. And now this great corporate enterprise, thoroughly uprooted and internationalized, is moving toward the exploitation of the whole world under the shibboleths of 'globalization,' 'free trade,' and 'new world order.' The proposed revisions in the GATT [General Agreement on Tariffs and Trade] are intended solely to further this exploitation. The aim is simply and unabashedly to bring every scrap of productive land and every worker on the planet under corporate control.
> *Sex, Economy, Freedom and Community,*
> Pantheon Books, 1992

Rose Maliaman's story

Rose Maliaman was one of my roommates on the Peace Train. She presented a segment of the train's alternative economics workshop. These are Rose's thoughts taken from a transcription of the notes I took during her presentation.

The 7,100 islands of the Philippines are very beautiful and rich in natural resources, yet seventy percent of our eight million people live below the poverty line while the other thirty percent are rich. We live in a country of fertile fields for growing food, yet we have to import nearly everything we eat.

How did our country get to be like this?

First we were colonized by Spain for 300 years. The Spaniards divided up the country among themselves, leaving the indigenous people the scraps. Then, after Spain was defeated in the war with the United States, the United States became our colonizer; then later, the Japanese. No matter in whose hands, almost all the land was owned by just a few.

Ferdinand Marcos began borrowing large sums of money from the World Bank in the 70s. He agreed to the World Bank's projects for our country, including three huge dams and a nuclear plant. The World Bank and the IMF imposed a structural adjustment program on us. They forced us to use their methods of agriculture. Before that, we didn't use irrigation, nor fertilizers, nor pesticides. The World Bank and IMF forced us to use all three and to buy them, of course, from the West. They told us what we could grow and what we couldn't. More and more of our land was taken away from the people so that crops could be grown for export, and repayment made of the debt we owed to the World Bank. As people were forced off of the land, they went to the cities to look for work. The cities became overcrowded. Slums grew because people could find no work and had nowhere else to go.

The debt grew and grew, until now we owe $38 million to the World Bank. Since we are unable to pay it, we are more and more at the mercy of the World Bank and the IMF and their programs for us.

They are forcing us to industrialize. We said "no," because foreign-owned industries would inevitably drive out our own local small businesses. But zones are already being

converted to industrialization. For example, the textile industries in our country are not Philippine-owned. They are
owned by huge foreign corporations who came to the
Philippines because they could find cheap labor here. These
sweatshops employ almost 100 percent women. The women
earn $1.50 a day! There is no protection in these sweatshops;
the rate of casualties is high. Women work up to 19 hours a
day. They have to put up with all kinds of disgrace, including
sexual harassment. The corporations don't have to worry
about protecting us or giving us our rights, because unions
are either non-existent or intimidated by the government-
backed corporations.

The number one export of the Philippines is human
beings. Millions of migrant workers, mostly women, go
abroad every year, for lack of economic opportunities at
home. Meanwhile, their children are left behind, so it breaks
up families. And of course you have heard of the sexual
exploitation of our children through sex trafficking. Millions
of children, the larger percent girls, are sold or kidnapped for
a sex industry that caters largely to Westerners. And we are
still unable to tackle the debt to the World Bank and IMF,
which just gets larger and larger. The IMF tells us we have to
accept "austerity measures," cutting back our social services—schools, health care, child care, vaccinations. Now we
have to accept "austerity" on top of poverty!

Consider Ladakh

I met Heléna Norberg-Hodge after she spoke at a workshop on the
global economy, sponsored by the Learning Alliance in New York.
Her speech, given without notes, had been brilliant, and I was somewhat shy about meeting her, but to my surprise she was completely
amiable and down-to-earth. She is a blond and blue-eyed Swede, yet
she seems half Ladakhi, speaking the language fluently after having
lived there six months out of every year for 16 years.

In those 16 years she saw the cultural and economic life of
Ladakh transform from a traditional way based on a nonmonetary
subsistence economy, a way that had sustained the community richly
for more than a thousand years, to a modern monetized monoculture
of Coca Cola, Nike, Rambo, and MTV. Sixteen years ago, she said,

the people were vigorous and their enjoyment of life was apparent. They lived in harmony with the land. Now, more and more, they are crowded into ugly cement apartment buildings in smog-choked Leh, the capital city, competing for scarce jobs in a money-based economy, and dependent on these paying jobs to provide them with money to buy food and other necessities that now have to be imported from other parts of the world.

The global economy has quickly invaded and transformed Ladakh, just as it has the Philippines. Caught in a collision with the modern world, the Ladahkis have lost their own culture and independence and have been forced to enter the global market system. The tragic results have been described by Heléna Norberg-Hodge in her book *Ancient Futures* (now also available as a videotape). "Everyone is affected by the global economy," she said. "Even a couple going through a personal heartbreak might be facing job loss through downsizing of their company, for example. Even kindergartners are being pressured to do well in math and science so they can get into Harvard and someday get a good job in the global economy."

She spoke of satellite dishes in front of tiny yurts in Mongolia, beaming in images of cars and Barbie dolls and all the other consumer items that the indigenous people (especially the young) soon feel they must have. She talked about the standardized global consumer monoculture that has invaded every corner of the earth like a cancer. "There are MacDonalds, Michael Jackson tapes, Rambos and Barbie dolls in every remote village, from Tanzania to the Tibetan Plateau."

She decried a global economy that slings products all around the world, while crushing local economies. "Mongolia has 25 million milk-producing animals," she said. "But when I went to Mongolia, I found imported butter from Kenya. When I went to Kenya, I found Spanish butter; in Spain I found butter imported from Denmark; in Denmark, I found imported butter from France. And it's the same with wheat and many other commodities."

It was fascinating to hear what she had to say about women's changing attitudes about their physical appearance. Many women in developing countries try to look Western, she said. Meanwhile, many women in industrialized countries hate their bodies and are often obsessed with losing weight, to the point of trying to starve themselves—anorexia and bulimia are widespread. In her own native Sweden, "blond, blue-eyed Swedes hate their bodies—and they have the ideal bodies"—according to the Western ideal!

What can be done?

So far we have considered some of the problems of our present economic system:

- Much of women's work is invisible and undervalued in economic terms.
- The systems of economic measurement (GDP and UNSNA) are biased against women and keep them at the bottom.
- There is a green light for the destruction of the environment and of traditional cultures and for the build-up of the weapons industry.
- It makes a few very rich, while keeping a quarter of the world's people in absolute poverty, and hides this from both the wealthy and the middle classes.
- It keeps "developing" countries in permanent debt, while harnessing them to Structural Adjustment Programs that benefit the rich and further impoverish the poor.
- It has created and spread around the world a global monoculture of Western materialism, typified by Rambos and Barbies.

What can be done to change this system? At the workshop in New York, Heléna gave five suggestions:

1. Pressure our governments to allow only democratically elected bodies to determine economic policies.
2. Work with corporate CEOs (Chief Executive Officers) and governments to make sure it is the governments who set the rules, not the corporations.
3. Pressure governments to put a ban on corporate mergers.
4. Reconnect with nature on a deep level; consciously open yourselves to the cosmos.
5. Reconnect to the human community on a deep level.

Heléna's suggestions are a beginning to thinking about how we can change the system. In the remainder of the chapter, we will look briefly at a few of the ways concerned people, especially women, are experimenting with alternatives. These are not long-term solutions to the major problems of the global economic system, but they are a start, and they reflect a growing movement of alternatives being tried by pockets of people all over the world.

The Ladakh Project

Let us look briefly at how Heléna put her insights to work in Ladakh. After many years of living there, seeing the destructive changes that "development" was bringing, she thought of a creative way to address some of the problems and get the local people involved. She and a Ladakhi friend, Gyelong Paldan, wrote a series of plays for the theater. They showed how the worst elements of modern Western culture and the global economy had invaded and transformed Ladakh, and how the ancient culture was in danger of disappearing. They emphasized the many values of the ancient culture. The plays were performed and were a resounding success, and many Ladakhis were led by their message to try to find a solution. The result was the Ladakh Project.

Promoting both the preservation of the ancient culture and the best elements of modern technology when it harms neither the environment nor the people, the Ladakh Project advocates such technologies as solar heating, solar ovens and water heaters, hydraulic ram pumps, and greenhouses that allow people to grow vegetables throughout the extremely harsh winter. As its own best advertisement the Project runs a restaurant that serves food prepared in solar ovens, operates a library with materials on natural technologies and also offers a handcrafts program to reinvigorate ancient crafts.

The Ladakh Project has had a significant impact on Ladakh, providing viable, sustainable alternatives to the wholesale Westernization which was ripping the culture apart. It has become an international organization, and staff members lecture all over the world on alternative economics and technologies.

Women's cooperatives

Ana Maria Valquez is a vivacious young woman with a great mane of thick black hair, a ruddy complexion and a likeable earthy manner. A native of Colombia, she was living with the indigenous people of Peru, studying their music, when a realization gradually dawned on her: the mighty Andes Mountains are dying, and with them, an ancient way of life.

Ana Maria had observed how the native trees of the Andes had almost all been cut down, burned, and sold for charcoal. She saw that these great trees were being replaced with quick-growing cash crops of pine and eucalyptus trees for exporting. This practice was not only destroying the delicate ecosystem of the Andes and the very land itself, but it was also wreaking havoc with the traditional way of life, which is intimately linked to the original forests and their creatures. She knew that this was happening in her native Colombia as well.

Deciding to do something about it, she went first to various government officials in Colombia to ask for help. She found none. Undeterred, she struck out as a lone individual determined to work for change.

She began visiting small mountain communities around Lake La Cochus, in one of the last remaining cloud forests in Colombia. First she made it known to the villagers (by means of a colorful mural at the Saturday market) that a meeting would be held about alternatives to cutting down the native trees. With that announcement she knew she was already on delicate ground, because the villagers themselves had been responsible for much of the extensive cutting for thirty years. They had forgotten the time when they had survived without cutting trees.

Still, many came to the meetings. Mostly women, they said they really did not want to cut the trees and they admitted that they knew they would one day run out of trees, but they were perplexed about what to do instead. It is interesting to note here that people in highly developed countries become impatient with such attitudes, forgetting that poorer people often do not *have* alternatives. They must survive, period. These women confessed that they needed the money even more than in the past because by now they had been penetrated by the global economy and were dependent on items that could only be purchased with money.

They began to explore alternatives. "What did we do before?" asked the women. "We wove." But none of them knew how anymore. The tradition had died out. There was one old woman, they remembered, from another village, who still remembered the old ways. Perhaps she could teach them.

The old woman was brought to the village, and she taught the younger women the ancient, traditional art of weaving, the careful movements of the needles through the intricate webbing of threads. The women pooled their savings, invested in several looms, and were soon producing colorful scarves, blouses, shirts and pouches, the very things for which they were once well known. They were able to sell them both locally and in markets farther away, including the United States.

Ana Maria continued to visit women in small communities all over Peru, Colombia, Brazil, and Panama. In eight years she has helped start eight different women's cooperatives in the rain forests from the Amazon basin to the Darien Gap. The traditional arts, which had almost died out, are coming back, parts of the rain forest are being preserved, and the women are making money.

"Why do the villagers listen to you, a stranger in their midst?" I asked her. "I am not getting paid for doing this," replied Ana Maria. "They know that I have to struggle, just like they do. They know I am one of them."

"Are you ever afraid that you will be targeted by the government or private groups for trying to subvert an economy which is destroying the rain forest?" I asked. "Of course one has to work quietly," she explained. "You just spread the word quietly. The more people who know, the more strength they have, the less likely the government is to take them on.

"It's my life's work. I knew this when I had the sudden realization that the Andes were dying. I knew I had to do something. Yes, it's scary sometimes. But what [was] happening to the land and the people is scarier."

Women's cooperatives, like the ones started by Ana Maria and her friends, are being created in many parts of the world. I have visited weaving cooperatives in Chiapis, pig- and goat-raising cooperatives in the Philippines, and food coops in California, and all are successfully operating by the basic principles of pooling resources in order to start businesses. Cooperation and community are the key concepts.

Women valuing their skills

Another idea is bypassing money altogether by simply bartering goods and/or skills. Some women in New York have elaborated on this idea by starting a project called WomenShare.

WomenShare is a venture begun by Jane Wilson and Diana McCourt in New York City. It is a skills bank which has 80 members, all women. Instead of dealing in currency, the bank deals in skills. Each member contributes one or more skills and in return receives other services from the bank.

Here's how it works: Myrna Lewis is a New York psychotherapist. The skill she has "deposited" in the bank is psychotherapy, in the form of 42 hours of free consultations to other participants in the bank. In turn she drew out 10 hours of other women's skills when she had her office painted, leaving 32 hours "in the bank" to draw upon for future services.

Listen to Myrna:

> My most frequent complaint as a working wife, mother, daughter of aging parents and parent-in-law, not to mention friend to a beloved circle of close buddies, is about the lack of time. Like many women—and men—I find it drives me nuts to be pulled in twelve directions at once. Moaning and groaning through middle age could be my fate, but I have found a solution: I now have 80 women of all ages with a splendid panoply of skills to call upon at any time to help with tasks ranging from repotting my plants to cooking my meals and ferrying my elderly relatives to their medical appointments. By simply picking up my phone, I can find someone to cat-sit during my vacations, coach me on a writing project or paint my office or kitchen. And it's all free!
>
> My secret is an organization called WomenShare, begun in New York City two years ago [in 1991] by two friends— Diana McCourt, a custom renovator in her 50s, and Jane Wilson, a health lecturer and cookbook author in her 60s. WomenShare was created as a cooperative 'skill bank' in which members list in a computer all of the professional and life skills they are willing to share with others, as well as shareable possessions such as cars, computers and book collections.
>
> These lists are circulated among all members to use as need dictates. One sacred rule: All work should be equal in terms of time spent—an hour of legal consultation, for example, is equal to an hour of electrical repairs.
>
> From "Personally Speaking: A Busy Woman's Wish Comes True" by Dr. Myrna Lewis in *New Choices for Retirement Living Magazine*, November 1993

The system goes beyond simple barter of labor and chores. Women who do the work earn credits for them. They can then use the credits to pay for work drawn from the larger pool of skills in the entire group. Women who have any work done for them are similarly charged with a debit in their account that will be wiped clear when they provide services for another member.

Barter systems and new money

Another group of pioneers is trying a similar experiment in New York's Columbia County, a rural community where many residents have lost their jobs, are between jobs, or have part-time jobs. Almost all have a difficult time making ends meet.

Virginia Osborn and Ann Greenberg became friends when they discovered a common interest in alternative economic systems. Together, and with increasing support from the community, they created a barter system in Columbia County. Based on a model started in Ithaca, New York, by Paul Glover, the system exchanges skills, while at the same time using a currency created just for the county.

In this system, each hour of work is given monetary value, using a unit of exchange, called a "county hour." Each county hour, or hour of work, is worth $10. So, for each hour of work the member does, she gets credit of one county hour. And when she *receives* an hour of work, one county hour is deducted from her account.

The system has printed its own money, according to federal guidelines. The printed money cannot look like federal money, cannot cross state lines, must be tied to the dollar in value, is taxable, and must have a lowest denomination worth at least one dollar.

The "county hour system" printed $35,000 worth of local money. Then Virginia and Ann went out and started recruiting members. Within three years they had 1,000 individuals and 200 businesses as members. At the end of three years they had $50,000 circulating constantly.

Skills bartered include auto repair, dentistry, tutoring in almost every subject, bookkeeping, house painting, counseling, snow shoveling, music lessons, chiropractic services, landscaping, farm help, plumbing, photography, gravestone carving, junk removal, sewing, and real estate brokerage. Arts and crafts are given an outlet here, too, because payment for services can be made with ceramic pots, oil paintings, or flower arrangements!

The county hour system is working. People who cannot afford to pay for services in dollars can pay for them with their own services. Virginia and Ann are working on making available food and other commodities as well.

In Columbia County, as in New York City, the barter network also creates community. Members gather for weekly potlucks and other social events. Labor exchanges, too, generate friendships and build the sense of cooperation and connectedness among the network's members.

People's banks

Another alternative that is working is based on the idea of giving loans to people who do not qualify for loans by the terms of commercial banks.

The Grameen Bank in Bangladesh is by now a model for other people's banks which help those, especially women, who cannot get loans because they do not have the collateral to get credit. In rural Bangladesh, where custom and law dictate that women cannot own land, it used to be impossible for a woman to get a loan. Fifteen years ago, a young professor of economics at Chittagong University, Mohammed Yunis, started the Grameen Bank, which began giving loans to women who had no collateral and sometimes no source of income at all. The loans helped them to start their own businesses, and eventually to achieve a regular income.

Although the bank went further out on a limb than could reasonably be expected, it found that the women were very reliable in paying back the borrowed funds. The staffing of the bank, including management positions, was equally divided between women and men. The Grameen Bank experiment was so successful that it now operates 241 branches and encompasses some 171,000 members in 3,600 villages. For many women it has made the difference between extreme poverty and an adequate standard of living.

The Qirabj Bank in Indonesia is little more than a table and a chair, staffed by one woman, Nurul Aini. Located on the island of Selong, it was started with seed money donated by a small Islamic foundation. It operates along the same lines as the Grameen Bank, giving loans at low cost to poor women without collateral, who then start their own small businesses and are able to lift themselves out of poverty.

"We lend money primarily to women because women are more disciplined," says Nurul Aini. "Women are more worried about what people will think if they don't repay their loans." The male director of Indonesia's Foundation for Self-reliance and Development, Ali Dahlan, agrees with her: "In our experience, if women borrow money, they will pay it back. Men may not necessarily pay it back."

New York Times, Sunday, February 18, 1996

Interest-free credit unions

Credit unions that charge low or no interest are another alternative being experimented with in various parts of the world. Eva Stenius, a woman who lived in my wagon of the Peace Train, gave several workshops about the interest-free credit union she and her husband started in Sweden.

The idea for the credit union came to them during the Vietnam War when they realized how hugely the war was motivated by profiteering rather than by ideology. This realization led them to study and analyze the entire global economy and to consider alternatives.

In the Stenius' system, people put their savings in the credit union, rather than in a commercial bank. A woman might put $100 a month into her account, for example. In 12 months she would have put in $1,200. If 100 women did that, the credit union would have $120,000 in one year.

Although the money doesn't earn interest, it is available for interest-free loans. So when the woman needs to take out a loan, the credit union will grant it without interest payments. There is no charge to apply for loan. If the loan is granted, the fee for the loan is 9½ percent for a ten-year loan, 6 percent for a five-year loan, and so on. An initial fee of 3½ percent is charged for setting up and servicing the loan, and then an annual fee of 0.6 percent every year after that.

The Episcopal Diocese of Los Angeles set up a similar credit union in 1992 after the uprising following the Rodney King verdict. Gloria Brown, former Economic Justice Officer for the national church, was the founder and first coordinator of the Episcopal Community Federal Credit Union, which gives loans at very low rates to AIDS patients, low-income mothers, and others who would be rejected instantly by most financial institutions. The facility also lends to people on welfare as long as they have a verifiable source of income.

This church-based credit union experiment—the first and only one in the Episcopal Church—is owned and operated by the poor of Los Angeles. It has over 2,000 members and $1.4 million in assets. Already it has made a significant impact on the community it serves.

From a report by Marianne Arbogast, "L.A. Pioneers Diocesan Credit Union," *The Witness Magazine*, vol. 79, no. 3, March 1996

Gloria died shortly before this book went to press. We salute and honor our sister, who pioneered new ways forward for women, and gave hope and a second chance to many in Los Angeles.

Community supported agriculture
and a new spirituality

Close to the border between New Jersey and Pennsylvania, very near the Delaware Water Gap, sits a magical farm. It is staffed by a committed group of lay people and two religious Sisters. It is a cornucopia of flowers, fruits, vegetables, animals, and people. It is also a place of healing and good will.

Genesis Farm was started by two Roman Catholic nuns, Sister Miriam Therese MacGillis and Sister Jeanne Goyette, and their two newlywed friends, Liz and Vin McMahon. When 140 verdant acres near Blairstown, New Jersey, was unexpectedly bequeathed to the Sisters' order by a total stranger, they jumped to the challenge of figuring out what to do with it.

Prior to this, in 1978, Sister Miriam Therese had begun studying the works of Jesuit theologian and ecologist Father Thomas Berry, who got her started thinking about bioregions, alternative farming methods, and a new cosmological story of the earth and the universe. So it was a natural step to think of turning the 140 acres into a community supported garden (CSG) and a center for a new spirituality.

In a community supported garden, local families and individuals buy shares in the garden and receive a yearly supply of fresh vegetables and herbs in return. The families are assured of an annual supply of organically grown vegetables which are hand-picked on a friendly farm, and the gardeners are assured the money they need to grow the vegetables and expand the farm.

Aided by a hard-working and intensely committed biodynamic farmer from the area, the Sisters and their friends began a vegetable garden. Local people began to buy shares in the garden. As they received fresh vegetables, the farm received enough money to begin an orchard. Over the years since the garden began, three greenhouses, a root cellar, and a winterized distribution center have been built. Fruit trees have been planted. The acreage of the vegetable garden has grown and grown. Today, beginning to plan for its tenth season, the farm supports five gardens and almost 190 families.

A learning center has also been started on the farm, using the earth itself as the textbook. Courses in "Earth Literacy" provide children and adults with opportunities to reflect on the principles of responsible earth care, the miracles of life in the natural world, and a spirituality deeply rooted in the earth.

Since 1990 a guest house has been renovated and several straw bale structures created. One tractor shed was turned into a library/resource center. A meditation trail was created, snaking quietly through the woods and fields. People come to Genesis Farm from all over the world for learning, healing and growth. Sister Miriam Therese travels widely, giving presentations on subjects like "The New Cosmology" and "Sacred Agriculture."

Ann and I met with Sister Miriam Therese on a radiant spring morning. Sitting in a quaint old farmhouse on Genesis Farm, early morning sunlight flooding the living room, we listened as she explained the spiritual and practical basis for the new cosmological story (see especially Thomas Berry's *The Dream of the Earth*, Sierra Club Books, 1988, and another book he co-authored with Brian Swimme, *The Universe Story*, Harper San Francisco, 1992) and the principles of community supported agriculture.

In her own words (quoting from a Genesis Farm brochure) Sister Miriam Therese says:

> Community Supported Agriculture is a creative response to a crisis. It offers an opportunity for a community of people to take greater responsibility for their social and community relationships by mutually supporting their own farm. It sees their food source as an essential part of their lives. In turn, the farm supports them and provides them not only nutritious, chemical-free food, but an opportunity to grow in friendship, mutual support, and a commitment to restore the soils, air and water through their choices and decisions.
>
> The teeming life, the extraordinary beauty, and the sense of wholeness that a farm provides is a precious gift to nourish this spiritual hunger. The garden offers a way to experience the mystery of seeds and soil and to reconnect in an endless variety of possibilities for creating friendship, community, and the strong connections that historically tied farmers and communities into a harmonious relationship with the earth and each other.

A Women's budget

Finally, let us consider what the national budgets of the different countries of the world would look like if women could design them.

Marilyn Waring, in *If Women Counted*, gives some chilling statistics about the United States military budget, designed primarily by men: "The United States military budget... is larger than the GNPs of all but eight countries in the world... In 1986, the Pentagon was spending nearly $1 billion a day, $41 million an hour, $700,000 a minute. This statistic does not include expenditure for the manufacture of nuclear fuel and all things nuclear, which in the United States is paid for by the Department of Energy." If women could design the national budget, would they allocate this kind of money to military expenditures?

The Women's International League for Peace and Freedom (WILPF) has created its own "Women's Budgets," one for each of the countries with a WILPF chapter.

Each budget is similar in that, in each one, money is reallocated from defense to social, environmental, and medical programs. They call the process "conversion." You take the cost of a tank, for example, and you convert it to a school program. The funds taken from the military would be used to clean up the environment, prevent soil erosion, develop forms of clean, safe, renewable energy. Converted funds would create health programs for the poor, fund peace education, give poor women credit, and feed into local economies.

The Women's Budget Newsletter, addressing the United States budget, reallocates one billion dollars from military spending to civilian investment, creating a net gain of 6,800 jobs. A $350 billion transfer from military to civilian spending would create two million jobs in five years. Investments of $350 billion could be made in social investments over five years through military cuts. Here are some examples:

Education: $40 billion
Increase funding for Head Start, Compensatory Education, Student Aid, enforcement of Women's Educational Equality Act.

Infrastructure: $45 billion
Increase spending for highways, bridges and airports, Mass Transit, Amtrak, Wastewater Collection and Treatment.

Environment: $20 billion
Increase funding for Superfund cleanup, Municipal Solid Waste Program, Groundwater Protection, Forestry and Conservation, Renewable Energy and Energy Conservation.

Housing: $55 billion
Increase investment in Public Housing and support services for the homeless.
>   From *Women's Budget, Special Edition,* Women's
>   International League for Peace and Freedom, 1996

And so on.

What would be sacrificed to provide the $350 billion? Missiles, bombers, attack submarines! Do we really **want** these? In all of the encounters with women both on the Peace Train journey of seven thousand miles through nine countries and at the NGO Forum in Beijing, I met only one group of women who wanted war. Practically **no one** wants war—and the most opposed of all to it are the women of the world. So why are we allowing the real needs of women to be replaced by bombs that can kill us all and destroy the world?

Women's budgets, community supported agriculture, interest-free credit unions, people's banks, barter systems, new money, and women's cooperatives are just a few of the many new ways people have been trying economics. There are many more (see Barbara Brandt's *Whole Life Economics* for a comprehensive listing and a short discussion of each). All point to the need for a new economic order in which women are visible and valued; in which the primary objective is to meet the needs of all peoples, *not* to make a profit for the few; in which a culture of peace is fostered, rather than a culture of war; and in which we will use natural resources and systems in such a way that they will continue to sustain life in future generations.

Resources

Berry, Thomas. *The Dream of the Earth.* San Francisco: Sierra Books, 1988.

_____, and Brian Swimme. *The Universe Story: From the Primordial Flaring Forth to the Ecozoic Era; A Celebration of the Unfolding of the Cosmos.* San Francisco: Harper, 1992.

Brandt, Barbara. *Whole Life Economics: Revaluing Daily Life.* Philadelphia: New Society Publishers, 1995.

Genesis Farm. 41A Silver Lake Road, Blairstown, NJ 07825, (908) 362-6735.

Greco, Thomas H., Jr. *New Money for Healthy Communities.* Tucson, Arizona: Thomas H. Greco, Pub., 1994.

Human Development Report, 1996. Published for the United Nations Development Programme (UNDP). New York, Oxford: Oxford University Press, 1996.

Kennedy, Margrit. *Interest and Inflation Free Money: Creating an Exchange Medium That Works for Everybody and Protects the Earth.* Philadelphia: New Society Publishers, 1995.

Korten, David. *When Corporations Rule the World.* West Hartford, CT: Kumarian Press, Inc., 1995.

Norberg-Hodge, Heléna. *Ancient Futures: Learning From Ladakh.* San Francisco: Sierra Club Books, 1991.

Osborne, Virginia and Anne Greenberg. Columbia County Hours. PO Box 300, Philmont, NY 12565.

Sidel, Ruth. *Keeping Women and Children Last: America's War on the Poor.* New York: Penguin Books, 1996.

Vickers, Jean. *Women and the World Economic Crisis.* London: Zed Books Ltd., 1994.

Waring, Marilyn. *If Women Counted: A New Feminist Economics.* New York: Harper & Row, 1988.

Women's Action for New Directions (WAND). 691 Massachusetts Ave., Arlington, MA 02174. Tele (617) 643-6740, Fax (617) 643-6744, E-mail: wand@world.std.com; Web: www.fas.org/pub/gen/wand.

Women's Budget Newsletter. Women's International League for Peace and Freedom. 1213 Race Street, Philadelphia, PA 19107-1691.

WOMENSHARE. Diana McCourt and Jane Wilson, founders. 680 West End Avenue, New York, NY 10025. Tele & Fax: (212) 662-9746, E-mail: Wshare@aol.com.

Women's Health

Ann Smith

■ ■ ■ ▪ ▫ ▫ ▪ ▫ ▫ ▪ ▫ ▪

Women have the right to the enjoyment of the highest attainable standard of physical and mental health. The enjoyment of this right is vital to their life and well-being and their ability to participate in all areas of public and private life. Women and girls have the right to control all aspects of their health, in particular their own fertility, the right to equal access to and equal treatment of women and men in education and health care, and to develop their full potential at all ages. A major barrier for women is inequality, both between men and women and among women in different geographical regions, social classes and indigenous and ethnic groups. To obtain optimal health throughout the life cycle, equality, including the sharing of family responsibilities, development and peace are necessary conditions.

Half a million women die each year from causes related to pregnancy and childbirth.

Approximately 100,000 die each year from unsafe abortions.

Women now constitute 40 percent of HIV-infected adults worldwide.

Two million girls suffer genital mutilation every year.
Platform for Action

Wholeness is so difficult to achieve because we live in cultures that separate us from one another, from God, and from our environment.

Wholeness is something we talk a lot about in church, but it is rarely achieved. Holistic health care settings are still rare but more and more are coming into being. The hierarchical structures of church and society are designed to separate and control those they ostensibly serve.

Visions for wholeness are transforming old structures and creating new models of collaboration wherein everyone is valued and everyone shares work, resources, information, success and mistakes.

The word *health* comes from the Old English word *helthe* which means "wholeness." What is wholeness? What is health? I believe it is that state of grace in which the individual (body, mind, soul) is in balance with nature (environment) and society. It is so wonderful when those moments of wholeness exist, and so terrible when we are not in balance and experience disease. The *Platform for Action* states that health is obtained through equality (including the sharing of family responsibilities), development, and peace. Health can only happen in societies that respect the freedom of all individuals and have reverence for all creation, when women and men are in equal partnership, creating, nurturing, and sustaining healthy individuals and systems.

In writing this book, sometimes I felt very much in tune with the process of writing, and at other times I would talk myself out of writing with self-inflicted negative messages. The wonderful thing about writing as a team was that I could talk to Lucy, Nancy, or Sister Heléna Marie and rid myself of my negative thoughts, or I could change my negative environment by taking a walk, meditating, dancing, gardening, or reading.

I want to begin with a personal story of wholeness.

On February 14th, Valentine's Day 1996, I became a grandmother for the first time. At five o'clock in the morning I woke up from a dream of my grandson being born. In the dream I was going to see him. A woman driving a small transport vehicle like a train was bringing him into view. Just as I was about to see him, the train backed up, stopped, and moved forward to meet me. I saw my grandson propped up in a blanket and I woke up.

From this dream I knew to pack my bag even though my daughter was not due for another week. At five in the morning she woke up with her first labor pain. She gave birth to a seven-and-a-half pound boy in a birthing room in a Miami hospital. Her husband assisted her the entire time and two midwives, one from India and one from Ireland, helped in the miracle of birthing. They utilized the universal and age-old skills that brought forth Alexander, who was having difficulty passing through of the birth canal.

Goushen, the midwife from India, saved my daughter from having a Cesarean delivery by skillfully pushing on Whitney's chest, forcing the stuck baby out of the birth canal. If this had been a scene in medieval Europe, with mother and daughter intuitively in synch at the beginning of birth and Goushen's midwifery skills, we could all have been burned at the stake for practicing witchcraft.

When I arrived two hours after the birth, mother and father were beaming with smiles and a sense of wonder, enchanted by their newborn son and the miracle in which they had been full participants. Goushen was helping my daughter to feel relaxed about breastfeeding, handling Sacha, the Russian nickname for Alexander, like a priest presiding over Holy Communion. I was witnessing that state of wholeness (health) in which wife, husband, infant, and midwife had "co-created" with God a grace-filled birth.

My daughter had received the best health care, representing a combination of modern science with traditional women's health practices. She was not alone in giving birth; her husband was with her, doing everything in his power to maker her feel safe and secure. The male doctor was not threatened by the skills of the midwives, and when the ancient practice of birthing was needed, he moved out of their way.

Everyone who was a part of the birth was respected and shared information, resources and love. It became, instantly, a team with a common goal that united their efforts in providing a healthy birth and a healthy mother and child. Jewish, Christian, and Hindu prayers were very much present during the miracle of birth. It was a time of God's grace, a holy space, a holistic event.

Such visions of wholeness are what we need as our guide for women's health care. As we study the issues from global and local perspectives, the definition of wholeness can be a lens through which we measure success and analyze problems.

In the industrialized countries the average lifetime risk for a woman of dying from pregnancy-related causes is between one in 4,000 and one in 10,000. In contrast, for a woman in the developing countries, the average risk is between one in 15 and one in 50. These countries commonly have maternal mortality rates 200 times higher than those of Europe and North America, the widest disparity in all public health statistics.

In 1984, the Pittsburgh (USA) Black Women's Health Network roused city public health authorities to action when it disseminated a report showing that the black infant mortality rate in the city was 29.7 for every 1,000 live births while the rate for white infants was 10.1. Much of the difference was attributable to socioeconomic facts, teenage pregnancies and inadequate prenatal care.

We cannot experience wholeness in societies that tolerate such imbalances such as men dominating women, humankind's domination of the environment, and one race dominating others. The balance of the masculine and feminine will happen when equal relationships are created. Women's full participation as healers of their own selves, their families, and communities is a basic human right and key to the restoration of God's wholeness.

When I gave birth to my daughter in 1963, my medical experience was very different from that of my daughter. It was dominated by a male doctor and male medical procedures. My experience was very lonely and, as a nurse in the health care profession, very disappointing. I did not receive the tender loving care that I knew was vital to health care and had personally given to so many others. I was given drugs and left alone to wait out my labor in a darkened room in a hospital. My husband had been banished to wait with other husbands while the doctor took total control over my birthing process.

Several years after I gave birth to my first child, the Boston Women's Health Book Collective sparked a movement that transformed women's health care in the United States. Before the publication of the well-known book, *Our Bodies, Ourselves* in 1969, practically no women's health information was easily available and the field of women's health care was dominated by men. How did this happen?

In 1484 the publication of the *Hammer of Witches* by two German Dominican monks, Heinrich Kramer and Jakob Sprenger, began the systematic destruction of women's health care by torturing and murdering women healers. Hundreds of thousands of women were murdered for practicing their time honored-skills as healers and as religious leaders. Healers were called witches and condemned to death by the laws of religion. This oppression lasted 500 years and was carried with colonialism to every corner of the earth.

It took a long time for women to reclaim their power as healers and to begin to share information, create health care centers, author health books, and create healing liturgies and rituals. The book *Our Bodies, Ourselves* and other resources helped throw off the 500 years of oppression and empowered us to reclaim our role as healers for ourselves and other women, body, mind, and soul. "Old wive's tales," a term used to denigrate women healers by the male medical system, are now being raised up as traditional women's health practices. The medical profession which had played a major role in defining women's morality now is viewed as an obstacle, and women are beginning to bring back traditional practices and incorporate them into the modern technology.

The United Nations NGO Forum in Huairou, China, with all of its logistical and weather problems, was a healthy place for women because we were equally valued and equally shared the resources. Penny Wise, an Anglican woman from Canada, observed that the forum was a place where women became the subjects and not the objects.

The forum created sacred space in which women's perspectives, ideas, talents, issues, programs, art, music, dance, and resources were given center stage. Women's self-esteem was nurtured and enhanced. We treated ourselves and one another with respect. We created women's space, which became a healthy environment for all people. Health was seen in the greater context, and sexism was seen connected to racism, classism, and all the other prejudices. Poverty was declared the most basic cause of ill health and early death in all societies.

No country fosters a healthy society such as existed briefly in Huairou. But 30,000 women now have this vision for a healthy society and have carried this dream to their homes with a commitment to make it happen around the world. Understanding the interconnectedness of the 12 issues and joining with others in carrying out action plans will begin the healing process not only for ourselves, but for everyone on the planet.

The following stories are about health care workers who follow the spirit and wording of the *Platform for Action* document by providing:

1. full attention to the promotion of mutually respectful and equitable gender relations, particularly in meeting the educational and service needs of adolescents; teaching girls and boys positive and responsible ways of dealing with their sexuality; educating about discrimination against girls, which often results from preference for sons; teaching nutrition and the value of breastfeeding, and providing equal access to nutrition and health-care services.

2. safe and effective family planning methods and emergency obstetric care; providing women with information and services that give them control of their own fertility with prevention of unwanted pregnancies given the highest priority; teach shared responsibility in caring for family members.

3. information and services that prevent and treat HIV/AIDS and other sexually transmitted diseases. Women represent half of all adults newly infected with HIV/AIDS and other sexually transmitted diseases. Unequal power relationships between women and men are obstacles to safe sex, and education and training in gender equality is essential.

4. gender sensitivity that gives women and girls respect and guarantees them privacy and confidentiality, including up-to-date women's health research, prevention of overmedicating, and education and services that meet the needs of older women and women with disabilities; information and training based on a holistic approach; acknowledging and encouraging beneficial traditional health care, especially that practiced by indigenous women, with a view to preserving and incorporating the value of traditional health care in services and research.

5. advocacy for local and national legislation that reaffirms the right to the highest attainable standards of health care for women and girls; support for health service systems that train women to become health-care providers, especially for women and girls.

6. prevention of sexual and gender-based violence against women and girls, including trafficking and other forms of abuse and sexual exploitation.

Community health care workers in rural Kenya

Several United States Episcopal women attending the United Nations End of the Decade Conference in Nairobi visited a community health care meeting held in a rural village in Kenya near the Ugandan border. I was among those women. Traveling by jeep we had to cross private farm land to reach the village because there were no public roads. As our Kenyan driver maneuvered us through a farmer's pasture, the family came out to have a look. Several small babies seeing our white faces and blond hair became very frightened and began to cry. Others waved and nodded approval as they knew we were on our way to an important village meeting. When we arrived in the village, the meeting was under way in a tent provided for this special occasion. Gathered were representatives from the town, health care workers, and a representative from the United Nations World Health Organization.

Measles was one of the major health problems in 1985, killing a child a day in most of the villages. The problem was not that they could not get the vaccine, but that they could not store it because it required refrigeration and many villages were without electricity.

The meeting discussed the serious problem of keeping health care workers. There was no problem in recruiting women. Many women volunteered, and after receiving the training to do basic health examinations and teach health care they were very successful. Village women and men trusted them and would bring their children and their elders. They were accessible to people in very rural areas. The women loved their work, but because no one was sharing their regular work of caring for their family, they were having to quit because of exhaustion.

African women must walk miles for water and firewood. They also plow and tend the fields, raise the children, and do all the marketing, cooking, and cleaning. Housework is a burden in itself but, combined with another full-time job, they could not work two jobs for very long, no matter how physically strong and enthusiastic they started out to be.

"Change will require not just the liberation of women, but also the liberation of men, in their thinking, attitudes and willingness to take a fairer share of responsibilities and workloads that women carry," observed John Wolfensohn, president of the World Bank.

During the lunch break, we were invited into a nearby home where we were served the most wonderful french fries that I have ever tasted, cooked on a wood-burning stove. We were served their traditional village drink composed of seven grains. The woman from the World Health Organization said that outside health experts had told them 20 years ago that this drink was not healthy. The village people believed the health experts, who preached on the need of protein that only came in the form of meat, fish, and cheese. Now the health experts are "drinking their words" as they appreciate the value of this most excellent source of protein. The UN document encourages the acknowledgment and encouragement of beneficial traditional health care, especially that practiced by indigenous women.

Years later I heard about a leadership program for men conducted by the Anglican Church in Kenya. It aimed at helping men take a fair share of women's workloads, deciding what work they could do while still maintaining their sense of manhood.

The International Labour Organization estimates that women put in two-thirds of the world's working hours. Women work, on average, one to three hours per day longer than the men in the same society. Women often do the heavy work, dirty work, monotonous, unpaid, or low-paid work.

When the work load is shared and women are compensated fairly for both their paid and their unpaid work, then a healthy environment will exist.

Keep traditional practices which heal and remove that which haunts us

When we look back at the history of the witch burnings in the fifteenth century, we can understand the influence of the church which inaugurated the persecution of all powerful women, the women healers, and ended with the deaths of millions of women and domination by men in health care. The 1484 *Malleus Maleficarum the Hammer of Witches* referred to earlier told about the evilness of women and states that "all wickedness is but little to the wickedness of a woman" and when a woman thinks alone, she thinks evil. "Witch midwives cause the greatest damage, either killing children or sacrilegiously offering them to devils."

Messages that denigrate and diminish women healers still prevail in our cultures which support practices that discriminate against midwives and women healers. We can give these messages a proper burial while we lift up positive messages of wholeness. Punitive insurance rates or unfair and expensive credentials are two actions we can prevent. We can become advocates for nurses, midwives and indigenous women's healing practices. We can become healers of our selves and form healthy communities in which healing takes place.

Vision for wholeness

This next story comes from the South Bronx in New York City. The

Childbearing Center of Morris Heights serves the inner-city poor. Jennifer Dohrn, its director, received start-up money from the Kellogg Foundation, the very same company responsible for the manufacture of cornflakes, which spends millions on young leaders and new enterprises that can make a difference.

When the center was open for business, it took a while to break down all the myths about midwives and mother and baby-friendly birthing centers. It took the birthing mothers' personal stories to convince others in the community to help spread the word. The birth mothers along with staff created a women's support group that served as the official Community Action Committee, who were to be the advisory group and decision makers of the center.

The Childbearing Center is connected to and supported by the Clinic, which provides health care for the South Bronx. Between these two health care services, women, men, and children are cared for from birth to death.

When Sister Heléna Marie and I went to visit the Childbearing Center, we met with Jennifer, the founder and director, and her staff. Jennifer's husband had been tragically killed in a traffic accident in South Africa just weeks before our visit. We did not expect her to be present to greet us, but her strength and the support of the women of the South Bronx sustained her in this difficult time. Just as Jennifer had guided these women—used to violent and unexpected deaths—into the acceptance of a natural way of childbearing, now they were holding her in love while she grieved, teaching her how to live with the loss of a loved one and to keep going. Every woman who enters this center is given love and respect. It offers the same high standard of health care that my daughter received in her hospital in Florida.

Holistic childbearing centers like these are the future. They will change unhealthy health care systems into living structures of health for the entire family. When they become available to all women in the United States and every country in the world, we will see the miracle of life-giving medical practices reducing mother and infant mortality and witness a maturing of educational opportunities for family planning.

Half a million women die each year from causes related to pregnancy and childbirth. Over half of all maternal deaths occur in South Asia. If women were able to have only the number of children they say they want, the number of births would fall by 35 percent in Latin America, 33 percent in Asia, and 17 percent in Africa. The number of deaths would decrease by at least one-fourth. The proportion of maternal deaths due to illegal abortion is 29 percent in Ethiopia, 64 percent in Bangladesh, 64 percent in Chile, and 86 percent in Romania.

Prenatal, natal, and postnatal care would greatly reduce unwanted pregnancy and wipe out the unnecessary childbirth-related diseases and deaths. Women's nutrition would improve, giving both girl and boy children the proper nutrition needed for good health. By the full participation of women as health care workers and integral partners in their own health and the care for others, malnutrition, disease, and environmental pollution could be drastically reduced.

We can become healers when we start to take our own health seriously, acknowledging that we are the experts of our bodies, mind, and souls. By working with both non-traditional and traditional health care experts, women are gaining important knowledge about women's health for themselves and for others. Living in the United States and employed full time, I have access to excellent health care facilities and resources. But if I were to lose my job I would be like the majority of the women in the United States, who do not have good health insurance. The goal of this issue is to have good health care information and services available to all women and girls throughout the world.

The Christian church is reviving its role in providing health ministry. The parish nurse is an ancient ministry and was an integral part of the early church, following Jesus' commission to preach, teach, and heal. Phoebe of Centura is mentioned in the sixteenth chapter of the Letter to the Romans as a professional nurse. Today there are thousands of parish nurses in the United States, often volunteering their time and skill, in almost every denomination.

Jean Denton is a Registered Nurse who serves as a health ministries consultant for the Episcopal Church. Her home parish is St. Paul's Episcopal Church in Indianapolis.

> Before the liturgy begins, I look over the congregation gathered to worship. They are wearing their Sunday best, giving the appearance that all is well with them and their worlds. As their parish nurse I know differently. For I have heard their stories. They have come to talk with me in the privacy of my office or home or over coffee in a local shop. Mostly it is the women who come. They say they seek me out because as a woman and a nurse, and as a vocational deacon, they can trust me. I am not an authority figure nor do I represent the hierarchy in a male-dominated institution. I am peripheral to

the system but in touch with it, and I speak its language.

They bring amazing stories. One woman recounts the domestic abuse she suffers at home in a 45-year marriage. Another tells of date rape and what it's like now to live with HIV. It is not uncommon for women to tell of the sexual exploitation they experienced in childhood. One speaks of the stunning agony of taking her teenager to have an abortion. Others share their fatigue and frustration in the dailiness of caring for elderly mothers. Another shares the angst of 'coming out of the closet' and integrating her sexuality into the rest of her life. Women come exasperated by juggling roles of breadwinner, housekeeper, and care giver. Single and married, they talk alike about the pressures of parenting, and the pain of finding they are doing no better jobs of raising their children than their parents did for them.

Addressing the health needs of the women of the church is a challenge that the church has preferred to ignore, being too often satisfied to address the rarefied issues of disembodied spirituality without recognizing that bodies (sexual bodies) are in need of salvation. The human trinity of mind, body and spirit is holy just as the Godhead is holy.

Health ministry within the local congregation is beginning to reconcile body with spirit and mind. Nurses often lead health ministries because of their awareness of both sickness and wellness issues. They are able to translate the jargon of the health care delivery system and to communicate with health care professionals. Seasoned nurses have a depth of experience that brings maturity of spirit, for they have been in the midst of death, crisis, poverty, violence, and suffering in their professional lives. Nurses have been hurt and have seen hurt and it is this above all that allows them to be healers.

A parish nurse knows how to listen actively to a parishioner's concerns and how to meet their needs. A parish nurse encourages. A parish nurse supports. She empowers others to find their voices and use them appropriately in the midst of health care crises. She gives information. She demystifies the system. She calls people to take action on their own behalf. She calls forth the Healer within each child of God, the source of all health and wholeness.

Perhaps most important is the role of a parish nurse as a spiritual friend, helping people explore where God is in the midst of their health or illness. She helps people to see that God looks for those vulnerable places in our lives, those cracks in our well-built walls where God can get a foothold and speak to us. Together with other spiritual resource people in the parish, a parish nurse creates containers for pain, liturgical containers of ritual, prayer, scripture, and the sacramental laying-on of hands or anointing with the oil of healing.

The parish nurse is bringing community health care that is free, accessible and holistic to people in the United States and the church is leading the way.

Health care information is available in books. The book *Our Bodies, Ourselves* has been revised several times and is one of the best books on women's health. Another one is *Women's Bodies, Women's Wisdom: Creating Physical and Emotional Health and Healing* by Christiane Northrup, a holistic physician and cofounder of a holistic health center, Women to Women.

After recognizing her own illness as a sign that her life was out of balance and that her medical practice was nurturing neither her own health nor her sense of being female, Christiane opened a center for women that is committed to improving women's health. Its credo is: "We are committed to living, creating, and enjoying health, balance, and freedom on all levels, personally and professionally, while providing educational and medical services which assist clients and patients in using their own power to create the same in their lives." She reconnects the split between the body, mind, and spirit so that we see ourselves as fields of energy with the ability to affect the quality of our own experience by getting in touch with our innate ability to heal ourselves. Because our bodies are influenced by our thoughts, it is very important that we change the negative thoughts we have about being female and create new images of health. "Hope, self-esteem, and education are the most important factors in creating health daily, no matter what our background or the state of our health in the past."

When hope, self-esteem and education are missing, women's bodies are given either by consent or by force to be used for pleasure by others. Unhealthy practices such as breast implants, foot binding, prostitution, female circumcision, bulemia and other eating disorders that cause extreme thinness deprive girls and women of their health. We can stop the misuse of women's bodies by passing laws that give women full equality and protection. We can help set up health care centers, write books and distribute information, provide classes and clinics, discussion groups and workshops. We can boycott products that have negative body images in their advertising. We can bring the parish nurse program to our community, start loving our own bodies, and teach other women and girls to love theirs.

Social structures are the problem

The next story comes from a woman prostitute whose life of mistreatment reflects unforgettable hardships. Her courage in becoming an advocate for prostitutes will, we hope, inspire a movement to stop the exploitation worldwide and to create healthy systems.

Maria da Gloria Rosa Miranda, well known in Brazil as Glorinha, was sold into prostitution when she was 11 years old. In 1992 she helped form an association for the rights of all women and founded the first Brazilian union for prostitutes. It took two years to have it officially recognized and in 1994 the union began working to stop child prostitution and fight for prostitutes rights. Following is her story:

> I lived with my family in Colatina till I was eight years old. My father worked as a clown in sales shops. He used to beat my mother when he was drunk and put beer bottles in my mother's vagina. He made us watch and prodded us to laugh at her. My father was kind to me and my brother, but the violence against my mother became intolerable and so my mother and the children ran away.
>
> We hid by a lake for three months, where we ate the vegetation, which consisted mostly of grass roots. We went to my grandmother's house but she did not want us. We worked in a rock quarry to pay for our food. The work was very difficult so my mother took us away and found work as a cook. I stayed home and took care of my two small brothers.

Glorinha spent most of her young life hungry and poor, and shifted from home to home. She learned to beg in the streets and her brother, when taken by the Children's Bureau, was taught how to assist with robberies. The mistress of one home in which she worked as a maid would hang her on a tree and beat her.

When she was 11 years old Glorinha ran away to Rio de Janeiro and lived in the parks.

One day I was found by a *cafetin*—a woman agent for prostitutes. This woman had a big car and was very well dressed. She took me to her apartment, bought me new clothes, and took me to the hairdresser. During Carnival she sold me to a Japanese man for $100,000 because I was an 11-year-old virgin, white, and had beautiful hair. I found out the amount of money because the woman told me she was buying a new apartment and a new car with this business.

Tanaka was 30 years old and a wealthy man who worked for a multinational company. He took me to live in Tokyo, Japan. When I was 13 I had twins. Because I was only a child myself, I did not know how to care for these babies and preferred to play with dolls that my husband had given me. I had two maids who took care of me and the children. When you are a Japanese wife you must always walk behind your husband, you can't eat as you please, you always have to smile and never complain.

When we returned to Brazil I had lovers, which Tanaka knew about and did not discourage. When Tanaka left to go back to Japan he took our children, whom I never saw again. I went to live with my lover. I lived with Laureci Lopes for 10 years and had six children. We both worked in a prostibulo in Vitoria. I worked in exotic dance and I only sold myself when we were out of money. In 1986, 180 women, most of them prostitutes, were killed. Nobody knows why and who did the killing, but everyone knows that big names and big money were behind it. Among those killed was a nine-year-old child named Araceli. All the women and girls had been physically abused before they were killed. I believe it was a group who did the killing, which included lots of savagery such as putting large wood objects in the women's vaginas. They were all abused before they were murdered. One woman was the godmother to my children. The last time I saw her was in a bar where we were waiting for our buses. She was happy because she had got good money for that night ($400) and it would help to build her house. She never got home. They found her 15 days later with three other prostitutes, including the money. They were murdered. Nobody saw, heard or knew anything. Laureci killed himself after this happened. In my heart I died with him.

Glorinha was one of the lucky ones to have been spared her life. A woman doctor helped her to send her children to school and together they started to denounce the conditions that prostitutes endure. It took two years to make the union for prostitutes official. Many people were against it. Her children were prosecuted because of her advocacy, and many times even the police have tried to kill her. She is now working in the tourist capitals of Brazil, trying to form prostitute associations all over the country. She educates people about the use of condoms and the prevention of AIDS and drug abuse.

Glorinha is one of the spokeswomen for the official union. Her life is in danger and she needs all the help she can get from women's organizations. She knows that the people who killed the girl and the other prostitutes are connected to two major prostibules in Vitoria. Two of them are judges. This is big business. It is very dangerous to become an advocate for human rights for women prostitutes. "I may be killed at any moment. I know too much."

If we organize we can stop all policies and actions that treat women's bodies as commodities; if we organize we can stop the violence and coercion of women and girls being used and abused for the sex industry. We can stop all advertising, all articles and other mass media messages that portray women's bodies as without minds or souls to be used for the pleasure of others. Otherwise women will continue to be abused, and sold into prostitution, and murdered.

New vision for wholeness

Feminist liberation theologian Mary Hunt states, "We push the conceptual horizons so that we shape what is beautiful, we name what is natural. This is a task for feminists in religion since we are responsible for molding foundational concepts and inviting belief. What better place to name the presence of the divine and to begin the work of justice than in our bodies, our beautiful bodies."

When I discovered that most women hated their bodies, we at Women in Mission and Ministry became intentional in addressing this problem. In our latest leadership program, the Creative Journey, we use most of the three-day intensive training to help expunge the negative body images and to create new ones that allow each woman to praise her body. Our goal is to see ourselves as whole and perfect beings (body, mind, and spirit), to recognize areas of disease and tension, and to celebrate healthy new images.

One of the ways we do this is by teaching dance so that women begin to experience body movement in many creative ways, all of which help them to express themselves physically, using the whole body to show anger, sorrow, joy and liberation. We provide body movement exercises that get in touch with hidden emotions and integrate feelings with thinking. We may be able to fool ourselves intellectually but the body does not lie. We teach one another how to listen to the body and to honor it.

The Creative Journey uses healthy rituals that cleanse those religious beliefs that give negative messages about women's bodies, such as the notion that women are unclean because of menstruation, and thus unfit for religious leadership. The negative messages are replaced by positive images of the ideal woman in an ideal world. Women are given the skills and the self-esteem needed to be transformational leaders, not leaders of the status quo, but healers of the old and change agents for a new church and society

When we become the experts of our own bodies, minds, and souls, and choose doctors, therapists, and ministers to be in partnership with our healing process, we honor the power within to heal ourselves.

Women are creating new rituals, prayers, songs, dances, images, stories, and information that bring health to body, mind, and soul. Women are re-imaging their bodies, mind, and spirit, as whole and constantly changing. It is exciting and healthy, it is the women's story for the new millennium, a health model for ourselves, our families, our community, and the world.

Resources

The Boston Women's Health Book Collective, *The New Our Bodies, Ourselves*, A Touchstone Book, Simon & Schuster Inc., 1992.

Christiane Northrup, M.D. *Women's Bodies, Women's Wisdom: Creating Physical and Emotional Health and Healing*. Bantam Books. 1994.

"Health Wisdom For Women" Newsletter, 1-800-804-0935.

Parish Nursing and Health Ministry contact:
    Health Ministries Association
    P.O. Box 7853
    Huntington Beach CA 92646
    1-800-852-5613

International Parish Nurse Resource Center
    205 West Touhy Avenue
    Suite 104
    Park Ridge IL 60068
    1-800-556-5368

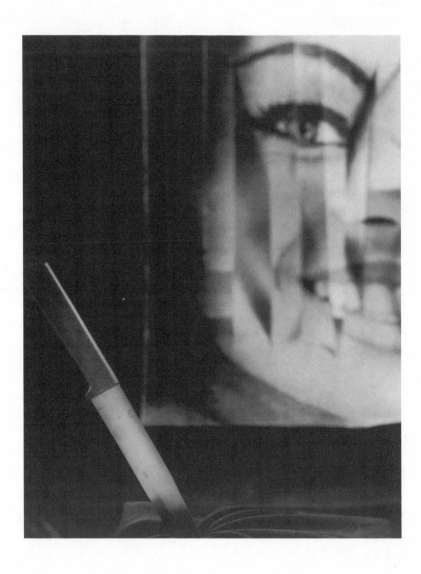

Violence Against Women

■ ■ ■ ■ ■ ■ ■ ■ ■ ■ ■ ■

Take integrated legal and social measures to prevent violence and protect women.

Adopt measures to eliminate trafficking in women and eradicate violence against women who are vulnerable, such as those with disabilities and migrant workers.

Study the causes of violence against women and effective measures of prevention.

Platform for Action

> Breast bruised, brains battered,
> Skin scarred, soul shattered,
> Can't scream, neighbors stare,
> Cry for help, no one's there.
>
> *From a poem by Nenna Nehru,*
> *a battered Indian woman*

Two men have struck me in my adult life, both times many years ago. I no longer remember the details, but I can still feel the physical pain on my face and neck. And I can still feel the humiliation, the shock and shame. I wasn't angry; I was almost embarrassed that I had become a victim of such fury, that I had known men who were capable of desecrating my personhood and changing my relationship with them. After the first incident I drove to my church (churches weren't locked in those years), went in, curled up on the floor, and spent the night. The second time I went into my room and didn't come out for two days.

In all societies, to a greater or lesser degree, women and girls are subject to physical, sexual and psychological abuse that cuts across lines of income, class and culture and takes place in both public and private life. Rape, sexual abuse, sexual harassment and intimidation are common conditions of the workplace just as systematic violence is integral to war. Sexual slavery, forced sexual acquiescence, sterilization, forced abortion, prenatal sex selection and female infanticide are also acts of violence that affect women; all such acts impair or nullify women's freedom and access to full human rights. Lack of sufficient preventive and protective laws and lack of effective enforcement by public authorities of existing laws only perpetuate violence against women.

Violence, of both natural and human origin, permeates our lives. We have little recourse in dealing with the violence of natural forces but what of personal violence, especially toward women and children?

A six-year-old boy in my city entered a neighbor's home and beat a month-old baby to death with a baseball bat in retaliation for what he deemed negative behavior on the part of the baby's parents. A Texas man raped a nine-month-old infant. Are we not outraged by such stories and are we not frightened because they seem to be becoming more commonplace in our society? It is true that all of us, especially women, are living in a time of terminal danger and terminal opportunity.

The *Platform for Action* recognizes the responsibility of governments to take action to eliminate violence against women. The United States response to that has been the allocation of $1.6 billion to fight violence against women, including domestic violence and sexual assault. A Presidential Memorandum has directed all federal agencies to educate their employees about violence against women. The Department of Justice held a post-NGO Forum campaign which included a Violence Against Women Information Fair and a subsequent Employee Awareness Campaign. The Advisory Council on Violence Against Women, co-chaired by Attorney General Janet Reno and Donna Shalala, United States Secretary of the Department of Health and Human Services, provides general policy advice for the implementation of the Violence Against Women Act. It also works to bring national attention to the problems of domestic violence and sexual assault.

There are more animal shelters than women's shelters in America, yet today women are determined to face the issue of domestic violence realistically, urgently and passionately.

Silence is something we learn

A friend told me she stayed with her abusive spouse because she "recognized that he grew up in a violent home and had a violent childhood." She said, "I thought I could change him." It is very difficult for a batterer to change. He doesn't want to give up power and control.

Silence is something we learn. Though our first instinct is to cry out for help or in anguish, we keep silent because we have been taught not to tell. We feel shame and don't want anybody else to know. The words, "I'm so sorry. I won't do it again" become the reason for staying with a violent spouse or friend. We desperately hope that things will be better.

In our silence we fail to name the problem. When we don't name it, we deny the connection between the people involved and our own responsibility. When a woman came to work with two black eyes, not one co-worker asked her what happened. When my sitter showed up one morning with a bruised and swollen face, I tried not to look at her or acknowledge that there was anything wrong about her appearance. I assumed she had been beaten by her husband. Later I learned she had had a wisdom tooth pulled the day before. This time I had come to the wrong conclusion, but still I wish I had acknowledged her pain and reached out to her.

As women we need to make a decision that domestic violence (upgraded since Beijing to "domestic terrorism") is not acceptable. We must speak out with conviction. Educating a complacent public and befriending victims of such violence must become our mission. When the TV film "The Burning Bed" was aired, thousands of women called in for help. Our stories, told in sincerity and truth, can ebb the tide of violence. When robbed, we willingly show police the spot where the TV used to be, but as victims of violence we have nothing to show except our damaged hearts, bodies, spirits.

In 1988 the *San Francisco Examiner* ran 24 stories on domestic violence. In 1995 the number was 298. Though the subject is no longer relegated to the back pages, there is the danger of consistent media distortion. Often this is done in subtle ways to favor the male perpetrator without giving any insight into the cause of the tragedy. For example, study the following headlines:

"COCKTAIL WAITRESS ASSAULTED BY FOOTBALL PLAYER"

"PROSTITUTE CHARGED IN CENTRAL PARK RAPE"

"VICTIM FILES SUIT FOR OFFICE PARTY HARASSMENT"

What words form negative images in your mind? "Prostitute"? "Cocktail waitress"? "Victim" rather than "Woman"? Reporters often use words inaccurately such as "lover's quarrel," "domestic dispute," or "date rape," words that imply a social faux pas rather than a violent act against a woman. News media even water down reports of child pornography, referring to it as "kiddie porn."

Women need to monitor the media and to educate journalists about issues of violence. Media need to know about the public policy initiative. In violence cases it is imperative that both parties involved be interviewed before the story is released.

As readers of newspapers and magazines and as viewers of television, we need to recognize our power and make it a duty to write and/or call the offending editors, TV channel managers or by-lined writers.

If the medium is indeed the message, we can become the messengers by counteracting corporate control. We can make our reply through informative brochures distributed by women's organizations. We can challenge ad agencies to produce posters or public service spots, ask newspapers to publish the name(s) of the perpetrators of violence, ask telephone directories to run a reference list in their Yellow Pages telling where help can be obtained. We can put domestic violence resources on the Internet, and ask for public service announcements on local TV and radio.

Three women die every day in the United States at the hands of violent men

Domestic violence is a global issue, occuring daily in homes, communities, throughout cultures, in all regions, classes, and religions. It leads to emotional, material, legal, and medical problems.

Often confined to the "privacy of the bedroom," domestic violence is literally invisible, difficult to observe and therefore readily trivialized. The ideal family is supposed to have internal mechanisms for coping with its problems, a supposition that makes it difficult for women to get outside help. Because women internalize fear, domestic violence restricts their freedom of movement and speech, undermines their dignity and abridges their rights.

"A chicken isn't a bird and a woman isn't a person"

On a cold, rainy morning, three women who had been part of the 200-woman Russian delegation to Beijing told a group of women crowded into the tiny office of The Global Fund for Women in Menlo Park, California, about the horror stories of battering and murder that were being called into crisis center hotlines in both St. Petersburg and Moscow. "Last year half the people murdered in Russia were women killed by their husbands," they said. "Only two percent of the battered women file charges with the police because in Russia the police 'wait for a corpse, then they investigate.'"

Yelena Potapova, Moscow hotline coordinator, quoted from *Domostroi*, a sixteenth-century Russian household guide, to give us some sense of historical precedence for domestic violence in Russia. The guide advised "caution with pregnant women and children so as to avoid damage to the stomach. Beat them only with a lash, in a careful and controlled way, albeit painfully and fearsomely." In everything from modern films to literature and colloquial expressions, Yelena said, "Family violence is as much a part of Russian culture as drinking tea with jam."

The St. Petersburg Center works six hours a day, five days a week, and receives more than 800 calls per week, mostly about domestic violence. Located in donated space in a local bank, the Center must close each day at 6 p.m. when the bank closes, but most violence takes place "after hours," so many calls are missed.

And the government is trying to close the Center down blaming it for "creating the problem that wasn't there until you people started the hot lines."

One Russian woman refused to take the counseling the police had suggested because "I was afraid my mother would find out." She wound up retreating into a shell, afraid of high buildings with elevators because the idea of rape in one haunted her. She ceased to enjoy sexual relations with her husband. "Women here are owned by men, and their power over women is unlimited," she said.

A St. Petersburg Crisis Center representative said, "We feel so negative about the new regime here, so isolated. People were not ready for freedom so they chose to return to communism. We need terribly to increase awareness of our self-esteem, responsibility, individuality. Eighty percent of our unemployed are women. Before perestroika there was no unemployment. Now women work as volunteers because they have no salaries."

Girls speak out: Stop feeling weak!

Following are excerpts from student responses to an art show at Berkeley High School, Berkeley, California. The title of the show: "Artists Against Violence Against Women."

As Latina/Chicana women, we need to overcome the machismo within our culture. Our partners must know that we are not animals, that we are human with feelings and most important, that we are women. You Chicana, Latina, White, Black, Asian women need to take action for yourselves. Stop feeling weak, stop feeling like you are nothing, that you are second-rate. Most important, stop the violence!

Males, stop beating your wife, girlfriend and children. Who gave you the right? Break the cycle, amigos! Machismo is the past. This is now. We need role models for our children. It is not right to show them how to hit women; that's not being a man.

Look at Mirala! Look at her pain! Look at her beauty that she carries. She should be respected. She needs the same love she gives to you, the same love with which she raises her children.

Look at us! We are Chicana, Latina women who have fought next to you, who have suffered and struggled next to you, who need the same things you do. Respect! Mujer... pick yourself up and rise! Hold your head high! Because you are a woman feel free to fly—spread your wings and reach the sky!

Then a Chinese woman said softly, "I am Selena Lee and I have been assaulted by my own father. I was beaten at a very young age and as I grew older, though the beatings subsided, still they were replaced by something more painful, something that did not heal in a few days. My father began to molest me. Incest is especially degrading in Chinese culture. Furthermore, my culture teaches me to keep my problems to myself, saying, 'Strength is within yourself.'"

She continued: "I will not call myself a victim of my father. We are both victims of a society that promotes violence and sexism in which women are supposed to be weak and men domineering and aggressive. The idea of men being the family leader is especially prominent in Asian families. My mother stood back and watched helplessly as my father wreaked havoc in our lives."

A sign of changing times

In 1996, Shanghai opened its first shelter for battered women. The Nnanfang Family Violence Protection Center is a collection of spartan rooms in a bare concrete building on the outskirts of the city. It offers 20 beds and a friendly but untrained staff. The privately sponsored (not government) center was made possible by a gift of $60,000 from Zhijing Baoye Ltd.

China Women's News reports that family violence is behind one-fourth of the nation's divorces which topped one million in 1995. Though China's constitution specifically bans the mistreatment of women, a new regulation in the city of Changsha in Hunan Province instructs the police to respond to complaints of wife beating thoroughly and sympathetically.

Mr. Zhang, the entrepreneur responsible for the gift to the center, said he got the idea for it when he read in the newspaper that among failed attempts by women to commit suicide by jumping off the Juangpu River Bridge in Shanghai, two-thirds cited unbearable family troubles as the motivation.

Most women who come to the Center say they have been beaten repeatedly. For example, Yin Jianqin, reported that she suffered violence at her husband's hands throughout her 15-year "arranged" marriage. "I tried to leave but my family and neighbors always urged me to go back." She found the women at the Center giving her a different kind of encouragement. "They say it's my decision what I do."

From a story by Seth Faison,
The New York Times, May 3, 1996

The constant anti-woman subtext

Marina Mahathir, daughter of Malaysia's Prime Minister, has spoken out against the "constant anti-woman subtext." In her country some religious leaders say females should not shake hands with a man who is not a relative. An article in Utusan Malaysia says, "If a man jostles with pigs smeared with earth and foul-smelling mud, it is still better than with women not allowed for him."

Better late than never, Malaysia's Domestic Violence Act finally took effect June 1996, two years after it was passed and nine years after women's groups began campaigning for laws against wife beating. But the legislation is not all the women hoped for: it does not make wife or child beating a crime. The crime is in disobeying a cease-and-desist order, and though it carries a fine of $2,000 and a two-year prison sentence, a repeat offender could spend just three days in jail.

In spite of the newspaper's comparison between women and pigs, women in Malaysia's diplomatic service shake hands with foreign guests. But women's groups, sensitive to the statistics—39 percent of Malaysian women are abused in a year—are tired of the stalling on protection.

From a story by Lewis Dolinsky,
San Francisco Chronicle, May 15, 1996

Church authority: "Don't wash dirty linens in public"

A woman judge in the Philippines advised victims when confronted with "it" during a rape incident—BITE IT OFF!

During a church convention in the Philippines, Episcopal Churchwomen presented a solidarity statement in support of a 14-year-old who was raped by a former mayor. The female presenter was known to be separated from her husband, who had taken another wife. The church representative verbally castigated her, telling her "not to wash her dirty linens in public." In this case the church gave more weight to her predicament as an abandoned wife than to her solidarity statement.

The Church position in the rape incident was to forge an amicable settlement under the guise of pastoral reconciliation. Episcopal Churchwomen of the Philippines believe that the church loses sight of the fact that reconciliation does not cancel the violation done. As reported in *Forward*, magazine of the Women in the Development Program, reconciliation is good for the rapist, but what about the victim who carries the feeling of "unpeace" throughout her life? Can the church say later that after an out-of-court settlement peace will reign? In her young age of 14 the rape victim cannot even seek solid support from the church. While the law metes out the death penalty to rapists, the church opts for amicable resolutions. Las Amigas, a team of friends of *Forward* readers, has an alternative resolution—castration!

A grandmother's crusade

Charlotte Boatwright, a Chattanooga, Tennessee mother, was fed up with her daughter's abusive marital relationship. Refusing to believe the excuse of overwork from law enforcement officials, Boatwright independently sought out other violence victims and heard innumerable stories about courts that "revictimized" the victim and rewarded the abuser.

Boatwright's mission led to the formation of the Domestic Violence Coalition of Greater Chattanooga, an organization consisting of law enforcement officials, social workers, attorneys, physicians, concerned citizens, and abuse victims. Through education, legislation, and coordination with social service agencies, the Coalition seeks to reduce the incidence of domestic violence.

There may still be states in the United States that continue the "rule of thumb law" which allows a man "to beat his wife with a stick no bigger than his thumb" but organizations like Boatwright's will keep the numbers down. She encourages other communities to tackle the task, even in the face of opposition and resistance.

From an article by Alice Clayton, editor,
The East Tennessee Episcopalian

What costs $29.95 and says "no way, O.J."?

Nobody at the Riley Center for Battered Women and Their Children in San Francisco could figure out why they kept getting checks for $29.95. The money was certainly welcome at the Center which, because of limited space, has to turn away four out of every five women applying to its two safe houses. Still, why $29.95?

Then a letter came from a woman in a San Francisco law firm: "In lieu of purchasing the O.J. Simpson tape, enclosed please find checks in the amount of the video's price from the following people..."

The unique crusade started with the Massachusetts Chapter of the National Coalition Against Domestic Violence, and is growing nationwide. People like Jennifer Grant, director of the Riley Center, would like to see it catch on big time.

The Nicole Brown Simpson Charitable Foundation, established by Denise Brown following the murder of her sister, is committed to stopping domestic violence through educational outreach to schools as well as personal counseling. It is doing commendable work

throughout the United States.
From an article by Stephanie Salter,
San Francisco Examiner

Boy meets girl, boy marries girl, boy beats girl
Moscow Times

An American woman named Lisa Hoffman recently returned from Russia, having served as a partner in their tiny feminist movement. She has spent the past few years assisting Russian women leaders in evaluating and designing effective strategies in dealing with problems of violence against women and children. Hoffman points out that there is still no word for "battering" or "batterer" in the Russian language. Consequently battering is generally not seen as such; it is simply the way one lives. Hoffman and the new Russian Association of Crisis Centers for Women (RACCW) hope that society will finally acknowledge this enormous social problem and thus will begin to change. The Association's research Project Team has begun surveying young people on their views about violence and interviewing battered women and rape survivors. The Association is conducting nationwide training as well as collecting, writing, adapting, and publishing helpful materials. It has also begun to lobby on a national level for legislative change and increased government and police accountability.

Hoffman describes her role as a foreigner as a very delicate one. She says that there is a fine line between wanting to help and imposing her own cultural values. "Americans can't assume that the way we have done things in the West is the best way in other countries. At the same time there is a certain universalism when one talks about human rights abuses on a global level; it becomes obvious that the problem must be addressed internationally. Westerners, in partnership with their sisters around the world, must support the work of the Russian crisis center." Hoffman recalls that in Beijing white American women often dominated workshop discussions and failed to hear what activists from other countries were saying.

Among questions asked by the Project Team were some concerning power and control in romantic relationships. "Is there such a thing as equality in your relationship? How does that work?" In one prison in the Urals region, team members interviewed several women who had killed their husbands in self-defense after years of abuse. One woman had been married to her batterer for 18 years. The abuse started early in the relationship. On her wedding day she had a black eye and a broken arm. For many of these women, it was their first chance to talk about the violence in their lives.

The RACCW centers are getting increasing press coverage and are part of a growing social movement in Russia. Still there are serious impediments: the draft law, developed this year on family violence, does not acknowledge that violence in marriage or in intimate relationships is a crime; the government has identified nonprofit women's crisis centers as a potential threat to their authority and is considering a licensing procedure for the centers. This would make it difficult for the small struggling centers to survive. Still, Hoffman notes, the movement will keep going in one form or another.

In the early 1990s there were no crisis hotlines in Russia; today there are 14. Still there are no shelters in spite of the attempts of many groups to establish them. Leaders of the crisis center are trying to educate lawyers on existing laws and survivors' rights, in order to change the currently entrenched position of many lawyers who assume that the battered woman or rape victim provoked the abuse. Alhough there is a general law against "hooliganism" which applies if one is mugged on the street, the police will do nothing in the case of a husband beating a wife in their home.

Hospital personnel are no better than police and there is no medical protocol for treatment and reporting of domestic abuse in Russia, Hoffman says. Women often won't report a rape or seek medical attention because of the hassle involved in getting a medical exam. Hoffman cites lack of accountability on the part of police, medical personnel, lawyers and legislators. Although there is a law against marital rape, the term is often considered an oxymoron.

Though the members of the Association are frequently asked if they personally have been raped or battered, Hoffman sees that as irrelevant because "any one of us could be raped or battered simply because we are women."

Many Russians describe their society as matriarchal because women do everything—they work in factories, take care of households, raise children, do the shopping. The impression is that women are in charge, says Hoffman. If this is the case, why the battering? Why do women have so little political influence? The truth is that women have all the burdens but, for all their work, receive very little respect.

Breaking the silence

An editorial in the *International Family Network* newsletter states: "Violence against women represents a hidden obstacle to economic and social development. By sapping women's energy, undermining their confidence, and compromising their health, gender violence deprives society of women's full participation. At the Beijing Conference, the plight of millions of women was made more visible and a new imperative was identified—" rethinking the role of men and women must be considered a major challenge for this generation. Centuries-old patriarchal systems based on dominance and subordination are finally being questioned. "Let us break the silence of violence against women—in our prayer, in our preaching, in our practice. Let us proclaim the story of women coming out of the shadows." (Ballycastle Declaration, World Council of Churches/Conference of European Churches Consultation)

For the blood of women

- Raped
- Sexually abused
- Imprisoned
- Molested as children
- Subjected to starvation
- Beaten
- Victims of war

Tie a red thread around your wrist

- to give visibility to what is often the only tie that binds women together worldwide—their silent, solitary suffering in the face of violence

- to insist this suffering must cease in our homes, churches, workplaces, world, streets

- to symbolize the blood of Christ, which ties us together in suffering and hope

Tell a story

Tell your story… tell another's story… but tell others NOW

AND DO SOMETHING TO HELP END THE BLOODSHED!

It was only a spanking

When my first grandchild was four years old, she was given her first (and only) spanking, actually just a whack on her backside. It surprised her parents almost as much as it did Lauren who, through her heart-broken sobs asked, "Whaaat waas THAT?" She was immediately gathered up into her mother's arms and reassured. Now my grandchildren, instead of being disciplined physically, are sent to their rooms until they feel they are ready to rejoin the family. We need to educate children so that they do not grow up in violent households, either as witnesses or victims. Boys need to know that it's okay not to live out a model of violence, even if that's what they see on a daily basis.

"Hands are for hugging... hands are for holding."

Resources for violence against women

Lisa Hoffman, 1480 Guerrero, San Francisco, CA 94110

Platform for Action, Section 4

National Council of Churches of Christ Commission on Family Ministries and Human Sexuality

Dutch Human Rights Reform

The Moscow Times

A Window Between Two Worlds, December 1995

Russian Association of Crisis Centers for Women (Research, Education and Advocacy Project)

Lora De Young, Teenage Abuse Counselor

Bonnie Campell, Department of Justice (202) 616-8894

International Anglican Family Network, Lent 1996

Action Guide for Girls' Education, San Francisco Bay Area Girls' Education Network, 1995

Human Rights

Sister Heléna Marie

■ ■ ■ ■ ■ ■ ■ ■ ■ ■ ■ ■ ■

The World Conference on Human Rights [in Vienna, 1993]
reaffirmed clearly that the human rights of women throughout the life cycle are an inalienable, integral and indivisible
part of universal human rights.

The International Conference on Population and
Development [in Cairo, 1994] reaffirmed women's reproductive rights and the right to development.

Both the Declaration of the Rights of the Child and the
Convention on the Rights of the Child guarantee children's
rights and uphold the principle of non-discrimination on the
grounds of gender.

Platform for Action

Our bags were packed and our tickets to Lhasa were issued. We were
celebrating our last night in Beijing when we got the word: "You can't
go to Tibet."

There we were, the four of us—Ann, Nancy, Lucy and I—ready
to be joined by nine other women who were to accompany us for a
women-to-women exchange in Tibet. Now at the last minute "go"
had suddenly become "no go."

The official explanation was that our visas were for the NGO
Forum only. No one acknowledged that some of us had regular tourist
visas. We were forced to accept our liaison officer's unofficial view; we
couldn't go because we had participated in the NGO Forum and were
therefore considered to be political dissidents. This reasoning was

strengthened four weeks later, when another group who had not attended the NGO Forum but were sponsored by the same tour operator and led by the same guide entered Tibet with no problems at all.

Some of our women were actually relieved. "I didn't really relish the thought of ending up in a Chinese prison in Tibet," said one. We were all very sharply mindful of the repressive measures taken by Chinese officials at the forum as well as of China's history of human rights abuses.

Others, like myself, were deeply disappointed. As a nun in a habit, I had wanted to stand in solidarity with my sisters, the Tibetan Buddhist nuns, who are being singled out with Buddhist monks for arrest, torture, imprisonment, and even execution.

Why this treatment? Because the nuns and monks wish to practice their traditional religion, which includes allegiance to their spiritual and temporal leader, His Holiness the Dalai Lama. They are speaking out for the free and independent Tibet that existed until the illegal invasion and occupation by the People's Republic of China in 1949. They are objecting to Chinese treatment of Tibetan women, which includes forced abortions and sterilizations.

"Women's rights are human rights" echoed throughout the NGO Forum and the UN conference, from blocks-long banners, to Hillary Clinton's addresses, to the forum and conference. This chapter focuses on some of the worst gender-specific human rights abuses suffered by women and girls today. Much of the following material is difficult and graphic.

A myth: freedom of religion in Tibet

One of the human rights violations most talked about at the NGP forum was China's treatment of Tibet. Although China attempted to cover the real facts with its official version of their occupation, none of us was impressed, particularly because we knew that almost all of the Tibetan women-in-exile who submitted applications to the forum and conference had been denied visas by the Chinese government.

What is it that the Chinese officials did not want 13 church women to see in Tibet?

More than 6,000 monasteries and nunneries in Tibet have been destroyed by the People's Army of China. A mere handful remain. Buddhist teachings have been systematically suppressed. Thousands of nuns and monks have been killed; many more are in prison for expressing the basic tenets of their faith. Both monks and nuns have experienced torture in prison; many of the human rights abuses suffered by the nuns are gender-specific. They have been reported over the last four decades with striking consistency and are in serious violation of international law.

In prison the nuns are brutally tortured and sexually abused. They are attacked by dogs and hung from their thumbs. Electric cattle prods are used on the most sensitive parts of their bodies. All are told to renounce their religion and their desire for an independent country. Few do.

The international community has not been allowed access to Tibet's prisons, but extensive interviews of nuns who have escaped into exile describe the abuses. A nun who was arrested after the uprising in Lhasa in 1987 reports:

> We each individually, and as a group, understood ourselves to be doing something for the people of Tibet... and we each were willing to suffer even death at the hands of the Chinese if it came to that. We made leaflets saying that Tibet is a free country, that China should leave Tibet and so forth. We decided to make the demonstration at 12 o'clock, when we thought most people would be at the temple. We were able to go around the Barkhor two times before finally we were all arrested and taken off to Gutsa prison. Each of us had two guards.
>
> When we arrived we were photographed and taken to an interrogation center... I was stripped naked and made to lie face down on a cold concrete floor. They beat me with a rope and stick and with an electric prod. They beat me as I lay fully stretched out on the floor. I thought at that time that I was about to die. The picture of Guru Rinpoche [a spiritual leader] appeared before my eyes and then I fainted. In order to make me come to they threw cold water on me. They were very insulting. They squeezed my breasts saying that there was much milk in them; that I was no nun; that I had at least two children already. They said that I was having sexual relations with the monks and that is why we were demonstrating together. I said that I was a nun. They pushed a stick in my vagina again and again hurting me so much that for three days I could not urinate. One of the guards pushed an electric cattle prod into my anus and left it

there. It was a pain that came into my heart and was unbearable. I fell unconscious.

This and subsequent quotes from Tibetan nuns are from *"Denial of Tibetan Women's Rights to Freedom of Religious Belief and Expression,"* published by the International Committee of Lawyers for Tibet, San Francisco, March 1, 1995

Another nun reports:

They threw us into the truck, like so many stones, and took us to prison, twisting our arms behind us. They took away our belts and body-searched us. Then they beat us and chained us to the wall. Later they stripped us and used electric cattle prods all over our bodies, several men at a time—on our eyes, mouth, vagina, everywhere. They used those cattle prods as though they were toys, enjoying themselves, especially when they applied them to our private parts... They actually laughed and joked among themselves while they were doing these things. "You are not nuns," they told us, "you are just garbage." They never called us by our names, but made us answer to names like pig, horse, donkey, and so on. They laid us down on the ground and stripped us and beat us. Sometimes they would trample our hands with iron-tipped boots. They kicked us in the face and stomach. Buckets full of urine were put on our heads while the guards roared with laughter as the urine and excrement poured down our face and bodies. *(ibid)*

Nuns have also been singled out for solitary confinement, a treatment usually reserved for special high-level cases. The extreme abuse of nuns is demonstrated by an anonymous description of the arrest of eight nuns after a peaceful demonstration at the Norbulingka Palace in Lhasa in 1989:

D.L. was treated very badly. In the jeep on the way to the police station a Chinese PSB agent cut off one of her nipples and almost severed one of her toes. She showed me the scars when I met her in Gutsa. The reason that she was treated so badly is probably that she was driven to the police station by Chinese PSB agents. There was not one single Tibetan among them. Apparently there was some language misunderstanding and a Chinese policeman got angry with her and attacked her with a pair of scissors... The eight of us were put in separate cells. I did not get anything to eat or drink until the next morning. For three days I had to sleep on the bare concrete. Two days after the initial interrogation I was called again. They asked the same questions and got so angry when I didn't confess that they hit me on the head with a chair. Again I was given electric shocks. The shocks on my gums and lips were particularly painful. (ibid)

During the interrogation, D.L. was made to stand for a long time while bleeding heavily. She was released in 1992 and was not allowed to return to her nunnery at Chusang. She did not have enough money to go back to her relatives in Markham. At present she is working as a nanny in Lhasa.

A Tibetan nun interviewed in India reports:

We had to empty out toilets with our bare hands and collect the feces. These toilets were all inside the prison compound. Sometimes we could wash our hands, but we were not given any soap. Many times we were sent back to our cells without being able to wash our hands. Every day we had to collect two buckets of feces and carry them to the prison farm. (ibid)

Is it any wonder, then, that Chinese officials denied us entry into Tibet, knowing that we had been participating in a conference advocating human rights for all people? Hearing the news that we had been denied entrance, I was angry that the Chinese government had taken away my opportunity to stand, in person, with my sisters in Tibet.

Yet, the Chinese government also *gave* us something: an even more impassioned desire to speak out and tell the world, "Look what's happening in Tibet!" The fact that we were forbidden to go made it instantly obvious that Tibetan liberation is not the success that China wants the world to believe.

Instead of visiting Tibet, we flew to Nepal where we met with Tibetans in exile who were not afraid to give the unofficial version of the "liberation" of Tibet: 1.2 million Tibetans have died as a result of the invasion and occupation. This is one-fifth of all Tibetans.

At refugee camps we heard more about sufferings, imprisonments, and daring escapes over the treacherous Himalayas into Nepal. The refugees were eager to hear from us how the plight of Tibetans had been presented at the NGO Forum. They were disappointed, but not surprised, to learn that the only version of the facts allowed at the forum was the Chinese one. The Tibetan Tent at the forum had been staffed by what the Tibetans call "GONGO" (government-organized non-governmental organizations; that is, women from Tibet who were forced to hand out the official propaganda).

At one point in the Forum, however, six Tibetans-in-exile, who somehow managed to obtain visas, presented a workshop that included an amateur video showing what has gone on inside Tibet. The video was suddenly seized by one of the ever-present Chinese officials, and then just as suddenly reseized by a woman in the audience who passed it on until it was safely smuggled out in someone's backpack.

"You tell the world what's really happening in Tibet," implored the refugees in the camp in Nepal. And so we are.

A coin that has two sides

Our mission included reporting what is happening to Tibetan women in the area of reproduction. The *Platform for Action* is clear that one of the basic human rights for women is the right to reproductive freedom. It is a coin with two sides. On the one hand, women must have the freedom to choose the number and spacing of their children, and be given access to birth control measures and, if necessary, abortion. On the other hand, women must have the freedom to be able to bring a pregnancy to term. In Tibet, this second freedom does not exist.

The Chinese government is striking at the very root of the Tibetan population with a family-planning policy that allows only one child each to urban Tibetan women. In some smaller villages women are permitted two children each. Women who exceed these limits are severely penalized.

A pregnant woman who is about to exceed the limit is required to have an abortion and sterilization. If such a woman gives birth, she is fined an exorbitant amount of money, and the child is denied a ration card, for school attendance and medical care. That child will never be able to work at any government job, nor will s/he be able to inherit property.

Mobile family-planning units travel the length and breadth of Tibet, performing abortions and sterilizations on many (if not most) of the village women. Many women are sterilized automatically, without their consent, either when they give birth or during an abortion. The perpetuation of an entire ethnic group is thus being engineered for extinction.

One Tibetan woman, C., from Amdo, escaped Tibet in 1993 and was interviewed in Dharamsala, India, on April 18, 1994. Her story follows:

> When I was pregnant with my third child, Chinese officials came to my house many times to convince me to have an abortion. They told me that it was not allowed to have a third child and that I should go to the hospital when I was about five months pregnant to have an abortion injection. I became very frightened and decided to leave home until the baby was due. I was afraid I would be forced to have an abortion if I stayed at home. I went to stay with my mother in another village. During the months I stayed with my mother the officials who had told me to get an abortion came to my home about ten times. They asked my husband where I was. When he said that he didn't know where I was they slapped him in the face, kicked him and beat him with sticks. They threatened to arrest him if he didn't tell them where I was and if I didn't turn up. They carried pistols and hand cuffs.
>
> When the baby was due I went home. About one month after the delivery the officials came to my house again and threatened that they would take away all our possessions and arrest my husband... I was given an injection in my spine. It was meant to anesthetize me, but in fact I could feel exactly what the doctors were doing [they were preparing to sterilize her]. The operation was very painful.
>
> There were four beds in the surgery room. I saw with my own eyes how they injected pregnant women with very long needles. They injected the head of the baby with some kind of poison. Later these women had miscarriages in the hospital. I saw many fetuses in the toilets. I saw how they were eaten by dogs. The parents weren't allowed to keep the fetus unless they paid the medical bill for the operation.
>
> From *"Denial of Tibetan Women's Right to Reproductive Freedom,"* published by International Committee of Lawyers of Tibet, San Francisco, March 10, 1995

Many Tibetan women are subjected to abortions without their knowledge. Pregnant women are encouraged to go to clinics for medical purposes, related or unrelated to their pregnancy, and then are given injections without being told the purpose of the injection—to induce abortion. Abortions are often followed by sterilization operations, also performed without informed consent. There are also reports of hospitals where, at the time of birth, lethal ethanol is injected into the baby's head, causing a stillborn birth. In other cases the mothers hear their healthy newborns cry, but within minutes the infant is injected with ethanol in the fontanel (soft spot on the head), which results in immediate death.

Report... or else!

Since most of Tibet's population lives in rural villages too small to support a hospital, the People's Republic of China has established mobile birth control teams that go from village to village to carry out the family-planning programs. Large numbers of women are operated on in a very short period of time. The use of force has been reported. Two Buddhist monks, Ngawang Smanla and Tsewan Thondon, witnessed a Chinese mobile birth control team that had set up its tent next to the monks' monastery in Amdo in 1987.

> The villagers were informed that all women had to report to the tent for abortions and sterilizations or there would be grave consequences. For the women who went peacefully to the tents... medical care was given [following surgery]. The women who refused to go were taken by force, operated on, and given no medical care. Women nine months pregnant had their babies taken out...We saw many girls crying, heard their screams as they waited for their turn to go into the tent, and saw the growing pile of fetuses build outside the tent, which smelled horrible. During the two weeks of this mobilization, all pregnant women were given abortions, followed by sterilization, and every woman of childbearing age was sterilized.
> Testimony of Dr. Blake Kerr to the United States
> Congress, 135 Cong. Rec. H448-49 daily ed. Feb. 28, 1989

These human rights violations are all the more grievous because Tibet, unlike mainland China, does not have a population problem. On the contrary Tibet has always been sparsely populated, and a significant percentage of the population is celibate due to the religious vows taken by monks and nuns.

In the People's Republic of China itself, women are allowed one child each. There is much prejudice against girl children. Pregnant women often undergo medical testing to determine the baby's gender. If the fetus is female, many women elect to abort (although it is also possible that this choice is made at the urging of their husbands). An echo of the genocide in Tibet is femicide in China.

Children have rights, too

We move now, as we did after the NGO Forum, from China, over the Himalayas, to Nepal. During the two weeks we spent in Nepal we travelled often by van or bus.

As we rode along dusty mountain roads we saw hundreds of women and children sitting by the roadside. They were pounding rocks with little hammers, making gravel from larger stones. They sat on their haunches in the merciless heat of direct sunlight, pounding rocks from dawn until dusk. Dust from the constant stream of trucks and buses swirled around them. So many children lined the roads that the sounds of their hammers hitting rock sounded like a sad percussion orchestra ringing out a symphony of despair.

Most of this poorly paid work falls to the lot of women and girls because the boys and men are engaged in the higher paid work of breaking large boulders into rocks of usable size. Breaking the smaller rocks into gravel is the bottom rung of the manual labor ladder, earning the workers approximately 35 cents (United States) for a day's effort.

Mainya is a Nepali teenager whose family moved to the capital city, Kathmandu, when she was four years old. Four years later, her father left to work with a timber company in the mountains, and she and her mother and younger brother went to work at the quarry.

At 17 Mainya has now worked at the quarry for nine years. She works 12 hours a day breaking rocks. Work is not regular, so they are often anxious. Sometimes they are lucky enough to be taken to the building site, where they can earn more (approximately $1.00 to $1.20).

Mainya's only recreation is an outing to the cinema now and then; her only luxury is an occasional cigarette. "My back aches and I injure myself in some way almost everyday. But it's no problem, really—I can 'digest' all that," she says with a smile.

Mainya and her family live in a small shack by the site. She was once admitted to school, when her father was still with them. She had to leave, however, when her father got an "eye sickness"—probably an injury caused by a rock fragment—and was laid off. So Mainya, then hardly eight years old, had to start work. Now she says she doesn't want to go to school. "What good is schooling for the likes of me?" she asks. (The story of Mainya and her family is based on a report in "CWIN, Voice of Child Workers," No. 9, 1990, Nepal.)

Over 200 million children worldwide under the age of 14 are working full time and not going to school, human rights experts estimate. Fourteen is the minimum age set by the International Labor Organization.

Although many of these children work to produce goods for local consumption, an increasing number are working to make products for gigantic multinational corporations to export to countries of affluence. In addition to sweatshops around the world for popular United States garment labels, children work in factories in China and Thailand making toys, in orange groves in Brazil turning juice into the concentrate which is found in Western supermarkets, and in Indonesia in assembly lines making $100 basketball shoes.

Sydney Shanberg and Marie Dorigny, a journalist/photographer team, traveled in Pakistan and India in 1995 visiting factories that use child labor, and subsequently wrote a report for *Life Magazine* ("Six Cents an Hour," June 1996). They went to carpet factories where children work in fly-infested shacks, 13 hours a day, six days a week, tying knots, cutting yarn, and pounding shuttles, making only six cents an hour—if they are paid at all.

They visited stitching sheds where, under similar conditions, children stitch hides for soccer balls that eventually bear the names "Nike," "Sublime," and others equally popular in retail stores. In some villages they found children sharpening scissors and surgical instruments for export to the United States. These children sat all day on concrete floors, inhaling metal dust as they bent over anvils.

Often children serve as bonded slaves, owned by the factory managers. The owner of one factory offered to sell 100 children to Sydney, who posed as a potential buyer. His asking price was less than $200 each. Parents had sold their own children for less than $15 each. Most of the children were illiterate; many have been beaten in the workplace for simple offenses such as making a wrong knot or asking to go to the bathroom. Some have been branded or blinded by their owners.

One of Marie's photos shows Silgi, a three-year-old girl, sitting on a mud floor in a Delhi shack. Her dress is filthy. She is stitching soccer balls with a needle that is longer than her fingers. Amazingly, reported Marie and Sydney, her stitching was more than adequate, but she couldn't yet handle a pair of scissors to cut the thread. Her older sister had to do that for her. The soccer balls she was stitching were to be sent to Los Angeles, bearing the name "Super."

Children who have been liberated by a human rights group, South Asian Coalition on Child Servitude, told the reporters of being beaten regularly by their owners, and of being slashed, branded, and tortured for crying for their parents. The Coalition has liberated some 29,000 children as of June 1996. Another 30,000 have been freed in Pakistan by another human rights organization called the Bonded Labor Liberation Front (BLIF). Primary schools have been started by these organizations so that the children can eventually have other options besides the sweatshops. Still, the owners, factories, and multinational corporations who contract for child labor remain unpunished.

Sex trafficking of girls: a major international industry

The human rights of millions of young Asians, especially girls, are being blatantly violated through a thriving business of international child sex trafficking. Girls are being sold by their families—or are kidnapped outright—and sold into brothels. Parents are often led to believe that their girls will be taken to another city or country to get a respectable job that will provide much-needed income for the families. But the girls are instead sold to brothels and forced to become prostitutes. Once this becomes known to the family the girls are sometimes disowned by the very people who placed them in this position.

Other families knowingly sell their girl children into prostitution. The district of Sindhupalchowk in Nepal, for example, is noted for having houses with tin roofs. Too expensive for a typical village family to buy, a tin roof generally indicates that a daughter in the household has been sold to a brothel.

Sindhupalchowk has become a market center for the illicit trading of girls to Indian brothels. The Child Workers in Nepal Concerned Center in Kathmandu reports that Sindhupalchowk supplies 5,000 to 7,000 girls a year to India. "The trading in girls is so commonplace that in many villages parents willingly send their daughter 'to Bombay' and the family with no daughter is disappointed."

"Voice of Child Workers," No. 23, October 1994, Nepal

When these young girls have outlived their usefulness in the broth-els—usually around the age of 30—or when they have contracted AIDS, they are sent back home to their families.

At the NGO Forum there were a number of Nepali NGOs who are working actively to eliminate child sex trafficking. One of these groups created a film shown at the forum called "Under the Tin Roof." It is based on true stories of young girls who have been swept into this trade by unscrupulous profiteers. Following is my synopsis of this very moving film.

Ten-year-old Batuli had grown up in Melamchi in Eastern Nepal. Batuli and her family lived in a straw-roofed mud hut which leaked throughout the four-month monsoon season. They dreamed of the day they could save enough money to buy a tin roof which wouldn't leak. Somehow the dream was always beyond their reach.

Every day Batuli worked in the fields picking tea leaves. It was hard work for little pay, but it supplemented the family income.

One day, as Batuli worked among the tea bushes she was approached by a man from a nearby village. Raul offered to take her to a big city in India where he would find her a respectable, well-pay-ing job. She would be taken care of, he said, by rich women who would provide her with food, a fine room, fancy clothes, jewelry, and even make-up. The money she made would buy her family a tin roof.

While Raul was thus soliciting the child he also talked to her father, suggesting that he might sell his daughter to him and describ-ing the benefits that would be theirs. Batuli's mother was plagued with doubt. She had heard that some of the village's girl children had been sold into unrespectable work and that some had become sick and even died. Still, she had no voice in the final decision making. It was all up to Batuli's father.

Raul's final message to the father—"do it now or you lose your chance"—prompted Batuli's father to consent. With scarcely time to kiss her parents goodbye the child was whisked by bus to a new life in Bombay.

The first night was spent in a cheap hotel room. Raul raped Batuli. The next day he took her to the market and bought her ear-rings, a fancy sari, and other trappings. He took her to a house in Bombay where she was given to the woman who ran the house. Raul demanded his payment, 1,000 rupees, and left.

Batuli discovered that she had been sent to a brothel. Alone and with no place to go, she was completely at the mercy of the woman who now owned her and who initiated her into the harsh life of a prostitute. At first Batuli refused to cooperate. She stopped eating. She didn't follow orders. When kindness didn't induce Batuli's cooperation, the owner of the brothel resorted to punishments, which finally became unbearable. Completely innocent about sex, Batuli's first experience as a prostitute was a nightmare of force, pain, blood, and the anger of a dissatisfied customer.

She worked for 14 years as a Bombay prostitute, exploited in such a way that, although she was able to send some money to her family in Nepal (with which they bought a tin roof), she could never work her way out of the horrible life into which she had been sold. One day the crushing news came to her that she had been disowned by her father when he learned of her disreputable lifestyle.

At 24, Batuli had already become quite sick with AIDS. The owner of the brothel, seeing that she was too sick to work, dismissed her. With no place else to go, she made her way back to her village in Nepal.

Although, tragically, her father did not want her in the house (not only had he disowned her, but he also feared contracting AIDS) her mother managed to persuade him to relent. She welcomed her daughter back; despite her constant care, however, the disease took its inevitable course. Nine months later, Batuli died.

Batuli paid for a tin roof with her life.

Whose body is it?

Every woman and girl should have the right to keep her sexual organs intact if she chooses to—and she should have a choice. An especially horrific human rights violation is practiced, most particularly, in Africa: the genital mutilation of women and girls.

At a certain age (which varies from region to region), a girl is pressured or forced to undergo a ritual operation that involves the removal of all or parts of her genitals: the partial or total removal of the clitoris; removal of the clitoris and labia minora; or the removal of all external genitalia, in which the two sides of the vulva are stitched together, leaving only a small vaginal opening. The operation is usually performed privately, often by a village "circumciser," usually without anesthesia, and often with a crude instrument, such as an unsterilized razor blade, knife, or glass shard. Cat gut or thorns are used for the stitches.

Although referred to as "female circumcision," it is hardly as harmless or superficial as male circumcision. African specialist Nahid Toubia compares the two: "A comparable operation in a man would range from amputation of most of the penis to removal of all the penis, its roots of soft tissue and part of the scrotal skin."

This and subsequent information about genital mutilation, except where cited differently, comes from *Women's International Network [WIN] News: All the News That's Fit to Print, For and About Women*, Frances Hoskins, editor; 187 Grant Street, Lexington, MA, 02173; Vol. 22, No. 1, Winter 1996; and Vol. 22, No. 2, Spring 1996.

Girls who have undergone this operation sometimes bleed to death. Those who survive suffer physical and psychic damage for the rest of their lives. Short term effects include infection, tetanus, septicemia, hemorrhage, and lacerations of the urethra, vaginal walls and/or anal sphincter. Long-term effects include chronic uterine infection, massive scars that can hinder walking, fistula formation, difficulty and severe pain during urination, menstruation, and intercourse, and hugely increased agony and danger during childbirth. The highest maternal death rates are recorded in countries where female genital mutilation (FGM) is practiced (Hoskins, *WIN News*, 1988: 116).

The numbers of mutilated women and girls in continental Africa alone surpass 127 million. These figures include 99 percent of women and girls in Somalia and Djibouti, 90 percent in Ethiopia and Sierra Leone, and 80 percent in Eritrea, Gambia, and Egypt. Another six to eight million women and girls have suffered mutilation in other African countries, while the practice continues in some Arab and Asian countries as well. At least 28 African, Asian, and Arab countries still carry on the practice, resulting in a total of two million girls mutilated every year.

African immigrants to Western countries often carry on the tradition. FGM is practiced, for example, in the United States, France, Italy, and Australia.

Why is this practice maintained, even after Africans have emigrated to other continents? Frances Hoskins of *WIN News* provides some of the reasons: It provides increased sexual pleasure for men, who find the smaller vaginal opening more stimulating; it prevents sexual pleasure for women, insuring that they will remain virginal until marriage and chaste afterwards; it is a tradition, and traditions are not to be questioned or tampered with; and it may even relieve men from any fear of not being able to satisfy a woman.

Meserak (Mimi) Ramsey is an Ethiopian woman who, 22 years ago, emigrated to the United States as a 19-year-old bride in an arranged marriage. Of her mutilation in Ethiopia at the age of six, she says, "The reason for my mutilation is for a man to be able to control me, to make me a good wife: make his bed, wash his clothes, prepare his food in the perfect way, give him children. It is to keep me in line."

At the age of 41, after Mimi had been through two marriages greatly complicated by the fact of her mutilation, she finally broke her silence about it. During a routine gynecological exam in Los Angeles, Mimi's doctor discovered her condition and expressed horror and dismay. For the first time in her life, Mimi talked to someone about what had happened to her. She poured out her story, including her pain, shame, and the fact that she had been unable to enjoy a sexual relationship with either of her husbands.

Mimi was surprised to learn on television that night about a bill being debated in Congress aimed at eliminating FGM in the United States. This seemed like an amazing coincidence, and it mobilized her to action. She called all of her female Ethiopian friends in the United States, and learned that almost every one of them (more than 90 women) had been mutilated.

The next day she called the office of Representative Patricia Schroeder (Democrat-Colorado), who had reintroduced the bill in the House after it had been defeated in a previous session of Congress. Schroeder referred her to Equality Now, a New York-based human rights organization working to eliminate FGM.

Equality Now paid for her to go to London for a month-long training with Forward, an international organization dedicated to assisting women who have been mutilated and to eradicating FGM through laws and education. (So far, Forward has helped in getting FGM legally banned in Sweden, Switzerland, and the United Kingdom.)

After her training in England, Mimi went home to Ethiopia. There she confronted her mother, who had arranged for her mutilation. "If you loved me, how could you let this happen to me?" she asked. Her mother explained that she had been pressured by her own mother. She begged forgiveness and asked what she could do to make things right.

Mimi's answer was to have her mother accompany her door-to-door in the neighborhood, talking to parents of young girls, trying to save them from this "surgery." Together, they told the parents that they had a choice, that it was not necessary to follow custom, that mutilation had horrible long-term consequences which they surely would not want for their daughters.

On the first day they estimated that they saved at least twenty girls. Mimi did not stop there. She spoke to parents in other villages, and after returning to the United States she continued to devote herself to spreading the word.

Now, often at her own expense, she travels to cities with large African populations. After poring through telephone books, she visits African-owned businesses, restaurants, beauty salons, and even garages. She tells parents that they do not need to harm their daughters. Because Mimi speaks from the heart, from her own painful experience, they usually listen.

Based on a report by Rita Henley Jensen in *Ms Magazine*, Jan.-Feb. 1996

Efforts are being made by other groups, notably the Women's International Network Grassroots Campaign (WINGC), to stop FGM. WINGC educates women at risk, partially through the use of the Universal Childbirth Picture Book, which teaches the basic facts about childbirth and health through pictures. The use of pictures enables women who cannot read to learn from the book. It has also made possible the use of the book in every culture throughout the world. A section on FGM explains that the genital organs of a woman are well-made for childbirth and cannot be cut or excised without endangering both mother and child. Favorable reviews have been received from women in villages and small communities all over the world, and especially in Africa.

Other individuals, too, have Mimi's courage and devotion to the task of stopping FGM. Zara Mahamat Yacoub, a Muslim woman from Chad, made a film called *Dilemme au Feminin (Feminine Dilemma)*, which shows an actual genital mutilation being performed. The film was shown to wide acclaim in Burkina Faso and in Canada. Thirteen days after it was shown on national television in Chad, a fatwa (a call for death that gives any person the right to kill with a clean conscience in the name of his or her religion) was pronounced by religious authorities against Zara, who now lives in danger of her life. Even the ten-year-old girl in the film has received death threats and has been taken out of school for her safety.

After the film was shown in Egypt, a fatwa was issued by the Grand Sheikh of Cairo, declaring FGM a duty for all women! The

Ministry of Health then reversed its thirty-five-year ban on FGM in government hospitals, and established special days when health-care providers could perform the procedures. Fortunately, human rights groups and women's organizations protested so strongly against this procedure that it was reversed in late 1995.

Based on a report by Frances Hoskins, *WIN News*, 1995: 94.

As of August 1996, FGM has been banned by the Egyptian Health Minister, but reports from Egypt indicate that most people are ignoring the ban because their conviction is so strong that women would be as sexually aggressive as men if they did not have their genitals mutilated.

New York Times, August 8, 1996

If you think that African women could protect themselves from the practice of FGM by emigrating, consider the case of Fauziya Kasingaa native of Togo. In 1994, at the age of 17, she came to the United States to avoid being mutilated and given in marriage (as the fourth wife) to a man old enough to be her father. Her own father, a wealthy businessman, had defied tribal custom by protecting her and her four older sisters from polygamy and genital mutilation. But he died suddenly when Fauziya was 15. His family, of the Tchamba-Kunsuntu tribe, took over the home and re-established the tribe's patriarchal customs, including genital mutilation. They arranged Fauziya's marriage, and the mutilation was imminent when Fauziya decided to flee.

In the middle of the night she left Togo by plane. She went first to Ghana, then to Germany, where she bought another woman's passport. Finally she flew to relatives in the United States. Landing at Newark International Airport, she pleaded for asylum, but was instead put in detention at Esmor, a detention center in Elizabeth, New Jersey, run by a private company under contract with the immigration service.

At Esmor, Fauziya was subjected to strip searches, isolation for long periods, and arbitrary cruelties by guards. A woman of the upper class in Togo, she was completely unused to such treatment. Because of an uprising by inmates who were protesting such treatment, Fauziya was eventually transferred to various prisons in Pennsylvania. Here, too, she was strip-searched and locked in maximum-security cells with American convicts. A week before a scheduled hearing with the immigration tribunal, Fauziya's story broke in the *New York Times*.

When the public learned of her treatment, there was an outpouring of concern and shock, which eventually led to her release. Said her lawyer, Karen Musalo, upon her release, "I don't want to sound like a curmudgeon—we're extremely pleased—but we hope it doesn't take this kind of outcry for justice to be done for other asylum-seekers who are being detained." Karen Musalo was able to take Fauziya's case to the highest administrative tribunal in the United States immigration system, where, on June 13, 1996, Fauziya was granted political asylum. She had been a prisoner of the United States for more than a year, but had managed to exercise a basic human right: to keep her sexual organs.

Based on articles in the *New York Times*, April 25, 1996 and June 14, 1996

In October 1996, after this chapter had been written, but before it went to press, Congress passed a law making female genital mutilation an illegal practice in the United States. It is through the efforts of women like Fanziya Kasingaa, Fara Mahamat Yacoub, Mimi Ramsey, and Patricia Schroeder that the practice of FGM is making headlines and is very gradually being eliminated in some countries.

From prison to sweatshop

It is sometimes tempting to point the finger at countries in which human rights abuses are blatant and obvious, but we must not ignore the fact that Western countries like the United States are committing abuses, too, although these are often hidden in places no one would think to look, such as sweatshops in the heart of major urban centers.

It is ironic that an elderly Chinese couple, immigrants to the United States where they sought a better life for themselves and their grandchildren, wound up in an urban sweatshop. Their story is based on a report by Helen Zia in *Ms Magazine* ("Made in the U.S.A.: A Special Report on Sweatshops," Jan.-Feb. 1996).

"Bibi" and "Zailung", as Helen Zia calls them in her story, immigrated from Shanghai, Bibi in 1992 and Zailung two years later. An elderly couple, they gave up office jobs in Shanghai, hoping to save enough money in the United States to bring their grandchildren over. Because their English is minimal, the only work they could find was in a garment sweatshop in New York City.

Bibi works for 16 hours a day in a dimly-lit, unsafe building filled with flammable materials. She is paid approximately $50 a day. Zailung also works 16 hours, but he is older and slower than

Bibi, so he earns less. Work is not guaranteed year-round, so they live in constant anxiety. In a good year, Bibi may earn $13,000, Zailung about $8,000.

Their living expenses are very high, although they live in the basement of a run-down rooming house. The basement has been sub-divided into three 12'x12' bedrooms, which rent for $250 per month each. There is no heat in the winter, because they cannot afford it. They cook on a hotplate and share a bathroom with the other base-ment occupants.

Their sweatshop work is tedious and dull; there are few opportu-nities during the day to take a break or even to go to the bathroom. There is only one open window in the entire factory. Bibi repeatedly says, "This job is going to kill me."

This sweatshop is operated by a major United States garment manufacturer. Clothing brands found in sweatshops include some of the best known labels in the country: Esprit, The Gap, J.C. Penney, The Limited, Liz Claiborne, Patagonia, Ralph Lauren, and Wal-Mart. Although sweatshops are most prevalent in apparel manufac-turing, they also exist and are increasing in other manufacturing and service industries.

The United States General Accounting Office defines a sweat-shop as "an employer that violates more than one federal or state labor law governing minimum wage and overtime, child labor, industrial homework, occupational safety and health, worker's compensation, or industry registration." More broadly, a sweatshop exists wherever workers are subject to intensive exploitation. This often means the absence of any benefits such as holidays, vacations or medical cover-age. Workers in sweatshops are also subject to arbitrary discipline and poor working conditions, including oppressive heat in the summer and lack of heat in the winter.

Although we are perhaps accustomed to hearing about sweatshops in developing countries, in the United States it is thought of as a thing of the past. Yet there are 2,000 sweatshops in New York City alone, out of 6,000 garment shops in the city. In Los Angeles, 4,500 out of 5,000 garments shops are sweatshops, and in Miami, 400 out of 500. (Figures from *Action Guide*, published by Partnership for Responsibility at UNITE, 218 West 40th St., 5th floor, New York, N.Y. 10018.)

"Today's sweatshop is a product of the global economy," states Helen Zia. "Large retailers and manufacturers, seeking greater prof-its in a highly competitive industry, contract production to thousands of contractors located wherever labor costs are low, whether in China or Honduras, Los Angeles or New York."

The industry's main workforce is immigrant women of color. "The whole subcontracting stratum lends itself to employing women," says Elizabeth Petras, Professor of Sociology at Drexel University in Philadelphia. It is a vast field of exploitation.

Where is the hope?

A surprising turn of events occurred between the time the manuscript for this book was submitted to the publisher and the time it went to press. The *New York Times*, April 9, 1997, shouted the headline: **"Apparel Industry Group Moves to End Sweatshops: Agreement to Bring Worldwide Inspection."** "A Presidential task force that includes human rights groups, labor union and apparel industry giants like Nike, Inc., Reebok International Ltd., and L.L. Bean has reached a groundbreaking agreement that seeks to end sweatshops by creating a code of conduct on wages and working conditions, including a maximum 60-hour workweek, for apparel factories that American companies use around the world," began the article. It went on to say that the companies agreed to abide by the code of conduct (which includes anti-harassment provisions), to be monitored by accounting firms working with human rights groups, and to not use workers under fifteen years of age. "The progress that's been made represents a unique and historic step here and around the world," said Gene Sperling, chairperson of the President's Economic Council.

Miracles happen. We were able to retrieve the manuscript before it went to press, in order to report two of them: the passage of the law in the United States making genital mutilation illegal, and the above move to end sweatshops.

We *can* make a difference. We can boycott companies who exploit others, and buy only from companies who don't. We can volunteer to help monitor the production facilities of large corporations. We can speak out against human rights abuses, especially the many hidden abuses of women and children.

If we are tempted to lose hope, we can look at courageous women who have dared to speak and to hope. Look at Hillary Clinton. She was brave enough to come to China during the women's conference in the midst of enormous controversy and to publicly denounce China's human rights abuses. Look at the Tibetan nuns who continue to make peaceful public protests against such abuses, knowing that their actions will result in imprisonment and torture. And remember their words of hope:

"There is no chance of loosing heart and feeling discouraged," says a Tibetan nun who was tortured by the Chinese military and now lives in exile in India. "The Chinese make things harder and harder for us, but we never feel discouraged. Instead it encourages us to work harder. So, the harder the Chinese push us, the bolder we become. So there is no time to lose heart and become discouraged."

Resources

Partnership for Responsibility.
> National Consumers League (202-835-3323),
> UNITE—Washington, D.C. (202-347-7417),
> UNITE—New York, NY (212-819-0959).

Tibet: The Facts. A Report Prepared By the Scientific Buddhist Association for the United Nations Commission on Human Rights. Dharamsala, India: Tibetan Young Buddhist Association, 1984; second revised edition, 1990.

Tomasevski, Katarina. *Women and Human Rights.* London: Zed Books Ltd. 1995.

United Nations Department of Public Information, *Universal Declaration of Human Rights.* DPI/867-40911-November 1988-100M: Reprint DPI/867 Rev. 1-93601-August 1993-100M.

"Women's International Network News: All the News That's Fit to Print." Fran P. Hoskin, ed. 187 Grant Street, Lexington, MA 02173, (617) 862-9431.

"The Women's Watch: Reporting on law and policy change in accordance with the principles of the Convention of the Elimination of All Forms of Discrimination Against Women." Published by IWRAW (International Women's Rights Action Watch) project, Humphrey Institute of Public Affairs at the University of Minnesota, USA. Marsha Freeman and Sharon Ladin, editors. 301 19th Avenue South, Minneapolis, MN 55455.

Power and Decision-Making

Ann Smith

■ ■ ■ ■ ■ ■ ■ ■ ■ ■ ■ ■

Power relations that prevent women from leading fulfilling lives operate at many levels of society, from the most personal to the highly public. Achieving the goal of equal participation of women and men in decision-making will provide a balance that more accurately reflects the composition of society and is needed in order to strengthen democracy and promote its proper functioning... Without the active participation of women and incorporation of women's perspective at all levels of decision-making, the goals of equality, development and peace cannot be achieved.

Platform for Action

Power is the ability to bring about change. The perceived reality of power is that it is limited and must be controlled so that power over people, places, and things is maintained. But for whose benefit? Man's domination over woman? One race over another? The human race over all creation? "Power-over" assumes that humanity can and must control people and events, and the life force given by God to all living creatures, can and should be used for self-gain without major consequences. Two important tools needed to maintain a power over society are information and money, and when these are manipulated so that only a few have access, the illusion of controlling people, places and things is created.

The misuse of power is the root cause of poverty, violence against women, poor or no health care, rape of women and children, the rape of Mother Earth, war, economic injustice, corporate take-overs, exploitation of workers by multinational corporations, clergy sexual misconduct, poor or no education, poor or no housing, poor or no nutrition.

This chapter is about shared power, a model for positive change. The stories in this chapter illustrate shared power as proposed by the *Platform for Action* document, which provides strategies that will equalize the power between women and men, bringing women's perspectives and gender-specific concerns, values, and experiences to all decision-making bodies. The women's movement believes that a new model of power is needed. The circular model of power transforms old structures of domination and subordination such as men over women, one race over another, and man over the environment, into structures of God's co-creativity and grace. Shared power is about relationships.

Shared power transforms old structures. Women in Mission and Ministry works towards transforming hierarchial structures into circular models of power sharing and creating new structures that empower all people to fully participate. The women's movement is changing the concept of power from power as control over others to power with all creation. To do this our words and actions must be congruent. For instance, I cannot preach about shared power from a podium that is physically positioned above and beyond the people in the room. I need to organize the room into a setting in which we sit in a circle and everyone has a chance to interact. People embrace this model when they feel they have been included in sharing expertise, information, and resources. When we serve as both a teacher and a learner, then the setting is one of mutuality and power is shared.

Positive power brings positive results. People respond like plants to the sun; we turn toward the light, especially sunlight. This is called a heliotropic response. Positive thinking, prayer, and other positive actions restore health in individuals, families, groups, communities, and even plants. The power of prayer is now widely acknowledged by the medical profession to hasten healing, especially during surgery. Power is love for ourselves and for all creation.

Power is limitless. God's power is one of abundance; it is not limited. Jesus came to give life and to give it abundantly. We do not need to fight over a limited amount like dogs fight over a bone. As parents we experience how our capacity for loving our children grows with each new child brought into the family. When another child is born we increase that love so that it is equally shared with all. When we claim God's power within us and use it lovingly we become "transformational" leaders. We seek out the best of what is and help others to ignite the collective imagination of what might be.

Shared power is miraculous. When we organize around problems, we will have problems. When we organize around making our dreams come true, miracles happen. The Beijing prayer would have been limited in its appeal if the dream had not been shared by people of all faiths. If we dream it together, it will happen. The use of affirmation and appreciation theory and practice in community organizing is bringing about miraculous results.

Power heals. The early Christian church grew out of attraction for God's light. Jesus performed miracles and assures us that we, too, can be powerful if we believe. In the Bible story of the woman who had been bleeding for 12 years, the woman took the power from Jesus by breaking the taboo that forbade menstruating women to come close to holy people, and touched the hem of Jesus's garment. Jesus instantly felt the power leave him and asked who touched him. The woman was healed by her faith. This story gives women the courage to break through barriers that discriminate against them and to be healed.

Shared power is synergy. When we collectively use the power for our own healing and for others, the sum of the power is far greater than individual power or even the sum of all of the individuals. When we work together as a group toward positive goals, synergy happens. The 20-year-long research and dialogue that has created the *Platform for Action* document is now being shared throughout the world. It is our hope that every reader of this book will become a devout teacher of the circular model of power. The old model of power-over will no longer have attraction for men or women and will be discarded like an old shoe that no longer fits.

Shared power is sustaining. The Native American concept of the Seventh Generation in which all actions must consider the consequences to seven generations provides a new yardstick by which to measure potential consequences of decision making. The *Platform for Action* document encourages greater involvement of indigenous women at all levels. Sustainable development can best be taught by indigenous women who can draw on hundreds of years of experience in preserving the ecosystem. Indigenous people know how to become co-creators with all creation, providing the balance needed to heal our planet. As non-native people, we have much to learn and to share with native people.

Power is personal and political. In 1985, at the Third World Conference on Women in Nairobi, the personal and political as interconnected and interrelated replaced the dualistic concept of these two as separate and competing spheres. In most societies the political was designated for men only and the personal for women. The UN document seeks equal representation of women in the political and greater participation of men within the personal: "The unequal division of labour and responsibilities with households based on unequal power relations also limits women's potential to find the time and develop the skills required for participation in decision-making in wider public forums." Equality in decision making in the political and private and at all levels and all sectors will improve the quality of life for women and their daughters, for men and their sons, and for all creation.

Paragraph 29 in the *Platform for Action* is referred to many times throughout the document and is vital for understanding the importance of the integration of the personal and political:

> Women play a critical role in the family. The family is the basic unit of society and as such should be strengthened. It is entitled to receive comprehensive protection and support... Women make a great contribution to the welfare of the family and to the development of society... the upbringing of children requires shared responsibility of parents, women and men and society as a whole. Maternity, motherhood, parenting and the role of women in procreation must not be a basis for discrimination nor restrict the full participation of women in society. Recognition should also be given to the important role often played by women in many countries in caring for other members of their family.

Shared power is collective. "It takes a village" is an old African proverb and the title of Hillary Clinton's book on the raising of children. It takes a community of people who share resources, energy and love to care for children, the disabled, and the elderly. Just imagine how your own community could make a difference if power was shared and all individuals were truly nurtured from birth to death. God's power is unlimited.

I experienced a Native Alaskan village this summer and felt so at home because Sr. Heléna Marie and I were so readily accepted into the community. Here all doors are open to the stranger, and children are free to come and go, knowing they will be cared for by the community. I would have loved to have lived in such a community when raising my children. The people of the village are the care givers for everyone in the village. The elders are held in high esteem and are constantly being sought for guidance and knowledge. They are the keepers of the old ways and the guardians for the seventh generation. In native villages there is a strong sense of being interconnected—to one another, to God and to all creation. The feelings I receive by being in these experiences are very spiritual.

Power is love. Love is the universal message in all religions. Namaste—the greeting used everywhere in Nepal—means "The divine in me meets the divine in you." This greeting of love makes every moment of the day a religious experience. Love creates positive change.

Shared power is spiritual. Spirituality connects us to God, to ourselves, and to one another. Imagine if we created loving villages throughout our cities and rural areas, communities that embrace the divine in all living creatures. We would no longer exploit native cultures and other races, we would no longer exploit women or children, we would not rape the land. Mother Earth and Father Sky and all God's children would be held in reverence. We would live as if all life matters.

The power is ours to dream and to work together to make these dreams come true.

Can the old structures be transformed? The following story of the women in the Philippines tells how they are systematically changing their women's organizations and breaking the barriers to women's participation in established church structures.

Ten years ago I received a letter from a woman in the Episcopal Church of the Philippines. She was discouraged with the existing Episcopal women's organization, the Episcopal Church Women (ECW). She wanted to know if the younger women and those who worked outside the home should begin a new women's organization that would more clearly meet their needs. I suggested they work within the ECW structure to transform it to meet the needs of all women, and wrote about the problems of competition among women when they must choose between two separate groups.

When I next heard from the women in the Philippines it was with greetings and a formal report from the national Episcopal Church Women. They had reorganized their structure by creating a national organization and were engaged in developing a women's leadership training program. The report contained a survey of the membership in the church documenting that their membership (women) comprised 80 percent of the adult members in the church and in some places as high as 90 percent. Although women make up the vast membership of the church, there were no women in decision-making positions in the patriarchal structures of both the local parishes and national Episcopal Church of the Philippines.

Their plan was to provide women's leadership training for their own members and to all women regardless of religion throughout rural and urban communities.

Several years later I visited the Episcopal Church Women in the Philippines. I attended their national board meeting in Manila and then traveled with Rose Maliaman by public transportation to a rural region in the North. As a guest of the women of the Episcopal Church I was treated differently than from a colleague of mine who served in children's ministries. Because he was invited by the bishops he rode in private cars that were purchased with money from the United Thank Offering, the women's granting program of the Episcopal Church U.S.A. Episcopal Church Women in the Philippines collect, in blue boxes, the pennies and dollars offered in thanksgiving and turn it over to the central fund managed by a committee of the National Board of Episcopal Church Women. The women who comprised 80 percent of the church and who actively engaged in development work were denied access to these private cars. How could this happen?

In the late 1960s, the Episcopal Church Women of the United States gave up their national structure and within several years lost their control over the management of their own funding program. Bishops decide what United Thank Offering grants will be sent to the granting committee for consideration, and in many situations women are entirely left out of this decision-making process, even though they raise the money. When women do not have an institutional mechanism within the patriarchal power structures, women's concerns are not given equal consideration.

The Episcopal Church Women of the Philippines, with help from their development office, received a substantial grant of money from the Church of Sweden for their leadership training program, which provided sufficient money for staffing and resources. The Church of Sweden routinely invests in women of developing countries because they are the development workers and with them real change can be implemented. "To train a man is to train an individual. To train a woman is to train a nation," is an African proverb, and, like "It takes a village," it stresses power sharing.

The *Platform for Action* document declares leadership training to be one of the most important actions to be taken by governments, national bodies, the private sector, political parties, trade unions, employers' organizations, subregional and regional bodies, non-governmental and international organizations and educational institutions: to "provide leadership and self-esteem to assist women and girls... to strengthen their self-esteem and to encourage them to take decision-making positions."

I experienced their leadership program in a rural town in the northern part of the Philippines. Both well-educated women and women who were illiterate took part. All gained leadership skills and self-esteem needed to become community and national leaders. What I learned from them is their openness to learning. They are eager participants in role playing, especially when this involves acting out non-traditional leadership positions such as mayor. In the United States it usually takes some warm-up exercises for people to engage in role play and other creative forms of learning. The women in developing countries quickly and enthusiastically jump into creative learning methods and the energy is so high that the facilitator usually has trouble getting participants to stop what they are doing in order to engage in a reflective dialogue.

Having experienced the effectiveness of this leadership training program and other experiential models when I was in Africa and in Latin America, I have incorporated this spirit of enthusiasm for creative adventures into a leadership program for women in the United States called the Creative Journey.

Experiential learning integrates the teachings of the programs into women's everyday lives so that they transform gender-specific roles into roles for both women and men. This is also true for men so that they can learn to accept non-traditional roles in supporting family life.

Rosemarie Maliaman directs the Women in Development Office for the National Episcopal Church of the Philippines. We first met in England in 1988 at the Lambeth Conference, a meeting of the Anglican bishops. These were very difficult days because women's equality was seen as a threat and women were viewed as a problem instead of an asset for the church by the majority of bishops in the Anglican Communion. In the midst of this very negative atmosphere, Rose and I became friends and spent a lot of time with women from Kenya, Haiti, Brazil, and Uganda discussing common issues, problems, and strategies.

Rose went to the Beijing conference by way of the Peace Train along with Sr. Heléna Marie. She wrote to me after the conference when she heard I was working on this book, and gave me an update on their struggles to change the old structures:

> Dear Ann, on the paragraph on the Ecumenical Decade, churches in Solidarity with Women... it is written: the women are in solidarity with the churches, but sadly realize the churches are not in solidarity with women. I heard a comment from a bishop with regard to the above phrase. He said, "How could you say that the church is not in solidarity with the women—when women are the church themselves?" I am not so sure if he is only raising an issue for a debate, but I think it proper for us to qualify the statement to say that it is the church hierarchy or the church structure that is not in solidarity with the women.
>
> One of the major roles of the Women in Development Program is to ensure the participation of women in decision-making bodies of the church. This work began in 1985 when we had a three-year leadership training program for our women.
>
> Much effort, sweat and tears have been invested in this endeavor, which at this point in time, only trickles of success could be gauged. Participation of women in the local vestries and mission councils are noted, although in a very minimal number.
>
> As the years rolled by, a result of our assessment proved that no amount of leadership training would set in place the women in the appointed and elective positions in the church bodies, unless there are changes in the structure in the church that would create the conditions for the women to participate.
>
> In 1993, during the Church Synod (governing body), the Women in Development Office sponsored a resolution calling for an "equal representation by sexes in the church committees and commissions." The resolution was amended to include youth and was adopted. Following the adoption, we have been very vigilant from then on, monitoring its implementation by the dioceses (regions).
>
> We are happy that most of the regions did implement the above action, and women's participation in the appointed church committees reaches up to 40 percent at the present time. There is one region, however, that has difficul-

ties in implementing this action. Their reason, they state, is that women are too busy attending to their home and families to be involved in these decision-making activities.

To ensure women in the elective positions of the church is a different struggle, a lot of conscientization activities and advocacy to this effect have been implemented. A series of women's forums before conventions, as well as during the national meeting, had been conducted to develop strategies around the election of women in the committees and commissions of the church.

In the Synod (national meeting) of 1993, two women delegates were elected to the Executive Council, through the lobbying of the women.

Admittedly, we still have a long way to go. There's a need to continually educate the women on leadership and assertiveness skills for us to be effective participants and members of these bodies.

Women's solidarity

The *Platform for Action*—"Build and strengthen solidarity among women through information, education and sensitization activities" is a strategy that the World Council of Churches enforces, and because they are an international organization, they are able to influence many churches.

In 1987, the World Council declared a Decade of Churches in Solidarity with Women because of the lack of support churches had demonstrated during the 1975-1985 United Nations Decade on Women. Shortly afterwards I attended an international meeting to plan for the beginning of the decade. I was asked to represent the National Council of Churches in the United States and was joined by women from national councils all around the world. The meeting was facilitated by the director of the women's desk of the World Council of Churches, Anna Karen Hammer.

We lived together for a week in a beautiful French chateau that had been transformed into a religious conference center. The chateau was in a quaint village outside Geneva, Switzerland; the setting so perfect it was like living in a postcard. Not only was I in the perfect setting, I was also in the company of highly intelligent and sensitive women, learning about women's issues, programs, resources, and concerns and working on common strategies for women's empowerment.

Our setting became the women's room, a place of shared power. We sat in a circle during our formal sessions listening to each woman as she told about her region. We had professional translators who transformed the diversity of language into a common symphony of different but blending melodies that we all understood. We shared stories, prayers, songs, dances and jokes during the informal times. In the circular model of shared leadership we quickly grew into a solidarity of sisterhood. It was amazing how quickly we let go of our sense of accountability to each country or region and became unified in our common goals of improving the status of all women around the world.

We discovered that the single most important strategy that has worked worldwide is grassroots leadership training of women by women—experiential learning using role play as the teaching method for integrating self-esteem and practicing leadership skills. This information was music to my trainer's ears. From personal experience, I knew this to be true for women in the United States, Kenya, and the Philippines, and now I learned that it was universal for all women in all regions of the world.

During the week we had a formal meeting with the General Secretary of the World Council of Churches and the general secretaries of national councils of churches around the world. This high-powered group consisted of all men. Our group presented our hopes and fears about the importance of women's equality in all decision-making bodies within the church. The tension in the meeting was intense and the questions asked of us were challenging. We did our best to bring forth several important issues related to women's equality and soon realized we were not talking to the converted. Afterwards we spoke about the reality of resistance to women's equality not only with this body of decision makers but at all levels.

Shared leadership is women helping women. During this meeting the woman representing Africa said she did not feel equipped to speak in such a male-dominated setting and was impressed by how well some of us could hold our own. When we returned to our chateau, we assured her that it is only a matter of practice. We spoke about the importance of mentors who coach women in speaking up in intimidating and hostile environments and provide gender analysis of political settings. This dispels the feelings of inadequacy and provides training to improve verbal skills in conflict management.

The following statement in the *Platform for Action* reinforces this need for a mentoring system: "Build and strengthen solidarity among women through information, education and sensitization activities… create a system of mentoring for inexperienced women in particular, offer training, including training in leadership and decision-making, public speaking and self-assertion, as well as in political campaigning."

The Decade of Churches in Solidarity with Women comes to an end in 1998. The World Council of Churches continues to hold meetings addressing the frustrations and reaching for the goal of women's equality. Men are learning to be compassionate listeners and to share the leadership. Women are asserting themselves as leaders who demand that the churches show solidarity with all women.

Leadership training programs are making a difference

Transformational leadership is not about becoming a leader in oppressive structures, but a change agent for new structures that give voice and justice to the voiceless. Assertiveness skills, active listening and compassion are essential components. Assertiveness is getting individual needs met without taking away the needs of others. It is a win/win situation, a level playing field. Active listening is hearing others and assisting them in clarifying their meaning so that all who are part of the dialogue are understood and respected. Compassion is needed to understand fears and anger so that communication stays open and honest.

Shared leadership, the circular model of power, provides full participation in decision-making, resulting in innovative new ideas that dispel problems and restore creativity. Leaving the old way of doing business takes time and patience especially for those who have succeeded in the hierarchial structures and are committed to maintaining the status quo. Spirituality is the factor in religious training programs that frees individuals to give up trying to control others and to entrust the process to God. I will finish this chapter by elaborating further about creating and sustaining the circular model of leadership, but first I want to tell one more story.

The Swedish government was thought to be a successful role model in power sharing but numbers are not always enough.

In an article in the March/April 1996 issues of *Ms Magazine*, Susan Faludi describes the rise and fall of power of Swedish women in government in the 1994 elections. Faludi, the author of *Backlash:*

The Undeclared War Against American Women, went to Sweden to study the effects of having a 41 percent female parliament and a cabinet that was 50 percent female. She found that numbers alone are not the answer to women's equality: that "ultimately, changing the style of governance is of little impact if the substance doesn't change as well." The appointment of women who maintained the status quo and the false rumors spoken against competent women undermined the progress of the women's movement. "The one radical proposal that the ministry was able to put forward—a modest plan to create 30 new professorships for women, a mere 1.5 percent addition to the existing 2,000 posts—generated a firestorm of denunciation from academia and the media."

> If such hostility to professional women's advancement seems out of place in this supposedly progressive nation, that is because Sweden has a well-kept dirty secret: working women's strides have been almost wholly segregated and contained within the public sector. In private business, less than 10 percent of all managers are women. In academia, less than 7 percent of professors are women. The result is a "his-n-hers" work place, where 80 percent of men work in the private sector, while 60 percent of women supervise nurseries and change bedpans in the public sector.

Governments can make real changes, going beyond a numbers game by sharing the power according to the *Platform for Action* which states: "The equitable distribution of power and decision-making at all levels is dependent on Governments and other actors undertaking statistical gender analysis and mainstreaming a gender perspective in policy development and the implementation of programmes. Equality in decision-making is essential to the empowerment of women."

Changing the number of women in structures that do not value women is not the answer. A new model of power and new structures are needed for both women and men to achieve a just and free society. Absolute power and absolute "powerlessness" corrupt absolutely; but power sharing is spiritually, physically, and emotionally healthy. Becoming a co-creator of God's power is to choose life and to give it abundantly. Governments, business and the church are hierarchial structures that operate out of a theology of scarcity, limiting power sharing to a trusted few at the top and operating out of self-interest, a quid pro quo where we only give to a few who support us in return.

The global women's movement is providing us with models of shared power, creating new structures and working in partnership with men to transform existing organizations.

Power sharing is the dream, and actions that lead to this dream are being tried in both the public and private sectors. Many American businesses, aware that the old way of doing business is no longer productive, are rapidly dismantling their hierarchial structures. They are creating new structures that employ leadership skills that empower all workers and that truly listen to customers. In between the dying of the old structures and the creation of new is chaos. "Chaos is not a mess, but rather it is the primal state of pure energy to which the person returns for every true beginning" is a quote from William Bridges' book, *Transitions: Making Sense of Life's Changes*.

Women In Mission and Ministry (WIMM) worked in partnership with all the Episcopal women's organizations 13 years ago to form a "circular model" of power sharing called the Council for Women's Ministries. This structure allows every organization equal representation and equal sharing of decisions, information, and resources. The small staff of WIMM does not direct the 23 women's organizations but collaborates with them to carry out a common vision with shared programs and resources. We expect chaos at all of our meetings. It is in the struggle that we find new beginnings. Form follows function and we are constantly reorganizing.

The first joint project of the Council for Women's Ministries and WIMM was to produce a magazine, the *Journal of Women's Ministries*, and design and facilitate leadership training programs for women. The Episcopal Church Women, our oldest and largest organization, whose structure empowers women to be connected locally and nationally, works in partnership with WIMM to conduct a leadership program called Women of Vision. This grassroots program is transforming outdated structures into viable organizations.

After a decade of success, the Women of Vision module titled "Making Order Out of Chaos" has been changed to reflect the latest theories. Chaos is the order, and the circular model provides a creative structure that enhances productivity for all who participate. In developing a resource that would break down the steps in developing and sustaining the circular model, I came up with seven principles. Two colleagues, Ginny Doctor, a leader, educator, writer, poet, theologian, and Mohawk missionary to Alaska, and Katherine Tyler Scott, leader, educator, writer, poet, African-American, theologian and founder and director of Trustee Leadership Development, helped me develop the seven principles.

In closing this chapter, I offer to you the *Seven Principles that Create and Sustain the Circular Model.* Use it as your blueprint (Women*Print*) to transform old structures and to build new organizations.

Create sacred space in all settings so that spirituality is the focus. Help create a place where the Holy Spirit guides who we are and who we are called to become. Arrange seating in a circle or in a series of circles if a large gathering. Provide rituals, centering music, prayers, and meditations that enable everyone to be fully engaged from beginning to end. Provide a ritual that discharges the negative energy and allows the group to move forward. This can be as simple as asking everyone to write down any negative thoughts on a piece of paper that they have brought to this gathering, acknowledging that we all bring baggage that can be left behind. The papers are then thrown away or burned.

Share the leadership. Each person is equally valued for her- or himself and equally shares the power within the gathering. Decisions are made by consensus, and all information and resources are shared. Individual talents, skills, and gifts are recognized and empowered. Power is derived from the consent of others and the leaders act as facilitators modeling power-with and not power-over.

Create together a vision. When we dream it together, it happens. A shared vision owned and articulated by everyone guarantees excellence in leadership. The vision becomes the navigational chart for sailing into the unknown water of the future. The future promises to be as unpredictable as the weather, constantly changing, and with a clear vision the organization will stay on course—a divine path.

Establish together working norms, standards of behavior agreed upon by the group. They are reflective of the group's values, beliefs, and ethics. Norms invite members to share the responsibility for developing the kind of relationships in community that will foster circular leadership. Norms shape the way the group makes decisions and solve problems. They are constantly reviewed and updated. Assertiveness skills and compassion provide the emotional intelligence needed for a healthy and productive organizations.

Everyone is accountable to the vision, the shared leadership, and all tasks. Accountability is two-way and circular in structure. "First among Equals" means that the organization has an elected or appointed head who relates to outside structures and entities, and has oversight for the entire operation. This person is empowered by the organization to act on its behalf, honoring the consensus model of decision-making. All task-related groups also designate a head who reports and receives information. Mutual accountability is very important so that the quality of the interactions remains positive and creative solutions to problems are found.

Theological reflection and evaluation are done at all gatherings and meetings. What is working? What is not working? What are we called to be? to do? The process is the means and the ends, and is held in trust by all the members of the organization. Assertive skills in giving and receiving positive and critical feedback along with active listening assures that the integrity of individuals remains congruent with the circular model.

Creativity comes from God and resides within everyone. As co-creators with God, everyone receives the power and authority to carry out the vision. The creative arts—art, dance, writing, poetry, music, drawing with the non-dominant hand, drama, meditation, role playing, shower of ideas, and listening in new ways—bring out the divine spark of creativity. Creativity brings new thinking and new behaviors that transform established organizations and develop new structures that constantly change in relationship to the environment.

Institutional Mechanisms for the Advancement of Women

Ann Smith

■ ■ ■ ■ ■ ■ ■ ■ ■ ■ ■ ■

Ensure that responsibility for the advancement of women is invested at the highest level of government.

Integrate gender perspectives in all legislation, public policies, programs and projects.

Collect and disseminate statistics showing gender impact of policies and programs.

Platform for Action

When I first agreed to write about this issue, I thought, "Oh, how boring! No one will want to read this; it is too complicated and doesn't apply to most women." But as my involvement in it deepened, I began to better understand that institutions are not political machines; institutions are made up of people in hierarchial structures. People can change and patriarchal structures can be transformed. Rather than thinking of "machines" I began to visualize living systems made up of people who interact and constantly change.

Institutional mechanisms that are responsible for the advancement of women are successful when they have a power base that can influence and transform structures. They are about sharing power in decision making so that women's perspectives shape all policies, programs, and budget considerations.

The "new systems theory"—the new science—explains how we as women naturally relate to one another and our environment. The old, mechanical theory, in contrast, was based on the thinking of Descartes, the sixteenth-century French philosopher and mathematician who defined the world as a machine set in motion by God, a closed system that wears down and eventually stops.

The United Nations, governments, and the institutional church still operate out of this old sixteenth-century paradigm. Organizations and all systems within are machines, closed systems that, once in motion, continue to operate in the same way until they wear down and stop.

People make up institutional structures and we are not machines. We are living organisms that are whole and constantly changing within and interconnected with our environment.

With the breaking of the atom, a new science of living systems and relationships of interconnecting was born. The new science affirms the way women think and organize themselves in small circles, around kitchen tables and in a multitude of close settings in large gatherings.

From a mechanistic point, the NGO Forum in Beijing contained identifiable elements of chaos. For many it was an organizational nightmare. For most of the 30,000 women there, the inconvenience caused by the rain and inadequate physical space for meeting in Huairou was typical of their home environments. So most adapted quickly and were able to interact regardless of the comfort level of the setting. We met in small groups, in large groups, we met walking in protest marches, and waiting to get in line for plenaries. We met through translators, in dance, in art, and in poetry, and in all these encounters we were changed. Being a part of the NGO Forum was like being a small sliver of glass in a kaleidoscope, part of many different patterns, each setting being beautiful and whole and each one making some kind of sense.

The new science shows us how the wings of a butterfly affect the weather hundreds of miles away. It illumines the African proverb: "To train a man is to train an individual, to train a women is to train a nation." One women is changed by an event, she tells another who is also changed, and they tell a village, and the villages tell a nation and it is transformed.

Even though one may feel powerless, every person in a system has a vital function to perform. The paradox in every society, as English philosopher David Hume observed two centuries ago, is that while populations submit to their leaders, power nevertheless always resides with the masses.

When women claim their power and identify with these new images that embrace their natural way of interacting, they accept their role as leaders. We see ourselves as equal partners within structures. Like the wings of a butterfly, our power can influence and transform systems. When we work together the synergy of our collective efforts produces far-reaching effects.

In this new light we can see systems as living and continuously renewing themselves in the environment. Systems are made up of individuals and are interconnected so that the integrity of each is maintained and interacts with the wider world. Margaret Wheatley in her book *Leadership And The New Science* gives us a helpful word for this new concept: autopoiesis (from the Greek for self-production), which means a natural process that supports the quest for structure, process, renewal, and integrity. Structures include all life because every living thing expends energy and does whatever is needed to preserve itself and connect to the outside world.

Anne Wilson Schaef, writer and organizational consultant, defines this structure as a living process system in which God is the process and we are co-creators. A living process is constantly interacting with the environment and constantly changing; only God is in control. Schaef uses the 12-step program to wean people away from the mechanistic system. Because we are not God, our control of people, places, or things is but an illusion. She defines the mechanistic system as the white male system which operates out of this illusion of control over women, people of color, places, and things. By being a part of the white male system, the mechanistic system, we have learned co-dependent behavior which has maintained its oppressive power. To realize our part in this scenario is the first step to recovery and health. By giving up our addiction to the power-over model of control and manipulation for fulfilling our anthropocentric self-interest, we can become leaders in life-giving systems that create freedom for all. The circular model is a life-giving structure.

An interactive power base can include a number of forms: a department, a committee, a section. Within these forms there is, ideally, someone in the role of ombudsman—in our context, a person concerned with the advancement of women. The ombudsman is the advocate who brings gender factors to bear on policy and program planning.

Before discussing examples of effective interactive power bases, I will list the conditions necessary for success set out by the *Platform for Action*.

1. location at the highest possible level of decision-making;
2. a two-way system that involves grassroots women;
3. sufficient budget and professional staff, including education and training;
4. opportunity to influence all policies and programs.

I will use these four conditions as I a describe an ideal family system:
1. the mother is equal to the father and together they make decisions;
2. the parents take into account the rights of the children and thus establish a two-way system of communication;
3. mother and father appropriate sufficient money for everyone's education and training;
4. everyone may influence all policies and programs related to the family and works to ensure equality for all, especially mothers and girl children.

The mother and girl child are given special considerations because, although this ideal family provides equality for all its members, it is obviously not going to encounter similar equality in society's institutions—for example schools, medicine, religion, and business. We add a fifth condition and call it "affirmative action."

The Mother's Union in an African village

My example of an effective interactive power base concerns a women's organization that built a brick-making factory and changed the balance of power in an African village. This story is like thousands being told where women in developing countries are making a difference. I chose this story because I visited the Mother's Union in Kenya several years ago. The Mother's Union is the Anglican women's organization that works to improve the lives of women and their communities throughout much of the developing world, particularly Africa.

I was one of the several Episcopal women who were taking a break from the End of the Decade Conference in Nairobi by visiting Mother's Union gatherings. Traveling by jeep up Mt. Kenya, and leaving far behind telephones, electricity, and other urban amenities, we passed lush fields of tea, coffee and bananas. Although the village was without modern technology, the women's ingenuity had created a model program of sustainable development by using their natural resources.

The previous year the Mother's Union decided to get involved in a money making project that would help their village. They did not seek assistance for money or for technical assistance from anyone outside their village, but used their own expertise and resources.

What God had provided was earth—teracotta earth—rich and plentiful and of the right consistency for making excellent brick. Husbands and sons of the Mother's Union helped to make the wood forms for drying the bricks and the oven for firing. People were paid in bricks and when the women accumulated a reserve of money from the successful brick making-factory, they decided to build a bakery that would provide the village with baked goods and bring in additional money. The Mother's Union was totally self-sufficient.

We arrived first at the brick factory just off the dirt road about a mile before the village. We were greeted by women, men and children whose smiling faces revealed their joy in seeing us and showing off their work. After shaking hands and being formally introduced, we were led by the children while the women proudly showed us every facet of their operation. It was not sophisticated by American standards, but environmentally clean with no pollution or waste. The workers, both volunteer and paid, were treated with the greatest of respect and appreciation.

After we said our good-byes, several of us decided to walk through the lush fields up to the village. The air was hot from the summer sun and heavily perfumed by the bounteous vegetation. The children again gleefully led the way, singing, skipping and darting in all directions pointing out a multitude of sights. Being with people who live out a theology of God's abundance in a simplistic and natural setting rekindled my memories of the pioneer spirit as learned from my grandparents.

When we arrived at the village the road was lined with people of all ages waving and singing out greetings. The Mother's Union members in their blue and white uniforms were the official greeters of the village. After proper introductions and special handshakes that are given to important guests, the president of the Mother's Union showed us the work schedule of the bakery. This carefully printed work schedule written in pencil on tablet paper listed every volunteer's name and the time and the day of work. All members were trained in the running and the management of the bakery, and because all the members participated they had sufficient numbers to be fully operational and therefore highly successful. The bakery was made with their bricks. All other materials and labor were purchased from the money they had earned from their factory.

The tribal chief and his council of men are the decision makers in African villages. Because the Mother's Union members were now wealthy businesswomen, they became the decision makers in this village, deciding against the building of a beer parlor in favor of a health clinic as their next project.

The Mother's Union in this small remote village became a successful institutional mechanism located at the highest decision level, the tribal chief. The women came from the grassroots and stayed connected to all facets of village life. They provided on-the-job training for all members, their families, and others in the village. Because they used their resourcefulness wisely they had the influence to determine the next town project, a health care center.

The story of equal rights and Methodist women

From the 1800s to the late 1960s, Protestant women engaged in missionary work in the United States created highly successful institutional mechanisms within their church structures. Several mainline denominations except for the Methodist Women's Division dismantled their institutions because they wrongly believed they had received equal rights within the church. Today only the United Methodist women have a structure that is secure and a powerful force in advocating for the advancement of women and girls.

The United Methodist Women's Division story is told by Theressa Hoover, who served the Women's Division for 50 years, in her book *With Unveiled Face.*

> It is strange that the Women's Division finds itself unique in the closing of the twentieth-century church, since our predecessor organizations once belonged to a flourishing company of relatively autonomous women's missionary societies. Our predecessors were inspired to meet the combined evangelical, physical, and social needs of marginal people—especially women and children, who could not be reached by male missionaries abroad and who were ignored by church and society at home. Women in the Protestant traditions organized thousands of their sisters into substantial lay missionary corporations with their own officers, programs, and careful

ledgers. Our foremothers were social feminists in the late eighteen hundreds. In 1968, R. Pierce Beaver wrote a book *All Loves Excelling: American Protestant Women in World Mission* in which he stated that he could not chronicle the rise and the phenomenal success of independent female church corporations in the nineteenth century without recounting as well their co-optation and absorption by male-dominated general mission boards in the twentieth century.

While the women controlled their own organizations, female interest in and zeal for missions never declined. It was rather that the women's independence and evident success did not sit well with their brothers, who grew restive and envious. There was repeated effort made to subordinate the women's societies, and if possible to absorb them. The first decade of the twentieth century was a time of increasing agitation for their integration. It was frequently alleged that the women were competing as rivals with the official church organizations.

How readily churchwomen's organizations were seen as less than official in status, while male-governed agencies were taken to be the real church organizations. This thinking was an article of faith with the men earlier in the century and churchwomen acquiesced to it. Even today, do we always see it for what it is? A patriarchal assumption—one especially irrational and undemocratic for churches, where the majority of members are women.

Despite varying degrees of resistance and expressed outrage, the women leaders were in most cases co-opted. The formalities were of course courteous. Churchwomen were assured that they would now have a major impact on the whole denominational mission program; they were guaranteed seats on general boards; and initially they were given a fair share of executive staff positions. Laywomen soon discovered, however, that they had lost the major, and in most cases the only, real female power base in their denominations.

This is sadly true for the Episcopal Church. In 1969 the seven women executives of the National Episcopal Church Women were dispersed in seven different departments and when they retired or left, most were replaced by men or women who were not a part of the women's structures. As Episcopal historian Joanna Gillespie wrote in the *Journal for Women's Ministries,* "the lights went out in the national church" and did not return but with one small light in 1983, the formation of the Council for Women's Ministries. For 20 years Episcopal women had no national direction, support or network that would empower them to carry out mission. Today they are struggling to recover what they lost.

While the Episcopal and other Protestant denominations disbanded their women divisions, the United Methodist Women's Division maintained their organizational base.

> We know that any marginal group must draw into itself and create solidarity in order to push forward effectively to gain a share of real power. Women in and out of the churches are discovering, as Blacks and other minorities learned before, that a variety of arrangements serve to keep marginal groups away from real power even after legal barriers fall. For example, co-opting can be used to integrate new elements with relatively little loss of power to the old guard; and tokenism invites selected members to forget that authentic power is not just the right to help make major decisions.
>
> Female institution building is not separatist in aim. On the contrary, it is a strategy—one of the genuinely fruitful strategies available to women—for reordering gender relations to enhance justice, equality, and community between the sexes. In 1969 we wrote with passion: we want to be catalysts for the continued humanization of God's world, mobilizers of the resources of women, creator of new arenas for their participation throughout the Church and world, and in coalition with other women's groups, with youth and with people of color, to be reconcilers in all the rough places.

Methodist did bend to the pressure to restructure but they did not break. They retained full control of their funds and other assets. Theressa states:

> In retrospect, 1964 can be seen as our year of inoculation. A painful dose of integration insufficient to kill our separate women's organization was injected. This has helped protect us against further attacks of the disease. In 1963, the seminar was prophetically called "Women in a New Age." Women in

public life were program participants, and Betty Friedan's *The Feminine Mystique*, then just off press, was assigned to the 175 members.

The Women's Division commitment to women's empowerment has been greatly intensified by its reception of the second women's movement in the United States. I say reception. We did not create the movement. It emerged in the consciousness of hundreds of thousands of American women in response to the Black civil rights movement, to new employment patterns, new forms of birth control, and the writings and actions of able secular women of the New Left.

These intelligent, angry younger women articulated our frustrations also. Their analyses deepened our understanding of the systemic oppression of women and in 1968 the Methodist Women's Division created a study of the extent to which women were involved at all structural levels in general program and policy-making channels and agencies.

The commission's research showed what was already self-evident that women were grossly under-represented, sometimes to the point of invisibility, in decision-making positions in the general church.

The United Methodist Women used the model of consciousness-raising groups and focused on becoming a supportive community that addressed temptations to competitiveness among women and to stress the need to be inclusive in our support systems. Particularly important is the insight that in general women have sinned less through pride and self-seeking (sins that have preoccupied male theologians and therefore been impressed on believing Christians) than they have sinned by patterns of self-abandonment and self-neglect fostered in women by patriarchal morality. Everyone is both a missionary and a mission field.

Liz Verdesi of the Presbyterian Church wrote, "The church is caught in the same kinds of cultural binds as is society. It responds more readily to power effectively used and to political savoir faire than it does to just causes or to obvious commitments."

Both laywomen and the growing group of clergywomen need to bear in mind the cultural entrapment of the church, which refuels its sexism. They need to be tough-minded and not be lulled into believing that they have come farther than they have. Otherwise, they will find their hopes frustrated and discover their trustfulness being used against other women. Power is here to stay; it is neutral; it can be used for good purposes as well as bad.

The inclusive and incisive work of our predecessors demonstrated how a unified Christian purpose in conjunction with an unbroken heritage of separate female work had permitted the Women's Division to protect and expand women's power and status in a major Protestant denomination.

It is my contention that our recent history shows that a measure of financial and administrative autonomy enhances the power of women within an institution noticeably. I urge churchwomen to create and maintain separate female structures in our era even while they enter as fully as possible into the general decision-making channels of the churches. The two lines of action are deeply and positively connected rather than being incompatible. Only the empowerment of women can bring about a true community of women and men in the church.

Today the United Methodist Women's Division is by far the most powerful institutional mechanism found in any religion. Their purpose is to be an advocate for the oppressed and dispossessed with special attention to the needs of women and children; they shall work to build a supportive community among women; and they shall engage in activities which foster growth in the Christian faith, mission education, and Christian social involvement throughout the organization.

The United Methodist Women's Division has 1.1 million members in 28,000 local units, served by 40 executive and 40 general staff. Their annual budget is around $20 million.

Poverty

Lucy Germany

■ ■ ■ ■ ■ ■ ■ ■ ▪ ▪ ▪ ▪

To create social security systems wherever they do not exist.

To develop gender-sensitive national and international policies, including those related to structural adjustment.

To provide poor women with economic opportunities and
equal access to affordable housing, land, natural resources,
credit and other services.

To devise statistical means to recognize and make visible the
work including unpaid and domestic of women and their
contribution to national economies.

Platform for Action

I've never been poor. I admit it. I was born middle class and grew up
middle class. My experience of poverty has come through travel and
the church: through people in Christian feeding centers, women who
have come to my church's thrift shop, villagers in Africa, Haiti, Mexico,
and Central America where I have paused in travel. Because I help out
in a small-town community center that serves a largely poor rural population, I have come to know people who live on the margin or below
the poverty line. Mostly they are elderly, live alone, raise chickens and
mustard greens and come in once a week for a box of food which I help
other workers to pack. Cans of government surplus products labeled
BEEF or PORK with a picture of a cow or a pig on the label; dented
cans from the local supermarkets; strange items from the Food Bank,
such as flavored cranberry sauces and weight-loss products.

I have been touched by the courage and determination of these people. Had their lot been mine it is very likely that I would have died.

But they live with good humor and astounding patience. If I ask 83-year-old Jessie about her day, she responds with a crinkly smile, "God has been good to me." And Johnny, who is 94 and looks about 60, wipes his face with a paper towel and says, "I thank the Lord for my life." Johnny wears old-fashioned overalls with shoulder straps and brass fittings. He talks about his garden and how, since his wife died, he suddenly realizes how much she did around the house.

Connie, who at 65 is working on her GED, asks me to help sack sweet potatoes. We laugh together about the shape of the potatoes, some of which look like coiled snakes. Some weigh upwards of ten pounds. All are coated with the soft red East Texas sand. We drop them into paper sacks, three or four to a sack.

I wonder what sort of person I would have become had I spent my life in an unpainted wood house with chickens in the living room, a pile of mustard greens on the kitchen table next to a box of Food Bank canned goods. I wonder if I would be bitter and hostile and too proud to take the food. None of the people who come to the Center exhibit such characteristics. They seem, for want of a better word, happy. It's hard for me to understand. I guess it's one of those impossible to define things about the human spirit. Where it seems the least likely to exist it is most abundant.

Poverty: the number one issue

The Areas of Concern in the UN's *Platform for Action* are so closely intertwined, it might be argued that it is virtually impossible to examine one apart from the others. For example, poverty is almost universally a health issue; without education and health, women are condemned to poverty; without the ability to make decisions and to have opportunities for economic advancement, poverty is the wolf in the house. Poverty is an inevitable result of armed conflict on masses of people; environmental outrages reduce the productivity of farms, foul water sources, and decimate forests. Human rights must be assured for women who are abused, deprived of their ability to carry on basic family functions and, in many instances, forced into the role of breadwinner without the capability of winning bread.

Rights—be they economic or personal—must be in place and protected in order for women to function fully in whatever role they are cast. The alternative is poverty, in some cases so dire and abject that most of us living comfortably well above the crucial line cannot visualize the horrors imposed by such conditions. It is no wonder that the burden of poverty on women heads the list of recommended UN actions, which include the development of social structures to ensure food security, the establishment of social safety nets, the support of female-headed households and anti-poverty programs, the study of relationship between unpaid work and poverty, the establishment of programs accessing financial services for women, and the recognition of the human rights of migrant women.

In its detailed analysis of the 12 issues involving women, the UN report points out the challenges and opportunities for sustained economic growth and development in the world as well as its risks and uncertainties. Global transformation of what was once largely a region-by-region economy has been responsible for the increased poverty of women, primarily through the gender disparities of economic power sharing and the narrowing of those centers in which power is exercised. The eradication of poverty cannot be accomplished through anti-poverty programs alone, the report states, "but will require democratic participation and changes in economic structures in order to ensure access for all women to resources, opportunities and public services."

The culprits in the poverty drama are listed as ill health, lack of access to education, hunger and malnutrition, lack of income and the means to produce it, lack of decision-making power in civil, social and cultural life. There is also the "underbelly" poverty that exists in developed countries, the poverty of low-wage workers, and the destitution of people who fall outside family or social or institutional support systems and safety nets. Both of these levels of poverty severely impact on women and have resulted in the feminization of poverty.

Women and children living in poverty are not all suffering to the same degree nor from the same sources. Most struggle for the basic necessities, food, shelter, and health care. This kind of struggle is almost unknown to middle-class people, many of whom, when it comes time to face the public cost of dealing with poverty, are quick to place blame. Laziness, indifference, drugs, "handout hunting," are some of the unthinking reactions to the cries of the needy when in fact it is lack of education, full rights for women, racism, inadequate health care, and lack of available jobs or low pay that are at the heart of poverty in most large cities of the world. In rural areas the root cause may be natural conditions such as drought, soil depletion, or massive insect infestation, or in countries of uncertain political climate, it may be forced migration, military threat, or outright attack. But whatever the cause, poverty has one common face and it is ugly.

"They are us!"

Huge gulfs exist between the middle class and the poor, particularly in terms of basic understanding. "I know rich Christians who would write a check to help a poor child through an established program but would not sit down at the same table with a poor family," says a young woman from Soweto, South Africa. Do they not realize that "they" are "us"?

Statistics give the story its skeleton but it still needs flesh and blood. In the United States, 52 percent of women are in the labor force, two-thirds of them are single, widowed, divorced, or must work to keep their families above the poverty level. Two out of three adults who are poor are women. One family in three is headed by a woman who is poor.

Poverty is not only an existence, it is a trap. Juana in the Philippines is 27 and has worked in a sweater factory for six years. She shares a small room in a worker's boarding house. Her job requires her to be up at 4 a.m., shower, cook breakfast, catch public transportation and be at work at 6 a.m. She works usually until 2 p.m. but often until 6 p.m. After work she does laundry, markets, and participates in workers' union activities trying to improve factory conditions. "Life is too hard to think about marriage," she says. "I need to help my family and help other workers." Where is Juana's future? Where can she go in life? What of her dreams?

There was a time in the United States when women's work was generally considered to be optional. The assumption was that the family breadwinner was the man of the household and whatever the woman did in terms of work was either unpaid or paid minimally. The man, with his breadwinner's status, was given a just and living wage. The value of his economic work was acknowledged. Such history is valuable only as a glimpse into the past; it no longer applies in this time when more and more women are fully supporting families. Yet women are still below the level of economic reward given to men.

Behind the men who made it possible?

History gives us a picture of men able to carry on their political, military, economic, and artistic activities because of an invisible corps of people behind them who took care of the day-to-day survival work with the family. These people have been either women, serfs, or slaves. "One can legitimately question whether that work of caring for the needs of the human family became devalued because it is associated with the work of so-called dependent persons, women, serfs and slaves, in a male-dominated society," says Maria Riley, OP, in *Women, Poverty and the Economy, Ecumenical Decade Series I.* "Evidence abounds that men have created a system dependent upon the work of women to succeed." She quotes some of anthropologist Margaret Mead's research on village labor where in some areas "women weave and men fish while in others women fish and men weave but in either place the work done by the men is valued higher than the work done by the women."

Putting the issue into sharp global focus, Leticia Ramos-Shahani, senator from the Philippines, stated that poverty is the continuing heaviest burden on women. Truly poverty has a woman's face. "Among the world's 1.6 billion poor people, 70 percent are women, a cruel condition that must not be tolerated." Speaking at an NGO plenary session in Beijing, she called on nations of the world to give women what has long been their due, to stand by their pledge to allocate 0.7 percent of their GNP to development assistance with 0.15 percent directed to the least developed countries.

It is the responsibility of all nations, said the African American Women's Caucus (AAWC) at the NGO, to make a commitment to the elimination of poverty. "The consequences of the imposition of gender and other forms of discrimination have relegated many women in developed and developing countries to the lowest rungs of poverty. This encompasses particularly women who live in countries significantly debt burdened."

Pain in the country

Rural women have been the last to benefit from or have been significantly harmed by economic growth, says Bao Erwen in an edition of *World Woman.* "More than 500 million women or 60 percent of the world's rural population live below the poverty line in rural areas, an increase of 50 percent since the 1970s, compared with a 30 percent increase for men." Observes Leena M. Kirjavainen, director of the Food and Agriculture Organization's Division of Women and People's Participation in Development: "Factors contributing to the feminization of rural poverty include cutbacks in essential services resulting from restructuring policies, environmental and social degradation and increasing male emigration. The challenge of feeding seven billion people by 2010 is a task in which women will have a substantial role. Women outnumber men as producers of food in many developing countries."

One event of the NGO Forum that attracted press attention was a Poverty Day staged by Latin American women. Carlina Manque from the Home of Mapuche Women of Chile said that many Indian people have lost their lands due to the fast development of industry in that country. With little education and skills these women are permanently relegated to poverty, having no more opportunities for employment than cleaning or service work. More than 100 women from various Latin American nations gathered to ponder the problems of women in poverty. They said that women need to unite to fight poverty, to urge governments to spend more on training and material support.

On the surface boom economies such as the one in postwar Vietnam look hopeful for women. In Hanoi and Ho Chi Minh City, the removal of state subsidies and the growing openness to the global economy have given many women possibilities for wealth and independence they could never have dreamed of under socialism. Still, prices have risen and women suffer from new burdens and disadvantages. The streets of Hanoi are crowded with home-based businesses mostly run by women who work long hours with few possibilities for leisure. This is true in the rural areas as well, since economic reforms have transformed the country into a rice exporting nation with heavy new incentives for farmers to increase their yields. The labor power of each family member has become a critical factor in the family's economy which, for women in particular, means a far heavier work load. Often men migrate to the cities looking for work, leaving women behind to manage field labor, to run farm machinery, and to handle heavy work, as well as to sell produce in local markets in order to meet their families' daily needs. Since the market reform process has been instituted, the poor are working harder than ever to better themselves economically but women are often paying the full price. They are working 15 to 16 hours a day and their health is declining. Many eventually migrate to the cities to become street sellers, factory workers, bartenders, masseuses, and prostitutes.

Work but no rewards

Noeleen Heyzer, director of the United Nations Development Fund for Women (Unifem), said at the NGO Forum that it is not acceptable for women to work two-thirds of the world's working hours but earn only one-tenth of the world's income and own less than one-tenth of the world's property.

Maria Cantoa, who lives high in the Peruvian Andes and for much of her life experienced what it meant to live in poverty, became involved in Unifem's Andean Food Technology Project, where she learned how to operate a food processing business. As a consequence she has been able to install electricity and running water in her family's dwelling. Big change. But women like Maria won't stop there. She'll be about teaching other women how to get out on their own, to use their gifts and improve their lives. Sometimes all that matters is a sliver of light in an area of complete darkness. Women wait for that sliver and grab it and spread it. Countless stories from women of the Forum give truth to that metaphor.

A variety of empowering factors exist for women trapped in poverty. Support groups provide training programs and monitor results, church-related organizations offer assistance and spiritual strength and even, as in one case, train women in body movement and visualization therapy. A group of highly educated women from the United States including women of color, women of various professions and active in a variety of social programs, came to a special workshop sponsored by the Sisters of Mercy in St. Louis to become informed about a program called Capacitar. This program employs Tai Chi, meditation, music, and other creative techniques, reaching out to poor and marginalized women in Guatemala, the United States, Nicaragua, Chile and other Central and South American countries. Additionally, this event spawned a workshop for poor women from the colonias and border towns along the Rio Grande, using healing techniques to build trust levels and foster feelings of safety in therapy. Therapist Robyn Keough offers her reflections on the polarity which exists and divides women of different cultures and socio-economic conditions.

> "The sacred is a word that doesn't often enough emit from my mouth or shine forth from my fingers. We women witness the sacred seasonally, daily, hourly, yet in our lives we've lost it, unlearned it, simply forgot what we once knew, stuck

its power and perfection away from our shadowed selves and walked on without it. Sacred leaves me speechless, renders me mute in trembling peace."

Trust building

In Chile, a blind woman with others in a workshop on Tai Chi and Polarity told how she and the women's collective *Araucaria* in La Victoria were going to start working with families suffering from drug addiction. She described poor women and families as being victims of anxiety, drug addiction, alcoholism, delinquency, without hope of finding or developing the self, without a place for sharing, relaxing, communicating, playing or dancing. New realization of worth, of "life behind the tired faces," has resulted from such exercises. "We aren't just communicating techniques but are awakening the hearts and souls of the women, helping them to realize their own power and energy, helping them to see how we are all one. Now the women build a beautiful dance with their spirits. They dance for themselves and for others, they dance for life," says Keough.

What can help to improve the quality of life for impoverished women? The UN platform cites a number of possibilities such as restructuring and reallocating some portion of public expenditures to promote women's economic opportunities and give them equal access to productive resources: development of agricultural and fishing sectors through allocation of financial, technical and human resources; improvement of support of female-headed households through targeted social, economic and agricultural policies; improvement of access to food for women living in poverty through appropriate pricing and distribution mechanisms; ensuring the full human rights of all women migrants, facilitating their employment through greater recognition of their skills, foreign education and credentials; enabling women to obtain affordable housing and access to land; creating or reviewing social security systems with a view to placing individual women and men on an equal footing at every stage of their lives; strengthening policies for indigenous women with full respect for their cultural diversity, so they have opportunities to exercise choice in the development process by which they are affected. Other needed reforms involve low-cost legal services, medical services, education, encouragement of women entrepreneurship, increasing availability of bank loans, and implementation of legislative reforms to give women full and equal access to economic resources including the right to inheritance and ownership of land, natural resources, and credit.

A roof over our heads

Poor housing or lack of it is one of the basic ingredients of poverty. As many as 600,000 people are homeless in the United States on any given night, according to a report from Women of Color on Homelessness and Housing. About 39 percent of those are women with children and an additional 15 percent are single women. On a global scale homelessness looms as a major problem with over 100 million people homeless, according to recent UN figures currently under study by the UN Center for Human Settlements. Seventy to 80 percent of the 23 million refugees and 27 million displaced persons are women and children, according to the UN figures.

"We talk of human rights; well what about the right to have a safe, affordable place to live?" asks Zenobia Nimmer, founder of For the People, a United States-based organization that fights homelessness. Nimmer says that the homeless population in the United States is disproportionately made up of people of color. Though African Americans comprise only 12 percent of the population, they make up nearly 50 percent of the homeless. Latinos and Native Americans, she adds, are over represented in this category as well. "When we see homeless people, especially those of color, we must understand that they're homeless not because they're lazy, but because the roots of their problem are embedded in events of history," Nimmer says, referring to the displacement of Native Americans from their land and the enslavement of Africans in the United States. Women are particularly vulnerable to homelessness since they are more likely to be unemployed or underemployed and they are often forced from their homes due to domestic violence, one of the leading causes of homelessness. Nimmer cites other chilling statistics: from 1992 to 1993, one million people who had been living above the poverty level, fell below it. Two-thirds of the working poor do not earn enough to rise out of poverty. Homeless women have no property rights, a third of them are heads of households who, if employed, are earning less than men. They cannot get bank loans due to low-paying jobs and lack of collateral. Often they cannot find government-subsidized housing, one million units of which have disappeared over the last decade. The government is being called on to provide safe, affordable, permanent housing, job training programs, child care centers and an increase in the minimum wage which, in 1996, became for the first time in over a decade a visible political issue. Nimmer's group calls for organizing on the grassroots level through churches and other organizations, supporting networks that offer leadership development as well as activities which enable homeless people to demonstrate their skills and share their experiences.

In Southeast China's Yunnan Province, a Chinese press report noted, some 1.2 million people have been helped out of poverty by government assistance. In 1995 some 1.24 million people in the province were living in poverty; the majority of these are now enjoying better food and housing. One of the problems was poor handling of local projects. The Chinese government sent many of these local officials to larger cities to receive training and to "change their outdated concepts on economic management." New techniques to help agricultural workers get higher yields from their crops were instituted. One of the most successful of these was the distribution of plastic film for covering young plants in time of stress from weather extremes.

Give them loans, get them started

Though unsung and unremarked, in many cases of extreme adversity and suffering women make changes on their own. They wait for no one to come in and help. In one of the many squatter communities of South Africa, home to between 3.5 and 7 million people, there was no easy access to running water and no sewers. The women lived in daily fear of their lives from vigilante attacks by nearby hostile residents. They lived in cardboard houses augmented with pieces of tin and corrugated aluminum. They felt the force of the wind inside these flimsy dwellings. The dust of the streets. The violence of life outside. All these were ongoing wounds. But as the traditional backbone of the community, the women began several years ago to realize that no one would help them except themselves. They organized themselves into groups. One of their first actions was to establish a revolving loan fund that enabled them to set up small businesses.

Women in Bangladesh had a similar story. Many of the local women "didn't even know how to count" and were afraid to accept money from the Grameen Bank, a project offering a revolving loan fund for local women. If they approached the bank at all, they asked that the money be given to their husbands. But gradually they lost their fear and began to borrow, first using funds to raise a communal cow and sell its milk. They expanded into processing rice, weaving baskets and sewing projects, things they had done all along as individuals and for which they had never been paid. The value of acting as a community becomes beautifully clear in the actions of these women. Now the money, instead of going to their husbands, goes directly back to them. It takes about ten loan cycles that is, ten times of borrowing before the women can rise above the extreme poverty line, project leaders said. The women who sign on to this banking project have to make promises such as neither to give nor to receive a dowry, to send their children to school, not to drink polluted water, and to plant trees.

Tourists who visit in parts of the world other than their own often do not see or recognize the poverty that exists. They spend time in cities or resorts, driving quickly through country where people's living conditions are but a blur from a car window. In countries like Honduras, Mexico, and other Central and South American countries, poverty has a "pretty face" because of luxuriant tropical vegetation. But they are looking at homes without bathrooms or running water, women carrying water from polluted streams, people eating tortillas and beans three times a day every day, women carrying their children to the nearest bus stop so they can get to a city where there is a doctor.

"I always look at the children of the rich," muses a campesina grandmother. "They have rooms full of toys while our children play with old cans and sticks. And rich children are so healthy, so full of life. They are smarter because they are better educated and better fed. It's not that ours are idiots. I want my grandchildren to have the same chances those children have. Why shouldn't they have toys? Why shouldn't they be well fed? Why shouldn't they go to school and get smart?" It is a cry from the heart and one to which there are no immediate answers. It is particularly hard when the mother, a strongly religious woman, cries out that God has deserted them. "God planned for us to be equals," she says. "Everybody in society has a right to a decent life." And then she adds, her voice lower, "I know it's too late for my children. But I'm fighting for my grandchildren. I want them one day to be able to enjoy all the wonderful things the world has to offer."

From *Women, Poverty and the Economy*, World Council of Churches

Terrorism: a neighborhood menace

Terrorism, like disease and hunger, is another unwelcome intruder in the community of poverty. A recent story in the *Dallas Morning News* by David LaGesse described how terrorism adds another dimension to the misery of poverty. In Peru, the story stated, quoting Lima social worker Jaime Antesna, "new wealth has failed to resolve social and political tensions that give rise to insurgency." The Peruvian government has over the past few years controlled inflation with an economic package that involved raising interest rates, cutting government spending, and removing price controls. The measures resulted also in the loss of thousands of jobs and raised the cost of most everyday items. The new economic growth, centered in foreign-backed projects, created a minimum number of local jobs. More than half of Peru's people live without power and water and four out of five have no full time employment. Because of the social conditions that persist under the new economic policy, such insurgents as Shining Path and MRTA are active and gaining strength. Meanwhile people like Maria Alvarez struggle not only with poverty but with death threats from guerrillas. She worries about her children's safety. Kidnappings, killings and bombings are everyday fare in her northeast Lima slum neighborhood.

No portion of the world today is exempt from poverty. It is in the midst of the richest cities, the most productive rural areas, on mountain slopes, beaches, plains, anywhere that human beings live, where concentrations of power cause some to be favored and others to be ignored. The fact that women and children are the most frequent victims of that poverty insures that it will continue, that it will be inherited as surely as eye color and bone structure. If a society could but recognize that it is made up of all of its parts and that no single part can be carved out without collapsing the whole structure, then those in positions of authority with responsibility for organization might reach down towards "the least of these" and bring them up to an acceptable level.

What we do not dare to acknowledge, those of us in our comfortable living situations, is that their struggle is ours, that if they go down, the world becomes a more precarious place for all of human life. We are part of their misery. Since the globe continues to shrink, since we are all closer to one another than ever before in history, it makes sense that we should help shoulder the burdens of people beyond our borders and that we should do it with our resources, our money, our creativity, our voices. This should not be a time in history for a resurgence of the Monroe Doctrine mentality. Any return to such a posture would be undertaken at our peril.

"Yet how lovely were the black, rounded pots, the long, hand-woven baskets borne firmly on shaven heads, the dignity of bark clothing falling to the ground. How picturesque and innocent-seeming were the naked dark figures and what strange animal-like shapes arose, on all fours, between the rows of young beans. But deformed bodies and minds resulting from malnutrition are not charming nor is a beheaded birth nor the ravages of bilharzia and trachoma, nor the general slavery of women, nor the hidden slave traffic..."

From "Kisoro-Kampala," in *Outback and Beyond* by Cynthia Nolan

Women and the Media

Nancy Grandfield

■ ■ ■ ■ ■ ■ ■ ■ ■ ■ ■ ■

Take steps to ensure women's access to information and the media on an equal basis.

Encourage the elimination of gender stereotyping in the media through studies, campaigns, and various forms of self-regulation by media organizations.

Platform for Action

"When film and all of society begin to depict women as complex, multi-layered persons, the effect will trickle down to every corner of every village of the globe... it happens village by village, woman by woman, conference by conference..."
Actress Sally Field speaking at the NGO Forum

Media is a second god. Twenty-three corporations control all of the media in the United States. It is time for a new information order for the world with a media network funded by the United Nations and controlled by women. We could reshape our image in the press, film and television beginning locally and expanding globally, touching sisters, touching shores, touching lives to bring about a celebration of sisterhood.

"In the wake of Beijing, what the media could have done and did not do was to highlight first this unprecedented widening of the global women's movement to encompass girls; second, the extraordinary unification of women across the North-South divide and third, the coming of age of women globally. I use that expression as a reflection of the genuine maturation of the international women's movement.

For the first time in history women have learned to renegotiate themselves and their rights. Above all, the open articulation of violence against women and girls within the society and in the family broke all walls between women and dissolved any artificial barriers that class, race, ethnicity and nationality had so cleverly and self-interestedly placed between them.

Women's access to media and communications technology is critical if women are to make their voices heard. Media has the potential to make a far greater contribution to the advancement of women and though today more women are involved in the communications field, few hold positions at the decision-making level. Without their presence on boards and governing bodies the projection of negative and degrading images will continue and society will not see a balanced picture of women's diverse lives and contributions to society in a changing world. Media's messages often portray women primarily as consumers. Children who watch "their" shows on major network television each Saturday morning will see about 123 characters but rarely, if ever, a role model of a mature female as leader. "When women appear at all they tend to be depicted within the home and are rarely portrayed as rational, active or decisive," wrote Margaret Gallagher, writing in a United Nations journal.

"Most women would like to see more women journalists on television and more female experts because these would act as significant role models for other women, would stimulate female interest in public issues and, perhaps, sometimes speak in the interest of and for women. As these women clearly recognize, access to the media bestows power. Those who produce its content can decide what information and images will appear and how they are to be presented."

"So much of the media operates from the neck up and in that realm you don't hear the personal stories. I want to find a balance between the heart and the mind."
Eileen Sudnet, California radio talk show host

The story of one woman found her power out of, in her word, "outrage." Eileen Sudnet is a talk show host on a commercial radio station in the Monterey, California area. She grew up in the 1960s, attending San Francisco State University from 1968 to 1973. At that time there was serious student unrest about the demand for a Black Studies Department, and an end to the Vietnam war. "I'd had enough of politics to last me a lifetime," she said, "and really wanted to be left alone." When the attack on abortion rights began getting more intense in the mid-80s, it began to "crack her open again politically." Eileen grew up when neither abortion nor easy access to birth control was an option, and now she looked upon "forced motherhood" as a form of slavery. She felt that men were attempting to assert dominance and control over women's lives.

There was a growing backlash to women's reproductive autonomy, and the more verbalized and violent the issue became, the more Sudnet's energy was "getting dialed up." She joined several women's organizations that were fighting to safeguard reproductive rights, and she decided to participate in a large pro-choice march in 1992 in San Francisco.

But "whenever I'd ask my woman friends to march with me, all but one said they were too busy. I'd say, 'yeah, yeah, you're too busy, but wake up! What about your daughters?'" Marching on the street, shouting, is not her style, but she was there to show support. "I know what was at stake here. I had heard many stories of women who gave up their babies for adoption, and who suffered illegal, botched abortions. I knew if not for pure luck that could be my story as well. I also realized that the fear of pregnancy under those conditions put me in great conflict with my own body, and the potential to become pregnant against my will or from contraceptive failure."

In January 1995 Eileen was listening to a local talk radio program with a "liberal" host. The murders of the abortion clinic workers by John Salvi (who has since committed suicide) was being discussed. "All afternoon men were calling in to argue that it was justifiable, that the ends justify the means. I was getting livid and disgusted at hearing only men's voices discussing an issue relevant only to women. Fortunately, there was a phone nearby, and the next thing I knew, I was dialing the station. As I was waiting for the connection my heart was pounding, and I felt like a vise was around my throat. I was scribbling a few notes to help me keep focused on what I wanted to say.

"When the host answered I somehow just let loose. I was so outraged at that point that the words just poured out of my mouth. I spoke out on several different levels, from a personal perspective, and from a general outlook. There are an estimated 40,000 children who starve to death every single day on this planet, and the population is still growing by 90 million every year, thus causing a pending ecological and environmental disaster. When I hung up the phone I felt dizzy from purging myself of those major feelings."

Eileen's words really activated the phone lines with other women callers who spoke about "deadbeat dads," and a mother's fears for her daughter who goes to a clinic for basic health care. Heretofore, it had been "all men talking from the neck up," but with the women's voices, stories were being told from the realities of women's lives.

As the radio show progressed, the host, Eric Schoeck, said, "Eileen, if you are still listening, please call back. I'd like to have you on for a whole show."

Her response was, "Is he kidding? What do I do now?"

"The long and the short of it is that here was someone opening a door of opportunity, and if I felt this strongly then I had to get past my fears and accept the invitation."

The host invited her to visit the radio station and left the invitation open. Meanwhile, she learned the statistics about who, why, and how many women seek abortions.

Several months later, armed with lots of information, she contacted Eric Schoeck, who suggested she involve two other women in a round table discussion on why women don't participate in talk radio. It was then Eileen realized she had no mentors. "I have a college degree, but don't know of a single woman who stands out in history who inspires me. It made me realize the importance and necessity of knowing one's history. I now understood the student struggle for a Black Studies Department, and the unrest of my college days now made sense. It was a struggle for identity. I understood the emptiness one feels when there are no specific people to look to for inspiration. On the round table show I brought up the name of Eleanor Roosevelt. All I had heard were about her looks, or how she got 'out of line' in the role of First Lady. I mentioned Loni Granier, who was dismissed as a 'quota queen' without our hearing her specific ideas to rectify voting imbalances and privilege. And I thought of Hillary Clinton, who tried to create a health care system that would accomodate all people, but who had been vilified as a 'ball-buster,' and who had to sustain endless comments about her hair-dos rather than her ideas.

"Our panel agreed that most women are not very comfortable with the typical style of talk show that tends to be combative, confrontational, competitive and argumentative. We are generally turned off by that style, and therefore choose not to phone in.

"As we talked about the 'style,' women started calling in. Eric knew he had hit a nerve when the whole phone board lit up. He heard from a vital and vibrant audience out there who were listening and wanting to be heard. The women callers said they didn't like the polarizing attitudes, the name-calling, and the blaming done by some male hosts. The feminine style was towards dialogue rather than debate, and towards consensus-building and networking to solve problems.

"As the hour was drawing to a close, the host suggested that we do a program on a regular basis, judging from the response of women listeners. I jokingly suggested we could call it "That Time of the Month." Everyone's eyes lit up and there was a resounding YES! Now, on the third Wednesday of each month, Eric and I have a feisty, humorous program, with decidedly feminist opinions on current topics with a largely conservative male audience. It's challenging, but being silent or victimized doesn't do women any good. I toughen up, jump in, add humor, a little well-planned sarcasm and good information, along with my own first person experience. Women are now being heard as never before, and they also inspire others to speak out.

"In January I was offered a weekly two-hour time slot in the early evening. It is called 'The Sunset Salon' where we discuss a single topic in depth and from many perspectives. My goal is to bring forth issues not usually discussed, especially those particular to women's lives. If I turn off the bi-polar thinking people, and encourage those who rarely speak up, then I have done my job.

"I often think of ideas in a circle; when I stand inside the circle I ask, 'How does this feel?' And then I step outside and try to assess the issue from the bigger picture perspective, analytically and comprehensively. Being inside the circle the subjective, personal perspective is the viewpoint that I feel is rarely addressed in the media. There is always this emphasis on objectivity as the only real truth, ignoring that we live our lives as a subjective experience. 'The political is personal and the personal is political,' as the saying goes, 'the integration of the masculine and the feminine, the head and the heart.'

"I'm not sure where this opportunity is headed, but one thing I'm learning is to let go and allow spontaneity to open doors. This tends to keep life a lot more exciting and amusing. I'm still reluctant to be too public, but so far I can say: I didn't die, it didn't kill me, and there's something that is saying YES. And if we don't speak out, we will get steamrolled by the prevailing voices.

"Did you ever try to sleep with a single mosquito in the room? One little mosquito can keep you awake all night long. It will not, and cannot be ignored! I hope I can encourage women to become like that mosquito. It's a great time to be a woman, to have the courage to be heard as well as the means to be heard, and to keep on being heard until we wake up the world to our presence and to our wealth of knowledge, compassion and experience."

Why is it important to be a media maker?

Bernadette Rounds Ganilau is a successful woman in the communications field and a Global Fund advisor in Fiji. She writes:

> I think that age has a lot to do with where I stand in the media at the moment. As I'm one of the older members in the profession, people have either gotten used to me talking in the background while they do chores, drive around the republic, sit at their desks, paint their roofs, plant marijuana or whatever every morning—or when I do say something, they express some surprise that I'm still around, still on radio. Maybe nothing more is ever thought or said about my presence. Or is it?
>
> Reflecting back to the early seventies when I started out in media, I felt intimidated by female members of our academe and the power sisters of our women's movement. While they talked of world-changing solutions to problems, I sat there and played music—the Rolling Stones, Tammy Wynette or Petula Clarke for 'Timaima Marama and the gang at Vunidawa and not forgetting mistress Sera of Rewa Street!' Maybe I'm still doing the same thing… but the difference is this time I believe!
>
> I believe that women in the media must highlight the work done by women in the community… because nobody else will.
>
> I believe that women in the media need to highlight as much as possible the disparities in all sections of the community where they are still being treated unfairly… because nobody else will.
>
> I believe women in the media need to fill the gap in the understanding between men and women regarding issues and concerns important to women… because nobody else will.
>
> I also think that to be a woman in the media is not enough—we have a higher goal to prove ourselves not only in the reporting of all issues but in ensuring that gender sensitivity is practiced.

Bernadette more or less "fell" into her media role. She studied architectural drafting in Australia and while on holiday in Fiji, she collected data on three of the island's woman leaders: a Fijian who was a government spokesperson, an Indian who was the opposition whip and a European, mayor of Fiji's second largest town. Her slant was that, although they all came from separate backgrounds, culturally, religiously, economically and emotionally, they were all working towards the one goal of the development of their country. For the resulting radio piece, "Women in Transition" that aired in 1975, Bernadette was awarded an international prize. She says, "I was fortunate to have entered radio in the early 70s when Fiji had only just attained independence." Even though at that time radio was a totally male-dominated media, Bernadette worked her way in and became the first local woman to present an evening news and current affairs program, "Fiji and The World." She was also the first local woman to do public presentations of national festivals and programs.

"Despite 1975 being declared by the UN as the first year of the decade for women," she says, "I did not think what I was doing at the time was only for women. I felt that everything that was coming out of my shows benefited both women and men and could actually be a means whereby men could understand the newly independent nation and its newly independent women..."

Bernadette, who had introduced Fiji to "Talk Back Radio," traveled with her microphone into the remote parts of the country including its many islands to hear from the people where they were. "This was wonderful strategy. What we got from the villagers were amazing stories of their lives. Communication at that time was three-way: the islander, myself, and the listeners spread out over 300 islands of our republic."

"Many of our women were still shackled to customs and tradition as well as the remnants of colonialism, and their conditioning was hard to break down. We had some very outspoken women in the islands including Amelia Rokotuivuna who brought the issue of nuclear testing in the Pacific to Beijing. Still a lot of women refused to acknowledge any of these spokespersons."

"Slow and gentle coercing" turned out to be the most effective way to bring about change. The women needed time to weigh the effects of custom on their rights and they needed time to absorb the novelty of participating in issue discussions.

As an illustration of the influence of customs on the people, Bernadette likes to tell the "whale's tooth" story. For many years in

Fiji it has been customary to present a whale's tooth (*tabua*) to someone to seal an agreement, celebrate a milestone, seek someone's hand
in marriage, cement friendship, or acknowledge a death. Tabua was
given to ask for forgiveness or to commemorate an event. It has been
used in the case of women who have been raped. Before the rape case
has been taken to court, the customary presentation of the tabua is
made to the woman's uncle (not the father—this is tradition!).
Everything then is supposed to be all right and the woman who has
been raped is supposed to accept this without question.

In recent years, women have been served by the Fiji Women's
Rights Movement and the Women's Crisis Centre, both of which
have done much to raise awareness of women's issues.

In 1994 a young woman was beaten at a local nightclub by one of
the so-called "golden boys" of sports, a football star who was doing
very well overseas. The police told her to "lay off" as he was the "gold-
en boy" and advised her to go home and forget it. She elected to go
to a doctor for a medical opinion and to get the details of her injuries
on file. Then she went to the media with her story—but nobody
would touch it! "He was too much of a star to have it twinkle the way
she painted it," said Bernadette, "But when I heard about it, I immediately talked about it on my radio show, mentioning the football star's
name only once. That was it! The community rang in non-stop, ques-
tioning the injustice of the whole matter."

As a result, the deputy police commissioner spoke on Bernadette's
show and promised he would act in the matter. The football star was
charged for the assault, and his family took the traditional presentation to the young woman's family, but they, on her insistence, refused
it! The accused was arraigned in court, found guilty, and ordered to
pay the victim $500. His visa was withheld for several months so he
could not rejoin his overseas team. He lost TV contracts with two
international companies. But best of all, says Bernadette, "it made the
community think."

Communicating for women in Fiji has brought with it a number
of problems. Bernadette published and owned the only woman's
newspaper in the southern hemisphere. *Fiji Women* existed for five
years after which, due to the reluctance of advertisers to support it, it
gradually ran out of money. She attempted television with three shows
but, although she enjoyed it, she admits that "I am a radio woman
through and through!"

The Pacific women's participation in the Beijing conference has
done much to stir interest in women's issues in Fiji. Bernadette pro-

duced regional newsletters and radio programs in the 18 months before Beijing and currently she is in the process of producing a film documentary tracing the journeys of Pacific women over the past two decades. "As a communicator I have worked with and felt empowered by, not the top level women in industry or government, but by the village women who know nothing of Beijing but who have struggled on silently to feed their families and maintain their God-given right as guardians of their environment and of their children. Their voices need to be heard more, not just as token case studies but as the communications movement of our industry."

In a workshop at the NGO Forum, women agreed that the use of media as a business-for-profit has been harmful since it has relied on a mixture of sex and violence for appeal. NGOs were urged to demand an end to the unwarranted exploitation of women, to call for media literacy at all levels of the education process and to carry on their own awareness and educational projects. There have been some exciting successes in this field—groups of women who have made huge differences in the transformation of their nation's female environment, who have given women hope for the future.

Making a difference

The Women and Media Collective in Sri Lanka is a group of writers, artists, photographers, actors, and researchers who use their skills to help women develop their talents in communication. The group publishes a bi-monthly newspaper called *Shakthi* that freely discusses sexuality, violence against women, and women's roles in religion and family.

The group's initial effort was limited to a monthly media monitor circulated among women's groups and interested non-governmental organizations. "However," a spokesperson said, "we realize we needed to broaden our outreach so we began contacting women journalists, writers, both freelance and from the mainstream press. We formalized the contacts with a series of meetings in which we discussed women's images in the media, the portrayal of women by both male and female writers in extremely stereotypical and sexist ways and the need to critique such practices. The response was encouraging; however, our ability to influence male-dominated thinking in the newspaper world has been an uphill task. This led us to publish a strip newspaper for women with the women providing the creativity and being given space to use it."

The collective also publishes poetry by Sri Lankan women in the three national languages and makes slide shows and videos about women. These include "Victims of Conflict" about women and children who are displaced because of war, and "Pause," about a brief moment of peace in the civil war. In their work the group tries to develop a feminist perspective to deal with problems of culture and ethnicity in the Sri Lankan as well as the South Asian context.

New ways of thinking and seeing

Telemanita is an alternative video production and distribution network that enables women's centers throughout Mexico and Central America to make their own videos. The network trains women to use video as an educational and organizing tool, so that they may be able to present a new way of thinking and seeing for both women and men. Telemanita has a central office and production center in Cuernavaca, Mexico and national coordinating offices in Guatemala, El Salvador, Costa Rica, and Nicaragua. Its strategy is to establish a few very well equipped production and distribution centers with access for many groups rather than a large number of less well equipped centers. Decision making in the network is decentralized—national centers choose training strategies that are most appropriate for women in their particular societies.

In the future the group plans to offer regional training camps for beginning video makers, to produce a video magazine program with clips from many countries, and to produce a feminist soap opera.

The visions of two women

In 1988 two young Nepalese women recognized that "the media are very powerful and effective channels for creating awareness and changing social attitudes about women."

They founded the Asmita Women's Publishing House which produces ASMITA magazine every two months, as well as pamphlets, posters and flyers designed to reach semi-literate women.

ASMITA covers news, views and research findings about women and has apparently established itself as a strong alternative medium for women in Nepal. Asmita Women's Publishing House also holds media workshops and translates foreign resource materials into Nepali. It is developing a poster series to be distributed in rural areas about the trafficking of girls.

AGENDA is a racially diverse women's collective in South Africa that produces a magazine of that name four times a year. The journal was first published in 1987 by a group of young academics, students and activists who had a magical vision of bridging the gap between gender-issue research conducted in universities and work that was being done at ground-level by women's organizations.

AGENDA'S editor, Gil Harper, describes the magazine as "the only feminist journal in South Africa." Its circulation is "a small but concentrated group of policy-makers, parliamentarians, activists, researchers, health care workers, professionals, educators," to which rural readers are slowly being added.

"Our authors are not journalists," says Gil Harper. "We seek out women who are experts in their fields or have experience in particular areas. We encourage first-time writers and all women to share their views, successes, challenges and experiences with readers. AGENDA also promotes good race relations while discouraging all forms of discrimination including homophobia."

The magazine is sold throughout the country and also has subscribers in the Southern African region and in North America and Europe. Future plans include adding more issues and training more women in writing and analytical skills.

CIDHAL: good times and hard times for women

Rocio Suarez-Lopez is a Mexican feminist sociologist who has been associated, for the past ten years, with CIDHAL, the longest living organization in Latin America working with women's issues. She spreads the stories of the plight of Mexican women and the feminist solutions to their problems and also lectures extensively about women's rights, reproductive health, rape, sexual abuse, and domestic violence. She is a member of CIDHAL's Board of Directors.

CIDHAL was formed by Betsie Hollants, a Belgian journalist, who began early to write stories about feminist issues through which she hoped to enlighten the women of Mexico. Her first task was to organize a documentation center that would research issues and provide their findings to other publications. Journalists could base their writings on CIDHAL's documentation and did so on a regular basis. One of the publications that depended heavily on CIDHAL for material was the weekly *El Correo del Sur* that in 1978 was bringing a Christian message to the underprivileged sector of Mexico and encouraging people identified with the Liberation Theology Movement.

CIDHAL provided *El Correo del Sur* with articles on the health services provided by Mexico's public institutions, the expropriation of women's bodies, the ruling medical practices, midwifery, rape, national and international birth control policies, housework and its importance, and other subjects of interest to women.

In the beginning CIDHAL welcomed contributions from all of its members, journalists or not. A rotary calendar was set up so that everyone who cared to would have the opportunity to write articles. Feminist content and perspective were deemed more important than the style and quality of writing.

In 1975 CIDHAL joined a group of women from poor neighborhoods to create a monthly journal titled *Maria Liberacion del Pueblo (Mary, the Freedom of the People)*. A year later it became an independent project and it still exists.

CIDHAL entered the arena of radio in 1985 with a 15 minute weekly show on a private station, as part of a traditionally oriented women's segment. Out of this beginning came the idea for a network involving other NGOs.

In 1990 a four-year affiliation with Morelos Channel 3, a state-managed television station, began. CIDHAL participated in programs on rape and sexual harassment, women and AIDS, the environment, recycling, population policies, and the Fourth World Conference on Women.

CIDHAL is one of five organizations participating in the International Women and Health Documentation Center Network that links documentation centers for the member organizations which include Asian-Pacific Resource & Research Centre for Women (ARROW, Malaysia), Boston Women's Health Book Collective (BWHBC, U.S.A.), Centro para Mujeres CIDHAL (Mexico), Isis Internacional (Chile), and SOS Corpo (Brazil).

One of the goals of the Network is to provide journalists with information and to sensitize them on topics relating to women's health and specifically reproductive health.

Throughout its 28-year existence, CIDHAL has persisted in publishing its own materials addressed to different sectors with the object of educating, informing, and raising awareness.

FIRE!

The Feminist International Radio Endeavor (FIRE) was set up in 1991 as a means of communicating women's ideas to the world. The radio collective provides an opportunity for feminists to speak out on all issues, and it supports local and international feminist movements.

FIRE broadcasts daily women's programs in both Spanish and English via short wave from Radio for Peace, Costa Rica. Its programming addresses a wide range of issues from a gender perspective: poverty, women's rights as human rights, the environment, violence, racism, sexuality, education, art, and culture.

Maria Suarez Toro, a member of FIRE, attended her first international conference at the World Women's Congress for a Healthy Planet in 1992. "I hardly knew how to use a tape recorder," she recalls. That was the beginning of her dedication to women's concerns and her realization of the role women's alternative media have to play in "bringing our gendered lens to the world."

On September 16, 1995, Maria wrote an impassioned letter to Mme. Huang Qing, editor in chief of *World Women*, the *China Daily* publication circulated during the Fourth World Conference. Her letter is a witness to what one voice can do and say when empowered by justice, honesty, and courage.

In her letter Maria shares with Mme. Huang some unusual insights as to how the western press covered the several UN conferences that have taken place in the last decade; how the emphasis on accommodations—the inadequacy or undesirability thereof—was magnified in the press treatment given China but hardly noticed in the coverage of other conferences such as the ones in Vienna and Brazil. Maria analyzes for Mme. Huang's benefit the press's intention in each case, and how the coverage related to either the physical site for the conference or whether or not it was, specifically, a women's conference. It is difficult for outsiders to understand that such factors could prejudice press reports either in favor of or against a particular gathering but Maria makes it superbly clear that it does take place and how it works. In the following excerpts from her letter Maria takes us behind the scenes into the magical land of press bias and journalistic procedures.

In her first comment, Maria recognizes that Mme. Huang has taken the Western press to task in its coverage of the Beijing conference for "taking logistical issues for women's issues."

Mme. Huang, who made her remarks at a UNESCO Round

Table discussion which Maria attended (and which prompted Maria to write the letter), expressed disappointment that some pre-Beijing media reports made some women's groups seriously consider a boycott of the entire Beijing event:

"I feel (as you do) that some powerful media tried to obscure the Conference and its objectives around the issue of venue—first Huairou, then the visas, then the mud, security, transportation, apartments and who knows what else.

"While I also attribute this bias to Western media's play into geopolitics against China, at the same time I blame it on media's sexist bias about women's participation in these events."

Maria, who has been to every UN Conference since the Earth Summit in Brazil in 1992, has been in the rare position of witnessing and being able to analyze press coverage of these events in both North and South—Austria, Denmark, Brazil, Egypt and finally, China. She writes Mme. Huang that though there was not much that happened to the women participants in China that did not also happen at the other conferences, the Western press overlooked this fact in all except China, because, she writes, "it was a conference on women and it was in China."

Though many United States women had difficulty getting their visas to go to China, there were almost an equal number of difficulties for women who had to go through the United States to get to China. Among these she noted, "long hours under surveillance at airports, or having to pay extra for flights that did not require transit through the United States.

"I was one of the many women whose visa to China was not issued in time, though all my papers were in order. Together with my colleagues I missed my flight, raised hell to mobilize national and international opinion, diplomatic intervention, women's protests... and finally, got the visa and made it to China."

There was much consternation and negative press coverage about the distance between Huairou, the site of the Forum, and downtown Beijing where most participants were billeted. But, Maria writes, "at the Earth Summit conference in Rio 1992, the site of the NGO Forum was also separated by 40 kilometers from the official UN Conference. Did Western media portray this? No!"

In Rio, she said, "places were so far away from each other, bus services so scarce and taxis so expensive that very few were able to make it to both (the NGO Forum and the UN Conference). Most had to stay outside the process where decisions were made."

In Rio, Maria wanted to visit Favela Rosina, "the biggest slum on the continent," but it was impossible because the bottom of the mountain slope where the Favela ends and becomes the public road, was lined with military tanks permanently pointing their heavy duty machine guns toward the Favela. "So we can't get out to go to the conference," she quoted one of the women dwellers. She was told that if she tried to go into the Favela Rosina she "would not come out alive."

Her experience in Vienna in 1993 was similar to that in China in that "we also had security checking our bags and making us go through 'rays' every day that we attended the conference. In Cairo in 1994, during the Population and Development Conference, this happened daily even at our hotels! But it was picked up by the media and made news only in China!"

In Cairo, the security measures were ostensibly for the protection of women from fundamentalist religions. Yet, says Maria in her letter, "when the conference was over, security in Egypt was no longer there to protect women from the fundamentalist backlash in the communities where they lived!"

In Vienna, security was selective and official. Maria tells of Emma Hilario, a Peruvian woman now living as a refugee in Costa Rica and one of the 33 testifiers at the Global Tribunal on Violations of Women's Human Rights at the Vienna conference, who had been a victim of death threats by members of the Shining Path guerrillas in her country a few years earlier. In Vienna she was followed by members of that same gang. "Yet for her there was no security. UN police made it clear that they were not there to undertake such a case. The women who were with her had to get her safely out of the situation." Eventually the Austrian authorities did provide body guards for her, but the UN remained completely uninvolved.

When the UN tried to shut down FIRE's communications center in Vienna, declaring it was "illegal," they had to be inspected and approved by security guards. In China the difficulties were those of language and comprehension, but the issue was readily resolved and "we were able to broadcast every day. We cannot ignore these issues; we want a free press everywhere! We also want protection and safety for women everywhere!"

In Denmark in 1995, during the Social Development Summit and simultaneous NGO Forum, the budget for food for most NGO participants was so meager that "many of us ate only once a day," Maria wrote. Some women from a Danish NGO then opened a soup kitchen so that everybody could be fed adequately. "It never made the big news but when it was in China, the price of food was all over the world! Previous stories about the scarcity of food in China were so common in the media that many women brought food instead of clothes in their bags."

"The real 'Forbidden City' for women is the table where the global decisions about macro-economic policies are made! In conferences that were not about women," Maria wrote, "media focused on the issues; yet when it was about women they featured what you call 'logistics.' To me 'logistics' are not women's issues. It has been under the guise of logistics that many states, some powerful media and many international agencies have justified not paying attention to women's needs." At the Earth Summit, she said, "Most media highlighted the numbers—too many people on the planet, so much pressure on natural resources." Then they suggested that "resources be privatized in order to control and administer them more effectively." Then at the UN Human Rights Conference, the media again claimed that there were "too many human rights already to recognize new human rights. Women's rights should be just that. And at the Social Development Summit, media said there were too many demands being made, that a few should be selected and prioritized, but these should not be social and economic justice issues because the adoption of these would wipe out profit."

Maria offered her opinion that "we have to tackle Western media for its geo-political manipulation. That is a big task because it reaches around the world with its obscurantism. But as a feminist, I also believe that women in media have the immense responsibility of challenging sexism in all media even our local media. Why? Because it tries to keep women in their places!

"Did you know that I and many others told media that if women were to select the venue for a women's conference on the basis of a place where there no violations of women's human rights, we would have had to propose the moon for the venue? Women went to China out of deep interest in the country, out of stubbornness and out of a need to be where the women's movement was strongest. The women's movement has paved its way to the United Nations Agenda by overcoming gigantic obstacles, holding the States and the UN accountable to gender injustice in national and international politics and especially out of deep conviction that we have a right and a need to be there just as we have to be everywhere else where decisions about our lives are made."

We can't go the moon for our conferences, she says, "but we have to break geo-sexist policies on earth because this is our living space. Journalists working for mainstream media cover the way they do because they have to fulfill their medium's objectives and the media act the way they do because they respond to information market trends. If U.S./China geopolitics was what sold, they went for it!"

In her final plea for women's power in the media, she asks the question: How can we establish our own links, tell our own stories and contribute to ending the prevailing policies in the world? How can we tell the world that we learned that it is false, that the cold war is over, that it has only taken a different shape? Vivian Wee from DAWN told FIRE in Huairou that after this world conference about women and its results, the women of the world should think about convening our own Women's Conference about the World.

"Let's begin it now. Let's begin it in the media."

And she signs the letter, simply, "Thank you."

This is obviously a letter not just to Mme. Huang but to all the women of the world. It is powerful and meaty, and its substance should fuel countless deep and earnest discussions by women all over the world in every hamlet, town, and city!

The view from here and now

As a 1944 graduate of a prestigious school of journalism in the American midwest, I was practically guaranteed employment upon graduation, and indeed found an excellent position in advertising. I later had two daily radio programs.

Today, women are still a minority presence within media organizations, whether electronic or print. No jobs are "waiting." UNESCO data show that women have pursued higher-level mass communication positions in increasing numbers over the past 15 years. Data covering 81 countries show that in 50 of them more than 50 percent of journalism and communication students are female. In Africa, Asia, Europe, and Latin America women's share of media jobs is less than 50 percent. The media employment that awaits women communication graduates is by no means commensurate with their training. When they do find jobs, they are mostly located in administrative posts rather than on the front lines of production and editorial writing.

Margaret Gallagher's research quoted in this chapter notes that "real power within the media remains largely a male monopoly." Out of more than 200 organizations studied in 30 countries across four regions, only seven are headed by women, and a further seven have female deputy directors. Most of these are small radio companies or news magazines. Women's share of top jobs in the media is still disproportionately small. The glass ceiling is hard to crack!

"Today, although blatant discrimination has generally been abolished, women's access to media power continues to be hindered by a plethora of invisible barriers—attitudes, working conditions, assignments, and so on that can impede career development in subtle ways.

"Women must still struggle to achieve recognition and respect as media professionals. But the struggle is a crucial one. For the assumption that media content will change for the better if more women are involved in its production has been an integral part of the debate. But clearly the numbers are growing to the extent that would have been unimaginable just a decade ago," Gallagher writes.

The strategic objectives of the *Platform for Action* to increase the participation and access of women to expression and decision-making in and through the media and new technologies of communication, to promote a balanced and non-stereotyped portrayal of women in the media; to promote extensive campaigns making use of public and private educational programs; to disseminate information about and increase awareness of the human rights of women, are certainly attainable through the commitment of governments and non-governmental organizations, national and international media systems and professional associations. But how much more powerfully can these objectives be resolved when women unite creatively, courageously, knowledgeably to find ways to attain equality and respect through truth, conviction and perseverance? The stories and successful ventures recounted here are a witness to women who see the goal and have the capabilities within themselves to carry it out.

BE A MOSQUITO!

Sources

Platform for Action J, Women in the Media.

The Global Fund for Women, *Network News*, Issue 8, May 1995.

Media, Catharine Sly, Montreal Council for Women.

Eileen Sudnet interview, March 1996.
Women and the Media, Margaret Gallagher.

Maria Suarez Tora, personal correspondence to author.

Beijing Conference Action and Resource Network.

California Women's Agenda Media Task Force.

Bernadette Rounds Ganilau, personal correspondence to author.

The Global Fund for Women, *Network News*, Issue 8, May 1995.

Resource information

AGENDA
Carolyn Newton
Room 29, Ecumenical Centre
20 St. Andrew's Street
Durban 4001, South Africa
Tel: 31 3074074 Fax: 011 27 31 301 0740

ASMITA RESOURCE CENTRE FOR WOMEN
Ms. Sabala
4-3-12 R. P. Road
Secunderabad Andhra Pradesh
500 003
India

FEMINIST INTERNATIONAL RADIO ENDEAVOR
Maria Suarez
Radio Pax Internacional
Apartado 88
Santa Ana, Costa Rica
Tel: 506 2 249 1821 Fax: 011 506 249 1095

TELEMANITA
Catherine Russo and Alejandra Novoa
Calle de las Flores No. 12
Col. Acapantzingo
Cuernavaca Morelos C.P. 62440
Mexico
Tel: 52 73 182058 or 140586 Fax: 011 52 73 182058 or 140586
E-mail: telemanita@laneta.apc.org

WOMEN AND MEDIA COLLECTIVE
Sepali Kottegoda
5 Jayaratne Avenue
Colombo 5
Sri Lanka
Tel: 94 1 584 350 Fax: 011 94 1 580 721

BERNADETTE ROUNDS GANILAU
Editor/Publisher
G.P.O. Box 15592
Suva, Fiji
Tel: 679 304 934 Fax: 011 679 304 935

Armed Conflict

Sister Heléna Marie

■ ■ ■ ■ ■ ■ ■ ■ ■ ■ ▪ ▪

An environment which maintains world peace and promotes and protects human rights, democracy and the peaceful settlement of disputes... is an important factor for the advancement of women.

Education to foster a culture of peace that upholds justice and tolerance for all nations and peoples is essential to attaining lasting peace and should be begun at an early age. It should include elements of conflict resolution, mediation, reduction of prejudice and respect for diversity.

Platform for Action

In the era of "peace" that began in 1945 with the end of World War II, more than 20 million people have died in armed conflicts. Only three of the 82 armed conflicts between 1989 and 1992 were between states. The remainder were wars in which the combatants were killing those of their own nationality. Ninety percent of war casualties at the beginning of this century were military combatants. As the century ends, 90 percent are civilians.

United Nations Development Program (UNDP),
Human Development Report, 1994

Twenty-three million refugees and 26 million internally displaced people have been forced to leave their homes because of conflict, massive human rights abuse, or the direct effects of conflict, such as famine and lawlessness. As a rule of thumb, more than three quarters of those destitute displaced

people are women and their dependent children. That proportion of women and children may rise to 90 percent in
some refugee populations, when husbands or fathers are
killed, or taken prisoner, or drafted as combatants.
United Nations Office of High Commissioner for Refugees
Report, United Nations, New York, 1995

Rwanda: can you imagine, sister?

Josephine (whose true identity and those of her relatives are withheld
for their safety) and her two young daughters had just returned from
a festive wedding in a nearby village. It was the evening of April 6,
1994, and the place was Kigali, Rwanda's capital city.

Although war was raging in nearby Burundi, the mood was merry
in the house of relatives Petero and Tawnda, where Josephine and her
daughters had been living for the past month. Rwanda seemed to be
untouched by the violence, and the past week had been spent in happy
celebration of the wedding. The firecrackers and shouting in the
streets outside enhanced the feeling of celebration. Everyone went to
bed with a feeling of contentment.

Upon awakening the next morning, Josephine was suddenly jolted
out of her happiness by the ghoulish view from the window. In the
middle of the front yard sat an array of artillery, pointing away from
the house, with several soldiers crouching behind. In a flash of realization Josephine understood that the previous night's "firecrackers"
had been gunshots; war had now come to Rwanda, too, and they were
suddenly in the thick of it.

Shooting began in their front yard. Josephine and her nine family
members ducked for cover. Furtive glances out the windows revealed
that all the houses in the neighborhood were similarly surrounded by
artillery and soldiers.

Josephine made a dash for the telephone to call her husband's
family who lived a couple of blocks away. "Don't worry," counselled
her brother-in-law, an Anglican priest. "We have shooting here, too,
but it will stop soon and the whole thing will blow over."

But the shooting became fiercer and Josephine and her family spent
hours hiding under beds. Later, she tried to call her brother-in-law
again. There was no answer. There was never again any answer; the
entire family had been killed.

That was the last call possible. All telephone lines were subsequently cut.

Peering out the window once again, Josephine saw her next-door neighbor walk out of the front door of his house. He was shot on the spot. She noticed that other neighbors, too, had been shot near their homes, and remained lying where they fell. The soldiers had given orders that everyone was to remain inside their houses; whoever tried to leave was killed. So Josephine and her relatives remained inside, hiding under beds. They were there for three days.

Finally the armed soldiers called them out. "Leave the house with your hands above your head!" Josephine and Tawnda were the first to come out. Carrying nothing at all, they passed in front of the soldiers, their children clinging to their skirts. Petero removed his eyeglasses because wearing them might suggest that he was a member of the upper class. He disguised himself as a servant and followed the women and children. They left everything behind.

All of them were herded into a truck. It was then that they caught sight of Petero and Twanda's eldest son, Christian, who had been at a friend's house since the shooting began. He was being herded in a different direction but when he saw his parents, he made a move to join them. A soldier called out that he would be shot if he moved. He was forced to stand and watch his family being whisked away, perhaps never to be seen by him again.

The truck stopped at a gigantic sports stadium where Josephine and her family were jammed in with 50,000 others. They were forced to stay in one spot in the stadium for two days, without bathroom facilities or food and only a small amount of contaminated water.

Soldiers began selecting people randomly to kill or rape. At the orders of any soldier, a woman had to report to a place where she was then raped by as many soldiers as desired her.

Although a UN office was located right next to the stadium, officials did nothing, according to Josephine, to stop the killing and raping. Their only interference, after two days, was to announce over a loudspeaker that those who were not Rwandans should identify themselves.

Petero seized upon this opportunity. Speaking Swahili rather than Rwandan he told the UN officials that he and his family were Kenyans who had merely been visiting Rwanda when the attack began. Herded out of their house at gunpoint, he said, they had been allowed to take nothing, not even their passports and other identification papers. He pleaded that he and his family be allowed to return to Kenya.

The ploy worked. Petero and his family, including Josephine and her daughters, were allowed to board an airplane and were flown to

Kenya. The fate of the others left behind in Rwanda is now well known to the world.

Eventually, through the efforts of Josephine, Tawnda, Petero, and the Episcopal Migrations Ministries in the United States, all ten of the family members were able to emigrate to the United States, where they now live safely in housing provided by a local Episcopal church. Christian, who was conscripted into the rebel army, finally managed to escape and join his family in the United States after more than a year, due again to the efforts of the Episcopal Migrations Ministries. This family's survival is a miraculous exception to the rule of genocide that has plagued both Rwanda and Burundi for the last three years.

One report states: "In tiny Rwanda, in the space of less than four months, between half and two thirds of the country's population was killed, died from epidemic diseases, or fled. It was the largest and most catastrophic exodus the United Nations High Commissioner for Refuges (UNHCR) has ever witnessed. Among the hardest hit by the violence and uncertainly of displacement were young girls, elderly widows, single mothers—women" (*United Nations Office of High Commissioner for Refugees Report*, United Nations, New York, 1995).

Some reports estimate that nearly every woman and girl in Rwanda were raped in the course of the ethnic violence. "During the four month ethnic bloodbath, tens of thousands of... women... were raped by... fighters and neighbors," reports Joshua Hammer ("Children of Hate," *Newsweek*, September 23, 1996). He quotes Human Rights Watch lawyer, Bihar Nowrojee: "When the violence began in 1994, it was no coincidence that it was sexual violence. It was a very deliberate type of violence." Joshua Hammer goes on to describe the hellish cruelty: "Some [victims] were gang-raped; others were dragged off to Zaire with the defeated... army and held as sexual slaves in refugee camps. Thousands were savagely mutilated, psychologically maimed or infected with venereal disease or HIV. Perhaps worst of all, the living victims of the worst genocide since World War II must now endure ostracism from their own people. Rwanda's highly conservative Roman Catholic society considers rape a disgrace to its victims, who often suffer worse punishment than the perpetrators."

He describes what happened to Leonille Mukamagera and her family, who, unlike Josephine and her family, did not manage to escape Kigali. "Leonille Mukamagera never saw the face of her baby's father. She remembers him only as a man in military fatigues. His gang of... militiamen descended on the homes of her family and their... neighbors outside Kigali in May 1994. The gang torched the houses and slaughtered most of the inhabitants as they tried to flee. Mukamagera was dragged into a window-less hut and locked inside. For the rest of that day and through the following night, one of the militiamen silently and repeatedly raped her on the dirt floor. In the morning, after the men left, she crawled out of the darkness. Near the smoking rubble of her house she found the dead bodies of her husband, her brother and her mother."

A few weeks later she learned that she was pregnant. Like thousands of other Rwandan women, she gave birth to the child of the enemy—"children of hate," they are sometimes called—and is now raising the child of the killer of her family.

Josephine and I sat and talked one day in the small northeastern town where she and her daughters now live. Looking at the beautiful slender woman with the calm gaze, I would never have suspected that she had been through hell.

"Can you imagine, Sister?" she asked me. "Can you imagine?"

I had to admit that I could not. I couldn't imagine the horror of having my husband's entire family wiped out in less than an hour, of watching my son disappear before my eyes, of enduring the filthy conditions that surrounded the endless throngs of dispossessed and traumatized people.

Then there was the continuing horror of rape. "My two sisters were raped, I know," Josephine said. "Though they did not speak of such a thing in their letters, I know they did not escape it. Every woman, every girl was raped during that time."

"Can you imagine?" she asked again. "The soldiers come and rape you, one after one, 20, 25 times in one night, and again the next night and the next. Any time they want to. You are never safe. You even regret that you were born female, and wish you were dead."

I looked at Josephine's two beautiful daughters. The 12-year-old had already mastered English and was excelling in her new school. The five-year-old looked up at me with sweet, innocent eyes and a charming missing-a-tooth grin. It was hard to imagine that these two lovely girls might have been raped had they not managed to escape from Rwanda.

Josephine then offered me some of her reflections on men and on war, particularly as it affects women and children. Her poignant thoughts, born out of bitter experience, are relevant and useful to all women of the world, regardless of the measure of their current safety.

"It's the men who start war and spend all the money and get killed, leaving the women to cope with what's left. The men dominate. The men make all the decisions. The women in Rwanda have no rights. They cannot criticize, nor even suggest. As long as this is the situation, how can we have peace?

"Men and women need to be equal. There cannot be peace as long as women are not part of the decision-making. Men don't want peace; they want to dominate, to be king of the mountain. So what result do you have if you take a man like that and put a gun in his hand?

"The sad thing is that the women are the ones who suffer the most, watching all the destruction, watching their husbands get killed, their sons get killed, having unwanted sex with the soldiers because they have guns.

"Yes the women were raped. You have no choice but to submit. The soldiers say, 'Come here with us,' and the women have no choice or they would be killed. I feel sure my sisters were raped but are too ashamed to write about it in their letters."

Two pilgrimages inside Bosnia

Sister Elise, a Sister in my community (Community of the Holy Spirit, New York City), made a pilgrimage to Medjugorje in the former Yugoslavia in 1988. Sponsored by a layman who wished to have her assessment of the alleged miraculous appearances of the Virgin Mary to several teenagers in the village, Sister Elise spent ten days worshipping in the local church, climbing the rocky slopes to the mountaintop where Mary is said to have first appeared, and visiting with one of the teenage visionaries.

Convinced of the authenticity of the appearances, Sister Elise listened carefully to the messages the visionaries relayed. Back home she repeated the messages to the Sisters in our community.

Many of the messages seemed to be warnings of something catastrophic about to happen.

Five years later a woman from Little Rock, Arkansas, also made a trip to Medjugorje. Like Sister Elise, Kathy Wells was a devout Episcopalian, but she made her trip for an entirely different reason. She was invited by the Bosnian government to come to Bosnia and counsel some of the women and girls who had been raped by soldiers during the brutal war which by now was in full swing.

Kathy tells the story of her involvement in Bosnia:

I had worked for 26 years as a counselor for rape victims in

Little Rock and across Arkansas. On a Sunday, I read accounts of the rapes, mutilations and forced pregnancies inflicted upon Bosnian women and children. The next day, I called upon friends and colleagues in Little Rock to join my letter of appeal to President-elect Bill Clinton to send trauma-counseling aid as part of the humanitarian relief then being provided.

Two days later, one woman who heard my appeal invited me to a dinner party in honor of Bosnian government representatives passing through Little Rock. I repeated my concerns that American-style trauma counseling ought to be arranged for Bosnian women.

One week later, a Bosnian called me and invited me to come to Bosnia, as a guest of the government, and help set up that trauma counseling program. Then I called Dr. Marlene Young, the Director of NOVA [National Organization for Victim Assistance, a private, nonprofit organization based in Washington, D.C.], who liked the idea right away. One week after that, Dr. Young and I were on our way to Bosnia, in January, 1993.

As they walked the streets and mountain paths that Sister Elise walked five years earlier, they found parks turned into makeshift refugee centers and shell-shocked women, men, and children. They found that rape had been used as a deliberate weapon of war and that there were few services for the traumatized survivors.

Women and girls, they learned, had been raped repeatedly by soldiers, followed by local men and boys swept up in the frenzy of the times. Some of the rapes by soldiers were videotaped and later sold as pornography on the world market. Some of the girls and women were raped in front of their fathers or other relatives, the ultimate humiliation.

Kathy and her team, using skills they had practiced for years with rape victims in the United States, encouraged the victims to express their feelings through writing, art and dance. They were allowed to tell their stories; naming the demon was an important part of the healing process. Says Kathy, "When you call your demons by name, you gain power over them. Under the most appalling conditions, we found women... whose self-worth was restored by telling us what happened."

The war stories they heard were a litany of violence: killing, rape, thievery, brutality. "The pattern was repeated over and over," says

Kathy. "Men with guns came and killed the men who were going about their daily business. [They] raped the women, stole money and jewelry. Women were held and raped repeatedly, until they were pregnant, then held until the pregnancies were so far advanced they could not safely abort the fetuses. Then, before being sent away at gunpoint and told never to return, the survivors were ordered to sign over the title to their homes and businesses."

An expose in *Ms Magazine* ("Turning Rape into Pornography: Postmodern Genocide" [July-Aug. 1993]) quotes a Bosnian soldier who stole into a Serbian military camp and witnessed a brutal gang rape of a Bosnian woman. "The woman was tied to four stakes in the ground, in a lying position but suspended. While they were raping her, the soldiers said that Yugoslavia is theirs... that they fought for it in World War II, partisans for Yugoslavia. That they gave everything for Yugoslavia. The men laughed and chided each other for 'not satisfying her,' for not being able to 'force a smile out of her,' because she is not showing 'signs of love.' They beat her and asked her if it was good for her. The superior who was ordering them said, 'She has to know that we are chetniks. She has to know that this is our land. She has to know that we're commanding, that this is our Greater Serbia, that it'll be like this for everyone who doesn't listen.' Does it ever occur to them that the woman is a human being? I don't know if they ever even think this is a person."

Thousands of women were raped during the war in Bosnia. The European Union estimates the number at 20,000; Bosnia's Interior Ministry says it was closer to 50,000 (*Newsweek*, September 23, 1996). In Bosnia, as in Rwanda, a policy of ethnic cleansing has resulted in genocide and widespread rape. It is women, girl children, and the children born of rape who are the ultimate victims.

The majority of refugees from armed conflicts are women and children. As refugees, they are vulnerable to further violence. "Most take refuge in remote, poorly developed areas where there is little security... Sexual violence against women is widespread" (*Women: Looking Beyond 2000*, United Nations, New York, 1995).

The hardest part of Kathy's work with the Bosnian refugees comes when she asks the rape victims if they have a request (something she was trained to do as a rape counsellor in the United States). "Their first request is always... for peace—an end to fighting," she says, "which is hard because we can't give them that."

When Sister Elise walked the mountain paths in Medjugorje, and listened to the messages relayed by the visionaries, she heard over and over again Mary's call for peace. Though only partially heeded at this present time, it is a call that continues to be voiced.

As a Sister in a religious community, I tend to take revelations from Mary seriously. Not every woman will give the same credence to Mary's messages, but most women seem to share that deep and abiding desire for peace.

Women can step out and take the lead in peacemaking. Indeed, one of the strategies in the *Platform for Action* is to "promote women's contributions to fostering a culture of peace."

Demonstrating for peace

Many women in the former Yugoslavia have joined a worldwide movement called "Women in Black." Every Thursday at an agreed time the women, all dressed in black, assemble at public squares and hold lighted candles, banners, and signs bearing messages of hope for peace. These silent processions of women include Serbs, Croatians, and Bosnian Muslims.

A "Women in Black" Thursday was observed during the NGO Forum. Women of many different nationalities stood together silently, in solidarity, bearing witness to women's desire for peace.

Women anywhere in the world can make "Women in Black" processions. All it takes is a little organization, a few permissions, and some publicity. The more women stand together, the more we can raise awareness and effect change. Non-violent demonstrations are one effective way to raise awareness that violence is not an acceptable way to resolve conflicts—and more and more women and men are beginning to realize this and to literally stand and march for peace.

It was a powerful and moving experience for me to watch the hundreds of women dressed in black, silently processing through the forum grounds holding candles. It made me realize that we have strength in numbers. It raised my awareness and called forth in me new energy to work for peace.

Deconstructing negative images of the enemy

Patti Browning, the wife of the 24th Presiding Bishop of the Episcopal Church, is a peacemaker. As a schoolgirl growing up in the United States during World War II she saw posters of caricatured Japanese soldiers, "crazed and bucktoothed, bayoneting women and children just like my sister and me." It wasn't until many years later, when she and her husband were called to a ministry in Japan, that she learned to appreciate and love the Japanese people and culture. As she lived with them and learned their language and customs, "God was redeeming me from the suspicion, anger and racism that had taken hold of me."

She found herself confronting a similar stereotype before her 1987 trip to Israel, that of the Palestinian terrorist: "a black-and-white-checkered, head-scarf-wearing, bearded, deranged, bomb-throwing fanatic, a brutal and merciless hijacker." Suspicious of the media, however, she herself never depersonalized the Palestinians.

Visiting Israel and meeting with Palestinians transformed her into a strong advocate for their cause, particularly when she began to worship with them and to listen to their stories. She heard of families who had lived for generations on land that was suddenly taken over by force, its occupants shoved into a crowded camp that was now their "home." She visited children in the hospital whose legs had been broken in retaliation for throwing stones (later they would simply be shot). "I used to tell my children not to throw stones," one Palestinian woman told her, "but then I saw that the quality of life they were living… it would have been better if they were in heaven."

She visited hospitals in which tear gas had been thrown into the maternity wards. Tear gas canisters had also been tossed into schools. She saw young Israeli children swaggering on the streets of Jerusalem with machine guns, and young Palestinians taunting them with rocks. "It pains me greatly to see little Israeli children growing up learning to hate and fear little Palestinian children, and vice versa," she says.

Patti has been to Israel eleven times since 1987. She has come to see her role in the church as a peacemaker, helping people to deconstruct their negative images, helping to humanize the enemy, praying that, as a rabbi in Israel once told her in hope, "long-abused Israel may be able to resist, in turn, being an abuser."

Based on conversations with Patti Browning, and on her article, "Breaking the Other Icon," in *The Living Church*, October 1, 1989

Crossing borders for peace

The world's oldest international women's peace organization is the Women's International League for Peace and Freedom (WILPF).

Eighty years ago, as World War I raged, a group of women who want-ed peace chartered a boat which took more than 1,000 women from 12 countries across the borders of their warring countries to meet together in The Hague, The Netherlands. They reached out to their "enemy sisters" in order to work together for peace. These women became the founders of WILPF. (Their objectives include the achievement of total and universal disarmament; the abolition of vio-lence and other means of coercion for the settlement of conflicts; the substitution of some form of peaceful settlement; the strengthening of the UN and its family of Specialized Agencies; the prevention of war; the achievement of a sustainable environment, and of political, social, and economic cooperation of all peoples.)

Eight decades after organizing the historic journey to The Hague, WILPF organized the Peace Train as a means to accomplish one of its stated goals: "To bring together women of different politi-cal and philisophical backgrounds to help abolish the cause of war and to work for a constructive peace." Riding the Peace Train was an expe-rience that changed my life. I met women from all over the world, and discovered that we all wanted and were willing to work for peace.

As my Peace Train sisters and I attended Parliament in Kiev and addressed the members about nuclear disarmament, as we met with social activists in Almaty, Kazakhstan, and evangelized for peace in the Peace Tent at the NGO Forum, we were taking some small but important steps to achieve those objectives.

My roommate for a few days in Beijing was a Palestinian woman I had met on the Peace Train. Tahgrid Shabit was from the West Bank. I told her about an experience I had had on the train. An internation-al songfest had spontaneously erupted one night on the train. Women from all over the world sang songs from their own and other countries. I had my flute and at one point launched into a popular Hebrew folk song, "Havah Nagilah," which I thought everyone would know. I played one verse, but no one joined in the singing, so I stopped. Later, an Israeli woman on the Peace Train, Aliyah, told me that the song has been taken over by militant Zionists as a fight song; those who favor the peace process in the Middle East no longer sing it.

I asked Tahgrid if she knew the Israeli woman, Aliyah. "Oh yes!" she exclaimed. "She was my roommate on the Peace Train. Several years ago we helped to start a women's peace organization bringing together Israeli and Palestinian women who want to work for peace. We are supposed to be enemies, Aliyah and me, but we are working together for peace, and in that process we have become best friends."

Most women want and are willing to work for peace. I met and talked with perhaps 800 women during my two-month trip around the world. I met Finns, Russians, Ukrainians, Bulgarians, Kazahks, Chinese, Nepalese, South Africans, Ethiopians, Filipinas, Tibetans… and they almost wanted peace. The only exception was a group of militant women from Iran who, alone, expressed the desire to use weapons to resolve conflict.

In Bulgaria the Peace Train participants met women from the former Yugoslavia who told us the message they wished us to communicate to the world: "Stop the war! Stop selling the weapons that fuel the war. It's a war for profit, a war that is making rich those who sell weapons and ammunition."

In Russia we met mothers of Russian soldiers who deplored the actions of the Russian army in Chechnya. "We did not raise our sons to be rapists," they cried. These mothers have formed an organization to stop the abuses they claim the army commits against their sons, including forcing them to rape and do other things against their will.

A woman wins the Nobel Peace Prize

Alison Wright, a San Francisco-based photographer, has a knack for arranging to meet Nobel Peace Prize recipients. Several years ago she met and worked in Calcutta with Mother Theresa, and in the past six months she has met and interviewed two more, His Holiness the Dalai Lama, spiritual and political leader of the Tibetan people living in exile, and Aung San Suu Kyi, leader of the National League for Democracy (NLD) and elected leader in Burma (Myanmar).

Alison succeeded in hearing Aung San Suu Kyi in person, which all the women at the NGO Forum were unable to do. Aung San Suu Kyi was to have been the first speaker to address a plenary session at the NGO Forum. Perhaps two thousand women were packed into the rather small auditorium (the largest one made available to the thirty-thousand forum participants), and many more stood outside hoping to get in. The air was electric with expectation. Suddenly the lights went out, a screen in front lit up, and a videotaped image of Aung San Suu Kyi relayed a message. Due to the circumstances of her political situation, she could not leave Burma. She sent a message of hope for peace in the world, and for gains to be made by the women at the Forum.

Seven years earlier, Aung San Suu Kyi had risked death to speak for peace. In 1989 in Rangoon, she bravely walked past six armed soldiers who had been given the order to shoot if she passed. As she walked calmly past, the soldiers lost their nerve and the order was withdrawn. She mounted the speaker's platform and addressed the assembled crowd about something stronger than guns: peace.

She went on to endure six years of house arrest under Burma's military dictatorship, sacrificing her health and her right to be with her husband and two children. Elected to be the general secretary of the nonviolent pro-democracy movement in Burma (the National League for Democracy) she remained in the country to struggle on behalf of her people rather than accept safe passage to her family in England. Eventually she was awarded the Nobel Peace Prize for her courage and commitment to peace.

Four months after the NGO Forum in Beijing, Alison decided to make a trip to Burma to meet and interview Aung San Suu Kyi, whom she greatly admired. In spite of difficulty getting drivers to take her there, she was able to go to Aung San Suu Kyi's house three times, twice for interviews with this remarkable woman. Afterwards Alison was followed around Rangoon by undercover officials, and felt that she was watched constantly. But being in the presence of Aung San Suu Kyi made it well worth it.

"She sat ramrod straight," said Alison, "and her bearing was regal. She made me feel like I should sit totally straight as well. Her presence was just immense, and yet she was soft-spoken and peaceful.

"She has an incredible inner strength— to have endured the isolation under house arrest for six years. And yet, when I asked her to what she attributed her ability to endure, she said that she always had a sense of solidarity with others, that it was impossible to feel alone during those six years. She gained strength from her Buddhist faith, and from the example of others, especially her father and uncle, who were martyrs for the cause of democracy in Burma."

Alison compared her to the Dalai Lama, but Aung San Suu Kyi declined such a comparison. Although she admitted that the Dalai Lama was one of the leaders she most revered, she said, "I wouldn't have considered myself reaching the heights of such spiritual elevation." Alison could see a similarity, however. Both are peacemakers who are willing to endure violence and isolation and being ignored by the international community. Both have that strength and resilience, an inner strength, not just political strength.

"If you ask whether we shall achieve democracy," Aung San Suu Kyi told a rapt audience in Burma, "here is what I shall say: 'Don't think about whether or not these things will happen. Just continue to do what is right.'" In the videotaped presentation addressed to the thirty-thousand women at the NGO Forum, she said, "It is time to apply in the arena of the world the wisdom and experience [that women have gained] in activities of peace over so many thousands of years."

I asked Alison if she knew at the time that government officials were following and watching her. "I don't doubt that they were," she said, "but it didn't deter me." The urgency of getting the message out about what is happening in Burma spurred her on past her fears, just as it spurred on Aung San Suu Kyi herself.

There are many women, like Aung San Suu Kyi, making personal sacrifices for peace. Some, like Alison, travel to dangerous places at great risk in order to report to the world what peacemakers are doing to bring about peace. Others work quietly in their own communities to foster a culture of peace.

Many of these courageous women go to great lengths in their efforts to achieve peace. Dorothy Grenada gave up her home and comfortable lifestyle in Oregon to live among the poor of Nicaragua, a country that was being decimated by war between the Contras and the Sandinistas. Using her own funds and a grant from an interdenominational group in the United States, she opened a medical clinic in the village of Mulukulu.

A registered nurse, she began working with a volunteer doctor in the clinic. Up to 100 women a day streamed into the facility, many of whom had to walk for days to reach the clinic. Most were mothers with many children—sometimes 12 or more. They were unable to support them adequately and were sometimes forced to watch them die of starvation. Numbers of the women accepted birth control measures from the clinic, knowing, as they did so, that to use such measures would risk hostility from their husbands.

The war has brought poverty and hardship to the rural women of Nicaragua. It is a war that is not really over, although we seldom hear about it now. Dorothy herself was recently beaten and threatened with death by ex-Contra forces who have a base in Honduras. They asked her to pay them $230 a day in exchange for their "protection." "You can kill me right now," she told them. "I don't have the money, and if I did have it I wouldn't give it to you!"

She was not killed, and since then she has sought and received protection from the local military. She continues her work under constant threat. Her funds have run out. Medicine is hard to get, and the clinic is now teaching people to raise herbs and roots for medicinal purposes.

"Solo Dios," says Dorothy, reiterating a favorite phrase of the peasants. "We have only God." She learns daily from these people who, rather than cursing and doubting God, have a remarkable faith.

Asked why she gave up her comfortable life to embrace poverty in a war zone, she responded, "I was converted while listening to the Gospel in my church in Oregon. I decided I had to simplify my life and put it on the line for peace and justice. I have suffered the consequences of my dedication to justice, but I have never been happier in my whole life than here in Nicaragua. I am by far richer now than I ever was when I had everything in the United States."

From an interview of Dorothy Grenada
by the Rev. Nina Olmeda Jaquenod

Peace begins at home

Closer to home, I found hope in an incredible woman who uses gardens to create peace. Catherine Sneed, a self-assured African-American woman with a mission, cultivates peace in a violent San Francisco community by cultivating plants. While counseling women in prison, she started a garden for prisoners—both women and men. She felt that gardening would have a healing effect in their lives, bring beauty to trash-filled areas, and provide food for people in need.

The first garden project began in an old storage area near the prison. Without tools, or even a wheelbarrow, the jail gardeners literally tore down old buildings with their hands. The clean-up took three years.

Finally came the garden. Vegetables, herbs and flowers began to emerge from the carefully tilled earth which so long had been but a barren space. The women and men prisoners likewise sprang to life. They found contact with the earth healing, they discovered new abilities and rejoiced in seeing the fruits of their labor going to help people in need. They began to feel their lives had new meaning. Crews of prisoners began to plant trees around the community outside the prison. They began in neighborhoods with rough reputations; the residents protected the new trees, planted as they were by people like themselves who were trying to make a better life.

Catherine began new garden projects. She and her jail friends converted several vacant and unbecoming lots into verdant gardens. They began to sell some of their produce to health food restaurants and to give to people in need in the bay area. The Garden Project eventually proved so successful that large corporations began supporting it.

Prison gardeners who were released from jail expressed an interest in continuing to help with the garden. Schools began requesting garden programs.

"Every day I get calls from schools to make gardens. A garden can produce revenue, and for kids who have no way of getting money to buy sneakers or something they want, selling carrots beats the heck out of selling crack," says Catherine.

Where is the connection between gardens and armed conflict? Here on their knees in the good earth are warriors from America's most infamous war zones. Instead of carrying Uzis, they are wielding hoes and trowels, creating new life and a sense of self-esteem.

The Garden Project will not solve economic disparity, institutional racism, or the major problems that lead to urban warfare, but it is planting seeds of hope in the hearts of urban warriors and showing them a different way, a way of peace.

Based on "These Green Things: Catherine Sneed and the San Francisco Garden Project," in the magazine *Orion: People and Nature*, Vol. 13, No. 3, Summer 1994

Bullets or books?

Martha Overall had been a successful attorney in New York City and San Francisco for thirteen years when a fundamental change took place in her life; dropping a lucrative law practice, she enrolled in seminary. Several years later she was ordained an Episcopal priest.

Why would anyone make such drastic change? Because she wanted to serve in one of the poorest and most violent neighborhoods in America.

As an attorney Martha had done some *pro bono* work at St. Ann's Episcopal Church in the Mott Haven section of the South Bronx. Gradually she came to know some of the people there and to understand the crazy system that keeps them economically disadvantaged—the victims of poverty and violence.

The day after her ordination to the priesthood Martha began serving at St. Ann's Church. In addition to offering the traditional liturgy to the community, she began to think of ways to encourage children and young adults to seek out books rather than bullets.

She teamed up with Nelida Espina, a Latina who had assisted in creating a successful literacy and adolescent program for youth in East Harlem. Leaving that program in the good hands of a talented staff,

Nelly took a deep pay cut to join Martha in a new endeavor. The chance to help children achieve full potential and to provide an alternative to urban warfare would be far more rewarding than a big salary. "I like difficult challenges," she grinned. "I like to start something from nothing, overcome the obstacles, and leave it in great shape."

Together Martha and Nelly built up a literacy program for children from kindergarten through the seventh grade, which became part of St. Ann's after-school program. The program operates every weekday afternoon from 3:00 until 6:00, and provides a snack, study time, recreation, crafts, tutoring, intensive reading and writing skills, and finally, dinner. The multicultural curriculum includes education about the everyday realities of drugs and AIDS. The church program is attended by 60 children, all of them African-American or Hispanic.

The after-school program was written about extensively in Jonathan Kozol's book *Amazing Grace*, and subsequently received gifts in the form of books, art materials, and, perhaps most valuable, volunteered time. Eleven used computers were obtained to teach computer skills.

Why do children who go to school every day need a literacy program? Not because they are less capable than other children. The public school system there lacks funds and operates in a destructive environment where armed conflict has become a way of life.

"These kids come to us with a worldview most people wouldn't believe," explains Nelly. "They don't even know which borough they live in. One girl said she thought the name of her borough was 'Mexico.' They live in a world bounded by 125th Street and Fordham University [an area of approximately five square miles]. They've never been beyond those boundaries. When we take them for a trip into Manhattan to go to a museum or look at Christmas lights [less than a mile away], they feel they are in another world. Even to ride in a car is a totally foreign experience for many of them."

"Only 16 percent of the children at one of our nearby schools read at grade level," says Martha. "Inner city kids have to compete with their hands tied behind their backs." In the face of drug warfare, AIDS, and unremitting poverty, St. Ann's provides these children a safe place; a place to read, to learn, and to grow toward their full potential, where boys use books to build minds rather than bullets to bolster their egos, and girls learn that there are other possibilities besides joining gangs and having babies, a place that fosters a culture of peace and hope.

I sit at a table with five girls in grades two through four. Two of them are African-American, three are Guatemalan. The Guatemalan children already speak three distinct languages: Spanish, a Guatemalan dialect, and English. They tease me; although already an adult, I am still monolingual. All five girls sparkle with excitement about having a visitor. They show me their drawings and carefully explain their homework. A woman volunteer comes to praise them for their good work.

I think these girls will make it somehow. They will make it out of the degradation that surrounds them. St. Ann's will have been an important stepping stone.

A few good men

Ed Eismann is one of those men who desire peace and who are willing to do something to bring it about. After earning his Ph.D. and only months away from ordination into the Roman Catholic priesthood, Ed found that there was a wider sense of priesthood which he believed in. He wanted to bring his sense of spirituality and his training in child psychology to the streets.

Foregoing ordination, he walked the streets of the South Bronx. He talked to the kids as he walked. He listened and pondered. The walks and talks grew to an idea and a program called "Unitas," a Latin word meaning "unity." This is what Ed hoped to foster in the community.

They closed off one of the short streets in the neighborhood, and Ed got donors to contribute gym mats, books, art materials, musical instruments and basketballs. He put this arsenal of creative materials on Fox Street and invited the children to come.

And they did come. When potentially explosive or chaotic situations arose, Ed enrolled the older kids in helping the younger ones. Teenagers helped ten-year-olds resolve conflicts, ten-year-olds helped seven-year-olds, and seven-year-olds helped preschoolers.

Eventually they organized into "family" groups; teenagers (symbolic "mothers" and "fathers" to the younger kids) learned to become role models. The young ones had someone to look up to and to look out for them. All conflicts were resolved by the children themselves. In this way they were learning conflict resolution—the road to peace.

That was 25 years ago. Today the Unitas program attracts hundreds of children each week. They meet every summer day on Fox Street; in winter they meet weekly in a school gymnasium. Some of the program's early recruits are grown and have children of their own who come to Unitas. They believe in it because they know it works.

The day Ann and I visited Unitas it was pouring rain. Indoors, kids were shooting baskets, doing homework, or drawing. It was noisy and healthy. A sense of community pervaded.

Suddenly, with no clear signal that I could discern, the children packed up their books, put away their basketballs and crayons, and formed a huge circle on the gym floor. Nearly 100 children organized quickly into "family groups." Again, with no discernable signal, they became quiet.

Then Ed, who had been waiting patiently as the family groups formed and settled down, began to tell a story about how kids who had a "beef" with each other worked it out peacefully. The story was a kick-off point, an invitation to the children to tell their own personal stories of conflict and resolution in their own lives. A short talent show followed with acrobats, hoop shooters, clarinetists, and poets. The growth of a healing community was apparent.

Whenever a child got too rowdy, his symbolic mother or father helped him to become quiet again. If a conflict arose between two or more children, their older peers helped them reach a peaceful resolution.

There are hard times, too; a boy's watch was stolen while we were there but the community helped create a solution. We had to leave before the watch turned up, but not a child was unaware of the community's responsibility to make sure the watch was returned. These youth have learned to put peacemaking and responsibility back where they belong: in themselves and in each other. And they have passed the legacy of Unitas on now to a new generation.

Three strong women

It took me a long time to work up the courage to visit Lucy Kuemmerle's students. Lucy teaches homeless teenagers and adults in a special education program in New York. Her students live at the Regent, a hotel for homeless families at 104th Street and Broadway, only nine blocks from the Manhattan convent where I live. I traveled to faraway countries to learn about economic disparity and armed conflict more easily than I walked the nine blocks to the Regent.

Perhaps this says something how much easier it is to address poverty and the violence it engenders when it is anywhere else but home. It is easier to send a contribution for refugees in Rwanda than it is to walk down the street to be with sisters and brothers who are homeless in my neighborhood. And, while armed conflicts are far away in other countries, yet I live only blocks from one of America's major urban war zones (Harlem), complete with Uzi's and AK-47's.

When I finally did visit Lucy's classroom, I was surprised to find a roomful of vibrant, enthusiastic women who welcomed me warmly and were eager to share their stories.

One of them, a strikingly beautiful mahogany-skinned woman, wore a golden dot in one pierced nostril and shiny black braids in corn rows wound around her head like a crown. In her arms she cradled a tiny baby.

"Meet Terona Brown," said Lucy; then, picking up the infant, "and her new son, John Anthony." Terona beamed serenity and openness. Her two-week-old son slept peacefully.

After further introductions, Terona and I stepped into the room where our interview was to be held. I had my questions ready; I wanted to know about economics and violence and the realities of being a homeless mother in New York.

I never got to these carefully prepared questions; when I suggested that I was interested in what life was like for her, Terona began to tell her incredible story. I was speechless.

Terona is a survivor. She endured years of sexual abuse by her mother's boyfriend, battering by her husband, the murder of her brother on the streets of New York, and the violence of drug warfare. She lives with her three children in a society that provides few economic opportunities for homeless single mothers. And Terona is 23 years old.

It is not war *per se* that has caused Terona's hardships. It is economic disparity, institutionalized racism, domestic violence, and other realities of American society. Yet her story sounds very much like those of the women in wartorn Rwanda: family members have been killed, she has been the victim of sexual violence, and she is virtually a homeless refugee from the inner city war zone. Despite a lifetime of hardship, including periods of self-harm and suicide attempts, Terona is hopeful and resilient. How?

She says it is her three beautiful children who have brought out these qualities in her. Flirting with suicide after her estranged husband had beaten her, she suddenly realized that she had a reason to live: she could prevent her children from enduring what she had had to endure. Pulling herself together, she took her children away from her husband and began to make a new life. This involved entering the shelter system.

She is now steering her three children through the snares and pitfalls of "the system" for New York's homeless while somehow providing for their basic needs. She is a beacon of hope. Her inner strength is apparent, her spirit indefatigable.

Terona is an agent of peace. Although she is herself a victim of violence, she has made the decision to rise above her circumstances to protect her children.

It will not be easy. But Terona is a strong woman. She has an intense desire to make a more peaceful world for her children. And she has friends like Lucy.

Pat Finney is another of Lucy's students whom I interviewed. An African-American woman from Harlem, she is another stellar example of the strength of the women in that community.

Life had once been good for Pat, she felt. Although she had grown up poor in Harlem she was well-loved by her grandmother, who raised her. Her mother was only 14 years old when Pat was born; her father was never part of the picture. ("No father, really," says Pat, "but I didn't feel nothin' about it.")

Pat got pregnant at 17, and within a few years she had three sons. Her husband, unlike her father, stuck around, but he "hung in the streets." Pat and her sons lived with her mother-in-law. Still, life was good, says Pat, until 1991.

It was on August 11 of that year that Pat's husband took their oldest son to a Harlem bus stop to send him off for his first year of college. As they were waiting, a man took her husband's jacket, which had been placed on a bench. As the two men tussled for his jacket, the thief pulled out a gun and killed her husband.

In 1992, her brother-in-law was killed, also by gunfire, and her daughter-in-law was killed in a car accident. Two years later Pat's uncle and mother-in-law both died of illness.

This series of tragedies left Pat and her sons traumatized and homeless. She held her family together as they became, in effect, refugees of urban warfare. She dealt daily with "the system" as she tried to find housing for her family. She learned from bitter experience that "the system," which was supposed to help the homeless, often made it much harder for them. But she never gave up.

Through it all she kept her sons in school. She managed to secure food and clothing for them through various agencies. And she continued to look for housing and to hang on to her hope.

Eventually Pat and her sons came to the Regent. Here they finally had their first piece of good luck: they met Lucy Kuemmerle.

Hired by the Board of Education to help prepare her students for the GED (a high school equivalency test), Lucy teaches conventional subjects like language arts, math, and history, but, in unique ways, so that her students can claim with pride their cultural roots (most of her students are African-American or Hispanic). They also gain the practical skills they will need to survive beyond the shelter.

Lucy goes far beyond the requirements of teaching. She buys Kentucky Fried Chicken when her students have no money for lunch. She takes the mothers shopping at Christmas time with money that she has collected from friends at her church. She encourages her students to express themselves in poetry, posts their work on a special bulletin board and publishes a scrapbook of their works every year. She looks after the children and follows their growth over the years.

"Lucy is my best friend," exclaims Terona. "Lucy is the best person I ever met in my life."

The admiration is mutual. Lucy sees strong women like Terona and Pat as the light of her life. Who can resist the charm and vitality of someone like Pat, who, after enduring so much tragedy in her life, says of herself, with a twinkle behind her thick eyeglasses and no trace of self-pity, "I don't drink, I don't smoke, I don't do drugs, I just wear glasses!"

Women like Terona, Pat, and Lucy are our hope for a future without war, as are the Rwandan women, Josephine and Leonille, as are *all* whose stories are told in this book, whose stories were told in Beijing. *We* are the hope of the future, all of us, and we will create the future.

If we are going to overcome a culture of war and rape, we must be stronger than guns, bombs and physical force. This is the power of peace. This is "the peace of God which passes all understanding."

"When attending a church service in Beijing," writes an American delegate to the NGO Forum, Elizabeth Hobbs, "[a gift] of God-given friendship came. I distinctly remember listening to the beautiful choir singing during the service, which was attended by over one thousand people. I knew I was being called to give copies of our ecumenical Noonday Prayer to the choir members. Quietly, as the last hymn was being sung, I walked over and gave the prayer to members of the choir.

"Three days later, while waiting for Mrs. [Hillary] Clinton to speak, a group of Chinese women entered the auditorium while we were singing 'Keep on movin' forward, never turning back.' Suddenly, the whole roomful of people from 189 nations began joining hands, and my hand was placed in the hand of Zhang Jian. She suddenly recognized me as the one who had given out the prayer cards in her church, and she told me this in excited and broken English, with gestures. I was so happy to see her again that [I gave her] a copy of "One Over All," [a booklet I wrote] about the importance of international friendship.

"It was such a crowded room that I did not see her again, but much to my delight, I heard from her at Christmas and discovered that she is a senior lecturer in a Chinese women's college department of social work. My profession is in the same field! She wrote, 'I felt your hand was placed in mine, and I was no longer alone when I read your booklet.'"

Sisters, let us keep on moving, never turning back, and let us join together to create a culture of peace.

Resources

Eismann, Edward. *Unitas: Building Healing Communities for Children.* New York: Fordham University Press, 1996. Second Edition.

Martin, Susan Forbes. *Refugee Women.* London & New Jersey: Zed Books Ltd., 1995.

"Peace and Freedom: Magazine of the Women's International League for Peace and Freedom"
"Women's Budget"
"International Peace Update"
Women's International League for Peace and Freedom
1213 Race Street
Philadelphia, PA 19107-1691

"Toward Freedom: A Progressive Perspective on World Events"
209 College Street
Burlington, VT 05401

Women: Looking Beyond 2000. New York, United Nations Publications, 1995.

The Environment

Lucy Germany

■ ■ ■ ■ ■ ■ ■ ■ ■ ■ ■ ▪

Involve women in environmental decision-making and integrate gender concerns into policies for sustainable development.

Assess the impact of development and environmental policies on women.

Platform for Action

Story, says Madeleine L'Engle, is where we look for truth. Story in many parts of the world is the entire history of a people and of the earth. We wonder now, standing at this brink of a new century and a new millennium, what kinds of stories we are making today to tell the children of tomorrow. Will they be stories of parched earth, devastating ultraviolet rays, ravaging storms over deforested slopes, rivers thick with sludge, and oceans shining with belly-up fish?

The UN position on the environment strongly interrelates poverty and environmental degradation. The environment is degraded, the concluding paper states, by global warming which results in rising sea levels, by the use of ozone-depleting substances such as halogens and methyl bromides and products with chlorofluorcarbons, and by general deterioration and depletion of the earth's once abundant natural resources. Women are not widely recognized as leaders in the struggle to right the tilted environmental picture, even though it is accepted that they are the ones closest to the earth in many parts of the world; they draw the water, tend the family's food plot, care for the animals. In local situations women do take leadership roles, albeit largely unrecognized, to reduce the use of natural resources, to recy-

cle usable wastes, to minimize excessive consumption. Women are the
teachers of the children, who instill in the next generation the holiness of a blade of grass, the sweetness of a clear drop of water. As in
many countries men work on contract in distant countries, women,
the nest tenders, are also the keepers of the environment. It is
women, the child bearers, who suffer most intensely from flagrant
violations of resource purity. In the workplace, in their homes and
communities, they frequently face daily hazards to their bodies from
chemical substances and pollutants in their water and food supplies.
Often these hazards are passed directly to the forming fetus which
then becomes one in a whole generation of the underdeveloped or
improperly formed. As incursions into developing societies by
multinational corporations seeking sources of cheap labor and low
taxation increases, those hazards, unless met with public outcry, will
continue to increase. And where should the outcry be raised? At the
site where the suffering is escalating, of course, but also in the source
countries where politics and marketplace pressures can most effectively be brought to bear and where often the home offices of the
offending company are located. We all suffer when such indecencies
are permitted. It is time for all women to become warriors rather
than worriers.

The *Platform for Action* makes the important connection
between women's health and environmental protection by addressing the lack of information concerning women's susceptibilities
and exposures to environmental hazards and toxic substances. This
is particularly urgent in light of the increasing environmental hazards worldwide, particularly in rural and poor urban areas. The
platform is an important step forward in focusing global attention
on this issue.

United States Department of State Press Kit, UN Fourth
World Conference on Women, Bureau of Public Affairs,
Office of Public Communication

Development: "by" not "for"

As Aung San Suu Kyi, Nobel Peace Prize laureate, said at the Opening
Plenary of the NGO Forum: "The watchfulness and active cooperation of organizations outside the spheres of officialdom are necessary
to ensure the four essential components of the human development
paradigm as identified by the UNDP: productivity, equity, sustainabil-

ity, and empowerment. The last is particularly relevant; it requires that development must be by people, not only for them. People must participate fully in the decisions and processes that shape their lives.'"
NGO Forum on Women '95 Bulletin

Population, militarization, and other concerns

We must consider several revolutionary trends, recognition of which will shape our lives in both the near and distant futures.

One is demographic. Analysts predict a doubling of the earth's current 5.5 billion population before the middle of the next century, provided we are not faced with a global catastrophe either natural or human. More than 90 percent of that increase will occur in the poorest nations, creating massive migration pressures, changing the nature of many communities and nations, including the United States.

Another is the switch from resources to knowledge. The drivers of all life are shifting from resources to information, from a resource economy to a knowledge economy. Educational achievement and facility with symbols will determine a person's future economic well-being to a greater extent than ever before.

The global economy is bringing about closer ties between nations. The futurists predict a single worldwide production and exchange system, an erosion of national boundaries and increasing difficulty in the solving of problems by individual nations.

Instability all over the world comes about as nations large and small brim with weapons and endure new kinds of conflict. Exclusivist nationalisms challenge the world's hope for greater universality, tolerance and democracy. The future of the world depends on progress in demilitarization and in developing strong and effective multilateral peacekeeping institutions.

Worldwide interest in mounting threats to public health and long-term habitability of the planet continues to increase. Human numbers and appetites push to the limits life-support systems and the renewal capacities of the earth. The last generation's challenge to protect humans from the forces of nature has done an about face: it is nature now that needs protection. Human fulfillment must be reconciled with environmental protection and sustainable growth. (This data has been excerpted from a report produced by the Friends Committee on National Legislation as it appeared in the 1993-94 Winter-Spring issue of *Earthlight Magazine*.)

We talk a great deal about the hope of the earth. How wide is that hope? What are its dimensions? Syndicated journalist Mickey Guisewite, recently wrote: "If anything can give us hope about our world it's the thigh-high army of environmentalists (grade-school children) policing our communities. If we can keep the planet together long enough for them to grow up, it might just have a chance." Guisewite forms her argument around a visit to a preschool class in which the children made comments about over-packaging (her cheese and cracker snack was wrapped in plastic packaging, then in a second clear zip-lock bag, and finally in a paper sack), about styrofoam (seeing her take out a cup of that dreaded substance), and were dutifully placing recyclable materials into properly labeled containers.

Where are the ducks swimming?

"Today's preschoolers," Mickey Guisewite writes, "are learning about the rain forest, global warming, the ozone layer, landfills and the polluted waters the ducks are swimming in. If children are environmentally aware by age three, by age 12 they're full-fledged activists. They've learned about our delicate balance with nature. They've studied the polluted air, the contaminated water we drink and the pesticide-treated food we eat. They've learned about the wildlife that is vanishing from the earth." Then she cites such statistics as the worldwide deforestation rate 27 million acres per year) and the fact that the tiger population has decreased by 95 percent in this century. Though the latter may not appear significant, it does exemplify what is occurring in many areas of the natural world in terms of dwindling number of species and a shrinking wild animal gene pool. Considering the interconnectedness of species and the dependence upon variety in order to make nature work, it is no wonder that such statistics are seen as alarming and that well-informed people are rallying to conservancies and worldwide environmental efforts.

Meet Marcie the Marvelous Tree

Guisewite's hope for the environment through the awareness of young people is reflected in the story of the Tree Musketeers, three teenage girls in California who a decade ago, when they were eight and members of a Brownie troop, planted a sycamore sapling in their hometown of El Segundo, to "give something back to the earth" after having used paper plates on a camping trip.

Today the tree, known as "Marcie the Marvelous Tree," is 40 feet tall, the girls are 17 and have founded the "Tree Musketeers," a non-profit program run exclusively by young people which operates a telephone hotline, publishes a bimonthly periodical called *Grassroots Youth Magazine* with 50,000 readers, and has an informal network called "Partners for the Planet" with six million members. The original aim of Tree Musketeers was to plant enough trees to form a pollution barrier around El Segundo, home of an oil refinery, a major sewage treatment plant operating for the city of Los Angeles and within hearing distance of the Los Angeles International Airport. "I remember feeling empowered," said Sabrina Alimahomed, one of the trio. "I thought we could plant the whole world with trees." And indeed the group has planted more than 700 trees in its own community and has inspired tree plantings all over Southern California. They have also opened a recycling center, created the world's first Youth Summit of environmental organizations, and even have a television program called "Tree Stumpers." Their message to teens everywhere: "Don't ever let anyone tell you that you can't change the world."

Taken from "How The Tree Musketeers Grew... And Grew" by Seth Shulman, in the April 21,1996 *Parade Magazine*

Another case in point is the story of Elzeard Bouffler, told in the *Journal of Women's Ministries* by human relations consultant Virginia Swain who attended the 1994 Earth Summit in Rio de Janeiro. Bouffler, a Frenchman, went about his country, grieving his dead wife, accompanied only by his dog and his sheep, to plant trees, 100 acorns a day for over 30 years. "Bouffler transformed the landscape," reports Swain. "Once desiccated, wind whipped, forsaken regions have been brought back to life by his trees."

In Ithaca, New York, a program called "Ithaca Money" has been established which offers services for services, eliminating the exchange of money for many kinds of tasks and encouraging the use of local products. Products that originate at home do not have to be shipped by air, thus eliminating pollution from transportation. In the case of food, chemical preservatives are not needed to keep the product fresh for the long haul. "Ithaca Hours help build direct economic relationships between producer and customer. If you know the person growing your food or making the materials for your house, you stand a greater chance of affecting that person's environmental standards," notes Sean Kelly in the program's newsletter.

Think locally, act locally

Environmental writer Wendell Berry offers supporting arguments on the importance of retaining the viability of smaller communities. His position favors thinking locally rather than globally. "Global thinking can only do to the globe what a space satellite does to it, reduce it, make a bauble out of it. In order to make ecological good sense for the planet you must make ecological good sense locally. You can't act locally by thinking globally." Cities need supporting regions in order to survive: "a city in balance with its countryside is the only one sustainable." He describes such a city as one that lives off the net ecological income of its supporting region, paying as it goes, all ecological and human debts. Such a sustainable city, says Berry, is one that begins by increasing the amount of food bought from local farmers, which would help those farms become more diversified, and more productive, and eventually put them in a position to hire city folk to work on them. They would use the city's organic wastes as fertilizer, which would motivate city dwellers to be more aware of contamination, which would then have a direct effect on their food supplies. He calls this kind of interaction and common concern "economic intimacy."

"The American lawn is an atrocity. It is the largest crop in the world, a $17 billion per year industry, using more fertilizer than all of India and Africa, let alone pesticides, producing nothing but poisonous surfaces for our children" (From the 1989 edition, *Plants of the Southwest*, Santa Fe, NM, Michael Reed, Editor).

Of greater concern, because it affects life immediately in many parts of the globe, is the continuing salinization of once arable lands. At present, according to environmental scientist Edward Goldsmith, 90 percent of Egypt's land, 68 percent in Pakistan, 50 percent in Iraq, 38 percent in Peru, 25 to 30 percent in the United States and 15 to 20 percent in India, Russia, and Australia are suffering from salinization. Increased amounts of sodium chloride, sodium sulfate, sodium, magnesium, and calcium carbonates in the soil affect crops adversely at root level and turns formerly fertile, friable earth into sterile dirt under a hard crust. Such quick fixes as continued and increased irrigation, mining of fossil aquifers, and chemical desalinization of water turn out to be no answer to sustained development.

A salty desert is no place at all

Humanity's efforts, writes Dr. Monique Mainguet, professor of geography at the University of Reims, France, in the October, 1995 edition of *UNESCO Courier*, "to survive in arid regions have helped to sharpen the human mind. The 20th century, a time of fewer certainties, has seen the high water mark of one phase of development, then the first signs of decline. I wonder if great works, because of their vast scale and their sometimes disastrous consequences, are not symptoms of a kind of loss of control by human genius and the prelude to a disturbing decline? Will the 21st century be a time when the idea that small is beautiful is rediscovered?"

Desertification has been widely defined as land degradation in arid, semi-arid and dry sub-humid areas resulting from factors including climatic variations and human activities. Dr. Mainguet notes that from 35 to 37 percent of the world's land mass consists of dry areas inhabited by 15 to 20 percent of the world's people. Yet 69 percent of these lands used for agriculture are either degraded or seriously threatened by desertification. Among the culprits are such human activities as ill-planned cultivation practices, deforestation, overgrazing, and poor irrigation techniques.

Difficulties arise from poorly conceived outside intervention in local problems. Outside funding sources increasing public wells in parts of Africa, for example, without consultation with the local populations, has caused abandonment of traditional practices of animal husbandry and farming. In some cases, availability of water and improved veterinary practices cause herds to increase with resultant overgrazing of available grasslands, encroachment onto arable lands or relegation to lands unsuitable for grazing.

Good techniques in Brazil

In the Nordeste region of Brazil farmers use organic matter for fertilizer and avoid plowing the land so as not to cause compacting of topsoil. Run-off water is captured in small ditches. Debris is spread over the ground to provide humus, which retains moisture. Grazing areas are protected by shelter belt trees and bushes. Fodder is stored in silos. These methods far outweigh the immediate benefits of increased irrigation which causes salinity of the soil and burden the community with prohibitive costs.

The Five Women Song

Five women could have stayed home
and sewed and did what their husbands wanted
or did what their neighbors thought well
They could have stepped over the garbage
On the public streets
They could have slept under umbrellas
Holding drops of acid rain
They could have walked in high heels
Through places where trees were dying
But they didn't
They took the evils by the throat
They drew their own bright knives
Stroking clean lines on arteries
Choked with the sud of greed
They stood waist deep
In wet places where the future's
children lay face down
Turning them over and up toward the sky
Pointing to forests and rivers
Of new greens and silvers
They could have stepped over the garbage
But they chose to look down
So the children to come could look up.

Lucy Germany

Five women have been included in a series of documentary films on women of the South made by American sociologist Judithe Bizot with UNESCO support. Two of them have won a Right Livelihood Award from the Right Livelihood Awards Foundation in recognition of their alternative contributions to the well-being of humankind.

Aminata Traore of Mali has founded a garbage collection co-op in Bamakko, organized cultural and study centers, and promoted community management of water supply points.

Pakistan's Khawar Mumtaz has set up a non-governmental organization, "Shirkat Gah," which encourages women's education and their participation in public life.

In Costa Rica, under the leadership of Marta Trejos, a program has been launched to build 6,000 homes for families living in the shantytowns of San Jose.

In India, Himalayan women under the leadership of Vandana Shiva have formed the Chipko movement which is dedicated to safeguarding the forests.

In Kenya, Wangari Maathai belongs to a group of women who in 1977 created the "Green Belt Movement," an organization that seeks to halt desertification by encouraging tree plantings and soil and water conservation.

In 1995 the Council of Europe, founded in 1949 and composed of 34 member states, inaugurated a year-long campaign called "European Nature Conservation," with an impressive list of events, pooling of ideas, and networking among established entities dedicated to conservation and to the principle of imposing civil liability for damage to the environment. The conference statement called for "integrating rural women's traditional knowledge and practices into environmental management programs; supporting women's consumer initiatives by promoting recycling, organic food production and marketing and produce labeling that is clear to the illiterate."

The question of soul

The subject of the environment is as multi-faceted as the interior of a baroque palace. It questions the finiteness of our resources, what we can live with and what we may have to do without. It includes the infrequently considered aspect of aesthetics and the human soul. How important is nature to our full development and the enrichment of our lives? What are our fears and guilts about being careless and inadequate stewards of the earth?

Our population continues to grow; therefore we face increased demands for agricultural land and land to grow other natural products considered essential to our well-being. We must face the always troubling question of integrating environmental with developmental issues. Some environmental issues are global in nature. Others affect only certain land masses or water resources.

Whatever our beliefs, whatever church, synagogue, mosque, or open space invites our meditations, we need to incorporate words about the environment into our prayer. We need to pray for God's mercy, God's protection of our fragile "nest," and for the strength and will to relate all we do to the good of the planet.

Wondrous Creator

Wondrous Creator,
Creator of mother earth and all that she holds
be with us in all of your ways:
In our mother earth where our ancestors rest
we stand on holy ground.
In shining sun we gather the warmth of your words.
In grandmother moon we feel the changes that you bring to honor all.
In thunder and lightning we are awakened
to open our hearts to receive your spirit.
In rain and snow your sacred water cleanses our bodies.
In river, lake, creek, stream
we are nourished by the life and peace you bring.
In wind we smell your breath
calling us to life with you.
In stars we see your presence of hope
that dances in our hearts.
In four leggeds and winged
we feel the humility of our being.
In plants and flowers we become
the beauty your strength gives.
In each other we feel the love
that brings us all to be with you.
In ourselves we hear your voice
gently calling us to you, Wondrous Creator.

Ginny Doctor

And city air

Part of the mosaic are other issues, smaller but of no less importance
to the people they affect. The subject of urban greenery is one of little moment to the family living on a subsistence farm or even in
poverty in a large city, but for many urbanites and suburbanites who
have achieved a measure of economic security it becomes a viable
concern. A study of the environmental and economic benefits of
trees in metropolitan Chicago measured the extent to which trees,
properly placed around homes and office buildings, can improve air
quality and reduce energy costs. Detailed studies were made, sin-
gling out large trees with open crowns that drop leaves in the fall

and sprout them again in spring. Not only do properly selected trees provide protection against wind and sun, they also tend to soften and refine neighborhoods so that developers have traditionally spent heavily to provide them as an ingredient in landscaping. Careful qualitative studies of tree species have been implemented in a number of large cities in the United States, among them Dallas and Chicago. Invasive species with characteristically rapid growth and a relatively short lifespan have been designated "trash trees" by the city of Dallas, and efforts have been made to replace them with more valuable species. This insures trees for the people on a long-range basis.

We have observed that women have received markedly few accolades for their work with the environment, even though they work in substantial numbers behind the scenes, in labs, on teams, in solitary research pursuits. With a few exceptions they are relatively unknown as champions of the environment.

Lady Bird Johnson is a case in point. She has appreciably raised the consciousness of Americans for the preservation of wild flowers. The validity of such efforts is not reduced by their specialization. Tree-planting efforts and civic beautification, roadside plantings and restoration of urban lots help to raise consciousness on environmental issues and bring that consciousness to a wider public. Such projects inform us of the seriousness of the loss of species, such as North American plants, which affects inhabitants both aesthetically and in terms of the loss of their role in natural cycles.

Fingers of guilt point to consumers of developed countries for overconsumption. Fingers of guilt point equally to developing countries hungry for ways to meet the needs of their ever-increasing populations so that of necessity they forge into virgin lands with little effort to preserve the richness of such areas. Many would argue that these guilts are not equal, the one being relatively easy to control, the other being driven by natural forces difficult to check.

An unlikely place for women?

One area in which women have received full credit for their work as scientists is in the Amazon forests. The plight of the Amazon has captured the imagination of schoolchildren, magazine editors, movie makers, environmentalists, and promoters anxious to prove themselves sympathetic to good causes. Women from both North and

South have done a great deal to unearth the secrets of the rain forest and to evolve plans for its preservation.

The new (and real) Amazons

In Roger Stone's doleful 1985 book *Dreams of Amazonia*, he gives liberal credit to such forward thinkers as botanist/ecologist Judy Rankin Jari-Carajas (*The Uncertain Future of Large Silviculture in the Amazon*, 1982), ecologist Susan Hecht (*Deforestation in the Amazon Basin: Magnitude, Dynamics and Soil Resource Effects*, and *Where Have All The Flowers Gone? Deforestation in the Third World*, 1981), Amazon basin scientist Betty Meggers (*Amazonia, Man and Culture in a Counterfeit Paradise*, 1971), Maria Teresa Jorg Padua, former head of the parks division of the Brazilian Institute for Forest Development, and Margery Oldfield (*Blowing in the Wind: Deforestation and Long-Range Implications*, 1981). Stone particularly credits Padua, whom he called "fiery and effective, a woman whose efforts to protect Amazonia involved fighting long odds to bring about a major expansion in the dimensions of the existing system of national parks and forest preserves." During her term of office she pulled some seven million hectares into the Amazonian parks network, an important milestone even in the face of skimpy budgetary resources for managing the total acreage. Stone's book also gives a warm nod to the work of Judith Gunn who has worked on increasing the knowledge of the forest's vulnerability, a fact now largely documented by a substantial number of scientists from several countries. Though largely pessimistic about the future of the great Amazon forests and their natural bounty, Stone finds some cause for hope in the expansion of scientific knowledge and the interest of scientists in the area as well as the increase in public awareness. Print and television coverage, he says, has shed light on rain forest destruction, the plight of doomed indigenous people, and the shared threat that global warming poses. All these have made billions of people aware of the plight of the Amazon. Stone suggests that the nations of the world must be involved in the future of great rain forests, but in taking up the challenge it is important to do so with careful respect for national sensitivities. The progress Brazil has made in attitudes and legislative programs favorably affects the future of the Amazon forests.

Ethnobotanist Mark Plotkin, author of *Tales of a Shaman's Apprentice* (Penguin Books, 1993) details the project of American businesswoman,

Lisa Conte, whose suggestion to return a percentage of profits resulting from the development of new pharmaceuticals derived from rain forest plants back to the indigenous peoples for their education, purchase of their traditional territories or other needs, has already effected some dramatic progress. Another percentage, she suggested, could be earmarked for the national governments of countries involved to support development and management of national parks and other protected areas. Finally, said Conte, a percentage could also go to support further ethnobotanical research. Her ideas led to the formation of Shaman Pharmaceuticals of San Carlos, California, which has a board of scientific advisors who work with staff scientists to help identify priorities and to offer advice on which countries, tribes, or plants to support. One of the company's first successes has been work on an extract from an Amazonian forest tree discovered to be useful in the treatment of herpes viruses. Conte has also set up a non-profit organization, the Healing Forest Conservancy, to return a percentage of all profits from Amazon forest derived products back to the indigenous people and to the countries in which the plants grow. Since that time other major pharmaceutical companies have supported similar efforts: Eli Lily, Bristol Meyers Squibb, and Merck, to name a few.

Plotkin urges the importance of understanding and safeguarding the treasure house of natural resources represented by the rain forests. If the rights of indigenous peoples and endangered species are to be protected, new foods discovered to feed the hungry and new medicines to cure the sick, "now is the time to act. We must develop a pro-active, holistic approach to the environmental problems we face, realizing that previously overlooked or even ridiculed world views like shamanic wisdom can help us find answers to some of the questions we face. If we don't, our children and grandchildren will inherit a world infinitely less diverse biologically and culturally than the one into which we were born."

One of the most impressive actions taken in recent years by a woman not a scientist is the earlier mentioned tree planting project in Kenya spearheaded by Wangari Maathi, who has become something of a national hero. Under her leadership and inspired by her enthusiasm, an innovative movement called "Green Belt" was started and some ten million trees planted under its aegis. Not only did this bold and innovative project halt the increasing desertification of Kenya, but it also provided income for many of the nation's poor women. Because in Africa women are the major food growers and firewood gatherers, it seems particularly appropriate for this project to have come from the mind and spirit of a woman.

So quiet and gray in Cité Soleil

The importance of tree planting becomes the text of a hymn when one visits a country suffering from the effects of treeless land, dead soil, and lack of fuel. This happened to me in Haiti in 1995 when I arrived in the middle of Cité Soleil, a shapeless, sprawling shantytown not far from Port-au-Prince. It was a moonscape without mystery. Not a blade of green was visible. There were only corrugated iron shacks, row on row, dirt paths, dirt alleyways, garbage choked depressions which had once been waterways. Without fuel for cooking, the women had to walk to feeding stations, carrying their plastic buckets, totally dependent on the largess of churches and other aid providers to feed their families. Equally shocking was the fact that without fuel they had lost the traditional center of the family, the hearth. At that point I saw no concerted effort being made to revive the calcerous soil, so hard and compacted that it seemed more of a crust than true earth. I saw no attempt at planting of any kind. I mourned for the future of this place and these people, living close to the glittering Caribbean and the picturesque mountains that appear on so many tourist pamphlets, so close to possibilities, yet so deprived.

Where do you get your tomatoes?

In the end the battle for the environment will be won (or lost) on two levels, Wendell Berry's localism and the global communications network. Neither one seems to be doing very well currently as cities continue to grow, consumerism to thrive, and agriculture more and more to resemble big business, while television trims away at the amount of coverage it gives to environmental issues. Coverage of the environment on the three networks has declined by 60 percent since 1989, a 1996 report in *Sierra Magazine* notes. Writer and executive director of the Sierra Club, Carl Pope says that the decline is certainly not due to a dearth of visual material or a lack of conflict. He blames it partly on the medium's love affair with celebrity exemplified by the trial of O.J. Simpson. Why bore people with America's assault on environmental protection when they can be entertained instead? Pope asks. He also suggests that because rightwing groups regard environmentalists as serious enemies and are willing to spend media money to counterattack, there is a distinct lack of balance between money being spent to help the environment and money to attack or to urge disregard of it.

Most foundations that give to environmental causes fund no media at all, Pope says. He suggests more letters to the editor (as have already been generated by the Sierra Club), more public expressions of interest and caring on the part of citizens generally. We need to speak out to managers, editors, and TV anchors and let them know that we are more concerned about our children's future than about the latest celebrity scandal. "If we don't make our voices heard," he warns, "the critical environmental issues of the day will remain buried."

All the great women

But they won't stay buried long if the public pays serious attention to such leaders as Bella Abzug (co-founder of Women's Environment and Development Organization [WEDO]), Anthropologist Jane Goodall (founder of the Jane Goodall Institute, sponsors of "Roots and Shoots," a program for teaching young people to be responsible for their actions), Wangari Maathi (coordinator of The Green Belt Movement, the environmental project founded by the National Council of Women of Kenya), Thais Coral of Brazil (coordinator of the Network in Defense of Humankind and cochair of WEDO), and local warriors (not worriers) such as Diane Wilson, a Lavaca Bay, Texas, shrimper who staged hunger strikes, public protests and legal challenges in order to clean up the Texas coastal shrimping grounds.

As a result of Diane Wilson's actions, reported by Vicki Monks in a story titled "Environmental Regulations: Who Needs Them?" published in the February/March 1996 issue of *National Wildlife*, Alcoa and other bay industrial polluters were investigated and discovered to be polluting the bay with mercury and other toxins which brought them under the jurisdiction of the Emergency Planning and Community Right to Know Act. Alcoa and Formosa Plastics both pledged to work toward zero discharge of waste water pollutants in exchange for Wilson's dropping a citizen's Clean Water Act lawsuit against them.

The National Council of Women of Canada recently filed a brief on the subject of the nuclear fuel waste disposal proposition drafted by the Atomic Energy of Canada Ltd. for a public hearing. The women asked questions and expressed concern over the safety of the proposals, particularly in the area of arrangements for safe transport of stored wastes from originating site to point of permanent storage. The NCWC is a 106-year-old non-partisan federation of voluntary women's organizations whose goal is to improve the status of women, families and society through education and advocacy.

There are hundreds, perhaps thousands of such protectors at work in ways large and small. Their names are known and unknown but their public exposure is irrelevant to the magnitude of the task they undertake, often at great personal cost. They are heroes and heroines to whom the world owes its gratitude.

We cannot leave this subject without once again mentioning the large responsibility that rests on the shoulders or in the laps of the world's women. Because women feel spiritually connected to the environment in ways unrelated to economics or power, the issues that attract men, it is women who must raise their voices in one prolonged cry for the earth. Then they must pick up new burdens, but because they will be working for the earth they love and with faith in the God they trust, their burdens will seem as nothing. The world, however, will long remember that no matter how immense the challenge, the women of the world did not shrink from the task.

The Girl Child

Nancy Grandfield

■ ■ ■ ■ ■ ■ ■ ■ ■ ■

Eliminate all forms of discrimination, as well as negative cultural attitudes and practices, against girls.

Ensure that girls develop a positive self-image and have equal access to education and health care.

Protect girls from economic exploitation and eliminate violence against them.

Platform for Action

The girl child

Some years ago a story was told about a doctor in Japan. Delivering newborn babies was a central part of his practice. When the delivery had taken place and the child been given to its mother, the doctor would talk to the new parents. Before he did this he always took one further step. He stood near the foot of the bed, facing the mother and infant and lowered his body in a profound bow, remaining there silently for a fairly long time, after which he would leave without saying a word. On one of these occasions, the father of the newborn followed him into the hall and asked him what the practice meant. "I do that each time I am a participant in a birth. It is a moment of awe and respect, for how could we know who has just been born. Who knows this child's destiny, her future greatness or the footsteps she will leave on the face of the earth?"

—The Rev. Roger Alling

In many parts of the world girls face discrimination from the moment of birth. They are often denied basic rights given boys and suffer from attitudes and customs that limit their potential. Cultures can be supportive and nurturing, but for girls cultures can cast a pall over talents, aspirations, and even survival itself. Girls often receive poorer health care and less education than boys, marry earlier and face great risks of dying in adolescence or womanhood from early or too closely spaced pregnancies. They are sold into prostitution by their destitute families; they undergo genital mutilation in the name of tradition and often, as females in the womb, they are aborted. They are forced into marriage without their free and full consent, often as nine-year-old brides.

The *Platform for Action* is concerned with girls' self-image, their access to equality of physical and mental health services and nutrition. It urges better education, skills development and training. It recommends action to eliminate economic exploitation of children as child laborers. It urges respect for the rights of the child to have access to information, privacy, confidentiality, and informed consent. It advocates legislation that ensures the equal right to inherit regardless of gender.

My source for much of the information in this chapter is author Neera Sohoni, who critiques the Webster Dictionary's definition of girl as "female child, young unmarried woman, female servant, sweetheart," calling that definition "out of step with the reality of a considerable proportion of the world's girls." Of the definition, she says, "the first part is a biological fact, the second a sad comment on the subtle semantic bias against girls or their labor and the last is too frivolous to deserve comment."

Before I went to Beijing I was only vaguely acquainted with the term "girl child." Because a friend had announced her pregnancy by saying she was going to have a "girl child," I thought of it as a quaint way of stating gender. Thanks to years of effort and lobbying by UNICEF and vast numbers of non-governmental organizations, particularly from Africa and South Asia, the girl child was not only visible but prominent on the Huairou agenda, having been the subject of over 50 workshops. During a "speak out" by girls aged ten to 18, we learned about the heavy workload and lack of respect that kept them out of school, their need for adequate sex education to prevent unwanted pregnancies, and the general inequality from which they suffered daily. Now I see "girl child" differently, especially since I learned that in my own San Francisco Bay Area there are hundreds, perhaps thousands of girls—some 12 or younger—who are among the city's 30,000 prostitutes.

To write about the pain, struggle, and despair of the girl child brings pain and despair to my own heart. My maternal lineage is overwhelmingly female. My grandmother, one of two children, had a sister. My mother had one sister and no brothers. I have one sister and no brothers. That sister has given birth to five girls. My own daughter has three girls and one boy. As I read and write about the heinous acts perpetrated against the babies and adolescents of the world whose seemingly only crime is being born female, I see the faces of my grandmother, my mother, aunt, daughter, nieces, and grandchildren. That they may be deprived of a fighting chance to lead healthy, productive lives because they are devalued as human beings from the day of their birth, gives me a sense of urgency in sharing stories of hope and success.

As I researched this topic, I was overwhelmed by the tragedies of millions of girls surviving insurmountable and intolerable conditions. How could I, by my writing, make a difference in their lives and mine?

I shared my pain with Lucy, Sr. Heléna Marie, and Ann as we sat one morning overlooking the Pacific, watching the serious pelicans go about their business of getting breakfast from the waves. After a time Lucy said, "We've all had to overcome the girl stigma. We have experienced discrimination even though we haven't been sold into sexual slavery or worked in factories at age nine. But there are attitudes out there that work against us and we have had to deal with them."

By including our stories I have a renewed connection with my sisters all over the world and have regained a sense of hope for the possibility of change and a better understanding of conditions that cannot be changed. The pain will always be with me, but it is accompanied by compassion and commitment to share our visions for a better world.

Why did you come, a girl, when we wished for a boy? Take the jar and fill it from the sea; may you fall into it and drown.

Karin Sham Poo, Deputy Executive Director of UNICEF, calls them "missing millions." The deep prejudices against girls mean that many are never born because of sex-selective abortions. She said, "Some are killed as infants; others die from neglect. Some 60 to 100 million fewer women live today than could be expected from demographic trends." Modern technology now enables the cultural preference for sons to be gratified before birth. The use of amniocentesis and ultrasound which can determine the sex of an unborn child, has resulted in an increased number of female fetus abortions. Some

Indian sex-detection clinics boldly advertise that "it is better to spend $38 now on termination rather than $3,800 later on a dowry."

Heise, 1993

A survey of 640 families in one South Asian community showed that 51 percent admitted to having killed a girl baby within a week of her birth. An official survey in China revealed that 12 percent of all female fetuses were aborted or otherwise unaccounted for, mostly as a result of ultrasound screenings.

In the May/June, 1996 issue of *Horizons*, a publication of Presbyterian women, Neera Sohoni states that traditionally mothers-to-be are aware that their motherhood stands vindicated only after they have produced a son. In many parts of the world, mothers pray and fast to have a son. They may resort as well to epsom salts, baking powder, and douches to influence the sex of the unborn. An English proverb compares girls to dead fish. A Dutch proverb contends that a "house full of daughters is like a cellar full of sour beer." An Orthodox Jewish daily morning prayer says, "Thank God I wasn't born a woman."

"I was born in a small hospital in Tokyo. Mama says she remembers two things. A mouse running across the floor, which she took as a sign of good luck, and a nurse whispering apologetically, 'I'm afraid it's a girl. Would you prefer to inform your husband yourself?'"

Liv Ullman, Ambassador for UNICEF

School before beauty

As a frequent baby-sitter for my five-year-old twin grandaughters, I often take them to "clay class" where they shape pots and animals from globs of clay. I have also taken them to gymnastics, music lessons, storytelling at the local library, an indoor park where they may ride fire engines or play in miniature replicas of grown-up houses. When they were but a month old I watched a teacher train them to balance by rolling them over giant plastic balls. They have had swimming lessons and finger-painting classes. They go to the children's museums and zoos. As a consequence of all this preschool activity, most of it free of charge, they are wholesome, healthy, interesting, happy, and creative kids. Only time set aside by their loving and enthusiastic parents is required. Note that these classes are for "preschool" children; their "primary" education is guaranteed.

Two-thirds of the estimated 100 million children ages six to 11 not in school are girls (UNICEF, 1993). Only 68 percent of girls worldwide have reached grade five. Between 1980 and 1988, girls' gross enrollment ratios at the primary level declined in 28 African, Asian and Middle Eastern countries (UNESCO, 1991). Eighty-six million girls—43 million more than boys—have no access to primary school education.

Girls are denied schooling for many reasons: they are needed at home to do chores, they are seen by their fathers, particularly, as "mothers and wives to be" and their education is seen as preparation for home-making activities. One hundred families studied in Peru revealed that 60 percent of adolescent males in households that hired help had their first sexual encounter with the house girls.

Girls are needed to care for younger children at home. No value is seen in girls being educated; it is thought that they can bring little or no financial help to the family. "Children come cheap, girls come cheaper," said Neera Sohoni.

If poverty demands that the girl child be sent out to work, her job will probably be the lowest on the pay ladder and most likely it will be in a factory. In India many jobs are gender-specific: while boys work largely in hotels and tea stalls, girls constitute 70 percent of the workers in the weaving industry and 63 percent in the production of matches. These girls, often between the ages of five and seven, work ten to 12 hours a day seven days a week. Girl laborers outnumber boys in agriculture, in making cigarettes and in construction. They face occupational hazards such as chronic bronchitis and tuberculosis from making cigarettes and tetanus and skin diseases from picking rags.

Mendonca, 1992

With marriage imminent, parents, particularly fathers, often consider schooling unnecessary. Girls who do manage to acquire a few years of education frequently drop out when pregnant. Few female role models exist due in part to a shortage of female instructors. The curriculum is often irrelevant in preparing girls for work or traditional domestic responsibilities.

King and Hill, 1993

In Malawi in Central Africa, teachers talk more with boys, ask them more questions, give them more academic support, and utilize teaching methods geared to boys.

Davison and Kanyuha, 1990

Books have few pictures of girls and women and always, when shown, they are in stereotypical roles. But this is not true only in countries like Malawi: Ann told us that her math teacher had labeled her "unable to learn" the subject because "girls don't have that ability." She was thus deliberately deprived of learning. Inferior education lowers a girl's self-esteem and limits her employment opportunities and her ability to take part in the world around her. And it follows that illiterate mothers usually have illiterate daughters.

Educating girls educates nations

"When I was little I wasn't allowed to go to school," says Chichani, a Nepalese mother of four daughters who married at age 13. Chichani had to take on adult responsibilities when only four years old. She took care of brothers and sisters, cleaned house, cooked, carried water and wood, and helped in the fields. There was no time for school or play. Fortunately a Nepalese program called Production Credit for Rural Women has helped Chichani improve her life. With UNICEF support she has been able to get a loan to buy seeds and a goat and has bought a stove for her house. She has learned to read and write and to earn enough money to send her four daughters to school. "My daughters don't want to marry early," she said. "They want to get an education."

UN agencies and NGOs, along with some local governments are, cooperating in many parts of the world, to bring schools closer to communities, to encourage them to hire more female teachers, use gender-sensitive curricula, lower school costs, and encourage girls' participation.

Listening to girls' voices

Two girls, ages ten and 14, from Bihar, India, are caught in conversation. Let's listen in:

Girl 1:   Do you go to school?

Girl 2:   Yes. Don't you?

Girl 1:   I'd like to but my parents won't let me. My brother goes to school and I wish I could. I see lots of girls going to school but my parents say my sister and I don't need to because we'll be getting married anyway. Don't your parents say that too?

Girl 2: They did at first. But my older cousin came to visit and she told my mother how she liked school, how she learned to read and write, heard interesting stories and made friends. Later she even wrote a letter from my mother to her mother that made my mother change her mind. She wanted me to write to her and give her all the news.

Girl 1: I've never been allowed to look at books. My father always snatches books away from me and say they are of no use. He says I must learn to cook and feed a family. I stay home and look after my brothers and sisters while my mother and father go out to work.

Girl 2: I'm lucky. I'm the youngest in the family and don't need to look after anyone. But I help my mother when I come home from school. There is a lot of homework and sometimes she doesn't understand but as long as I help her I know she won't stop me from going to school.

Girl 1: And what will you do after you finish school? Won't you have to get married?

Girl 2: Every girl has to get married. It's our destiny. My mother is looking for a boy for me and will marry me off soon but I hate the idea. I don't know why I was even allowed to study up to Class IV. It's opened my mind to many new things. All will be closed to me after I marry.

Girl 1: That's too bad.

Girl 2: Ever since my twelfth birthday my parents have changed. They are much more cautious and watch everything I do. I can't even stand on the road outside our village. I feel depressed and there is no one I can talk to, not even my mother.

Girl 1: That's so strange. I always thought going to school would make a difference in a girl's life.

Meeting the needs

In Colombia and El Salvador, the public school curriculum has been remodeled to allow girls to drop in and out of education, as opposed to dropping out forever.

Night classes in India and Kenya are full of teenage girls who do a full day's work, then squeeze into children's desks to catch up on their school work.

A study in Yemen found that girls' enrollment dropped to zero after Grade III because of a lack of women teachers. When a woman was finally recruited by one school, many girls who had stayed away returned and went on to complete their education.

Research in Bangladesh, Morocco, and Pakistan revealed that the lack of toilets was keeping thousands of girls away from school. Their parents didn't want their daughters relieving themselves in the open—an inhibition that did not apply to sons.

In Egypt, 94 percent of boys and 72 percent of girls were enrolled in primary schools less than one kilometer from their homes. But when the schools were farther away, girls' enrollment dropped to 64 percent because parents would not permit them to travel that far from home. Bhutan and Morocco are now building dormitories for girls with female oversight to reassure parents of their daughters' moral and physical safety.

After 80 percent of parents in Malawi indicated that school fees were the primary reason for taking girls out of high school, GABLE (Girls' Attainment in Basic Literacy and Education) was launched to pay the primary school fees for all non-repeating girls. GABLE is also redesigning textbooks to show women in professional roles and as decision makers in the home. Teachers are being taught gender sensitivity.

The Commission for Sex Equality in the Unified School District of Los Angeles presented a report to the Board of Education in 1991 called: "I Really Wanted to Stay in School: Recommendations to Support the Education of Pregnant and Parenting Teens." This was a result of a survey showing that 40 percent of the female dropouts in the district were pregnant teens. The Board subsequently told every middle and high school to identify a faculty member to serve as a teen-parent advocate.

The Daughters Education Program in Thailand is committed to informing and empowering girls who are at risk of being sold to village agents. The goal is to provide girls with a positive educational alternative and to help stabilize troubled communities by using the knowledge learned by these students. The girls, aged eight to 18, are offered training in computing, typing, sewing, and agriculture. They are taken on awareness trips into Bangkok's red light districts so that they might witness the dangers there. High school girls in the program gain work experience and are encouraged to open bank accounts. Older girls are invited to come to villages to undertake research on prostitution, AIDS, and the status of women and children. The group is also funding a leadership training project that will help former participants further their job training and education. Girls who have completed training are encouraged to teach their skills to younger girls.

Female genital mutilation

More than two million girls are believed to undergo genital mutilation each year in a practice carried out largely in Africa and some Middle Eastern countries. The practice is described graphically in this book's chapter on "Human Rights."

As populations migrate from Continental Africa, the practice has moved into Australia, England, France, Italy and the United States.

Neera Sohoni writes in her factual and compassionate book, *The Burdens of Girlhood*, "sexual tampering is not a trivial subject; certainly it is one on which there can be no ambivalence. It pits culture against country and religion against reform. Because these practices restrict and immobilize girls, they need to be tackled. Pressure must be mounted to confront those who believe the female benefits from culturally and biologically constraining practices." There are those who believe cultures have a right to carry out their traditions without having to answer to the presumed higher authority of Western behavior. It is hard to understand why such customs as foot binding at ages three to five of Chinese girls, child marriage and widow-burning should be renounced by some cultures while others are permitted the autonomy of retaining female genital mutilation.

Hoshen

In 1990, a group of women in Beni Sucif, Upper Egypt, formed the Care for Girls Committee that began using street and village theater, picture books, posters, slide-tape productions and brochures to address girls' lack of freedom and choice. The Committee has organized village leaders and others into consultative groups and has called for legislation to safeguard the rights of girls.

In the Luuq District of Somalia, 22 Islamic women have united to refuse to allow genital mutilation on the girls of their community. Aware of potential damage, and mindful of their own suffering they have determined that their children and grandchildren will be spared.

Even with the current generation of mothers being educated, a risk is still posed by grandmothers' strong ties to tradition. Women knowledgeable in the practice, serving as community "nurses" also still continue the practice. They are paid by the family of the girl children and though many do not subscribe to the old methods, some continue to use the "sunna" method that involves a small intrusion into the clitoris, enough to draw blood without cutting.

Girls on the streets: some lucky...

I first met Diana Frade at a Council for Women's Ministries meeting several years ago in Honduras. I was drawn by her strength, wisdom and compassion reflected in her intensely blue eyes. Over lunch she told me some of her personal story as the wife of the Bishop of Honduras, the Rt. Rev. Leo Frade, and as the founder and director of a home for abandoned girls called Hogar de Ninas Nuestras Pequenas Rosas (Our Little Roses) near San Pedro Sula. Diana's story is an incentive for those whose visions will not go away, who realize that complacency is the enemy and who dare to risk the high cost of perseverance.

"For the past 25 years," says Diana, " I have lived in this lush country known as Honduras where poverty is all but covered by the year-round natural beauty. One of the worst signs of poverty, which I encountered soon after my arrival, is the number of children begging on the streets, barefoot with dirty faces, dressed in rags. The government's inability to deal with this problem has created a culture of street children who perpetuate a cycle of illiteracy, abuse and deprivation.

"Eleven years ago, I was motivated, by the fact that the Episcopal church had established a home for orphan boys but none for girls, to begin a new ministry to the girls. When I initially asked about the disparity I was told that girls are too hard to take care of, and are the source of too many problems.

"I kept at it, finding more reasons to do this ministry than not to do it and in 1988, we acquired a suitable home which we formally opened as 'Our Little Roses.' Here, in a warm, homelike environment, girls are given a new chance for learning and a normal life.

They are given all the basics—food, clothing, health care, education, but above all, warm, nurturing Christian love.

"The home has expanded and grown over the years and recently we added a space to care for newborns, infants and girls up to seven years old, which not only doubles the home's capacity but also provides a day care center and preschool for neighborhood children. The home's 20 older girls, by helping with the younger ones, are able to continue their education, thanks to the new community funds.

"This is an exciting ministry, involving a whole new generation of Honduran women who will go forth into life armed with the tools of education and the power of advocacy along with an unswerving Christian faith. They will be a significant force in the new Honduras.

"I recommend this ministry to anyone who has knowledge of neglected or abandoned children. If each of us made a personal commitment to address the problem of children at risk, we would significantly impact our societies. Until we put our children first and focus on those in need, we will continue to perpetuate the pain, suffering and disadvantaged state that exists around us."

And others not so lucky

Other girls in Central America are not so fortunate. "After three months I was completely demoralized," said Rosa, referring to her life as a 17-year-old Colombian prostitute. "I lost contact with my family and remained apart from them for many years."

Many girls like Rosa turn to the streets to escape physical and sexual abuse at home. But the streets are not "Our Little Roses," as at least 100 million children worldwide are presently discovering.

Childhope US, an international NGO, estimates that girls constitute up to 30 percent of street children in many developing countries. In Brazil, SOS Crianca, an NGO, is turning to peer counseling and training in personal health and safety to help attack the problem. Thirteen-year-old Emma Emily Ombogo of Kenya had her story about family abuse read at a workshop on the girl child at the NGO Forum in Huairou, China. She said, "Children need a peaceful and united family. We learn from our parents. We beseech you, parents, set good examples."

Gifty Dowuna, of AWID forum said, "Our vision for girl children is to free their bodies so they are healthier, free their minds so they can be productive, economic players and free their time so they can be

children." Do not we all, as mothers, owe as much to the least of
these, our girl children?

Children of the night

Too often we assume that the horrors of sex trafficking happen only
"over there in poor countries." Clearly, girls in the United States are
at risk as well and often face the same kinds of prejudices and rejec-
tion by official agencies when they end up in prostitution, as early as
age five. Clients fearing HIV infection from adolescent girls and
women are seeking out very young girls, believing them to be free of
the deadly virus. There are an estimated one million child prostitutes
in Asia, including an estimated 300,000 in India, 200,000 in Thailand,
100,000 in the Philippines, 40,000 in Vietnam , 30,000 in Sri Lanka,
and many thousands in China.

Girls are tricked into leaving their families by agencies that
promise lucrative employment with their wages returned to their families. Atrocities abound: girls are burned to death while being held
captive by a brothel owner; others are forced to provide services for
up to 15 customers per day; and still others are required to offer services while pregnant.

Kurz-Prather

"Children of the Night" is the name of a program of help for prostitutes. The pioneer behind it is Lois Lee, an American sociologist, who
offered her insights in an article by Vicki Jo Radovsky. Lois is depicted driving on a sunny afternoon down Sunset Boulevard where she
spots young women plying their trade. "She's a hooker," she says,
spotting a girl who is about to get into a van with a man with whom
she is obviously negotiating. "She'll be in a hotel with hourly room
rates inside of ten minutes. She'll do that maybe a dozen times in a
night, making from $40 to $100 per trick. Her pimp will get most of
that; she'll survive on the rest. She probably isn't even 16 and there are
some 600,000 like her working the streets of America's cities.

"Everyone knows child abuse, wife beating and drug addiction
are problems," she says, "but with prostitution, people think kids
WANT to do it. If a kid steals or deals dope, it's considered a serious
crime, but child prostitutes fall between the cracks in the system. The
bureaucracy just dismisses them. The world's oldest profession will
earn more than $1 billion in the United States this year. The youngest

of them are on missing persons lists all over the country. Many are escapees from abusive families." Lois's "Children of the Night" has a 24-hour hotline, a walk-in crisis center, and a street outreach team that lets child prostitutes know there is help. It also provides medical attention, legal aid, counseling and placement in foster homes, and jobs.

Use me no more

"Sanlaap" was formed in Calcutta, India, in 1990 to "restore dignity and esteem of economically disadvantaged women from rural areas and urban slums." They work with prostitutes, especially the young ones, trying to get them away from the hard-core professionals and into skill training so they can earn a living another way. They also try to catch the evil before it takes hold, reaching the street children, the "pre-prostitutes," children eight to 12, many of whom are already selling their bodies. Sanlaap offers a home for short stays to abused and battered girls where they get counseling, classes in literacy and hygiene, and vocational training in block printing. A big part of Sanlaap's job is identifying the sex workers and getting to know them so that they will turn to this safe base for help.

Bonds of affection

In Santiago, Chile, prostitution is a major attraction for young street girls. El Rostro is one answer. It offers a service called "Servicio a Menores Explotados Sexualmente" which works with young women before they defect into this destructive profession, offering vocational guidance and counseling, education and tutoring. El Rostro believes young girls need a place of safety and comfort in which to meet and have some semblance of ordinary lives.

"Sempre Viva" is Rio de Janeiro's answer to the problem of adolescent girls on the streets. They form the girls into small group discussions in which each is encouraged to tell her story and describe how she would like to live her life. This input shapes the organization's activities. "Sempre Viva" workers have found that most of these girls "have a kind of ignorance about themselves as citizens." They have no idea of their legal rights or where to find information on contraception, resources that "Sempre Viva" tries to provide. The workers try to establish bonds of affection with the street girls. which is difficult to do since many of them have been shot or brutalized by police and gangs. Educators who have spoken out about the violence have themselves been threatened. One was murdered. Still the group goes on, broadening its base of support, educating people on the magnitude of human rights violations in their midst.

"You can do things that make a difference..."

Stuart Fowler

Stuart Fowler knows whereof he speaks. He and Rodney Burr, Australian attorneys, laid the groundwork for the First World Congress on Family Law and the Rights of Children and Youth. The pair has taken on the escalating practice of child prostitution and its increasing worldwide "markets," particularly Western tourists who seek sex. They have determined that more than 140,000 children under the age of 14 have been sold into prostitution in Taiwan, that 75 percent of children in some villages are HIV positive, and that in some cases children are deliberately mutilated so that they can be used as professional beggars. They have also exposed the practice of selling children for their organs and of abducting children for adoption.

As a result of their work, Australian travelers receive pamphlets warning them of the dangers of prostitution and informing them that laws have been enacted that provide severe penalties for pedophiles who have committed crimes on foreign soil. Since the law was passed, two prosecutions and one conviction of sex-seeking tourists have been handed down. New Zealand and Japan have passed similar laws and England has one under consideration. Where are other countries on this? The United States?

The Second World Congress, that takes place this year in San Francisco, has identified areas of focus: children in a violent world, family law, the effects of poverty, health of families and children, and the impact of culture and education. Hillary Rodham Clinton is the honorary chair for the Congress, which is also concerned about child labor. One way to tackle this, says Rodney Burr, is to pressure manufacturers to ensure that their processes are not employing young girls as cheap labor. "This is the route that's been followed with the environment and now even financial leaders want to make sure business is environmentally clean before they make a loan."

"If you talk to me about my mother, you will get my respect. If you talk to me about my wife, I will tell you it's none of your business. But if you talk to me about my daughter, you have my eyes, ears and heart..."

Old Egyptian Saying

Every woman's victory is a victory for the girl child

At the urging of Queen Silvia of Sweden a World Conference against the Commercial Sexual Exploitation of Children was convened in Stockholm in the late summer of 1996. It was the first international meeting of its kind, with over 1,000 delegates from 130 countries. They discussed ways to choke off the multi-billion-dollar pipeline that flows from the most brutal form of abuse of children. They recognized the rampant nature of the problem in Asia but acknowledged that it is actually a worldwide tragedy. The congress determined that although poverty is the root cause of such obscenities as families selling their children to be indentured servants or sex slaves, the equally guilty part of the equation is Western sexual appetites. In both Europe and the United States children are victimized by a lust for child pornography in pictures and films.

Declarations urged on governments by the gathering include making the sexual exploitation of children a crime while ensuring that the young victims are not punished; and promotion of stronger cooperation between states and societies to prevent children from entering the sex trade. Now governments need to adopt these standards and maintain continuing vigilance.

Our own girl child stories

We are women who were once daughters, who know what it is like to have been there, where so many now are, except that our experience was largely good. Still we understand, looking back, that even in our basically comfortable family existences, there were circumstances that made us know that girl children were not quite "equal."

Ann's Story...

I guess when I think of whom I am at 54 years of age, I see an eight-year-old child in me who was so full of hope and who believed she could do anything. I had to go through a time into puberty when I was not affirmed, not necessarily by my family so much but by society. It really stunted my growth for a while; I forgot who I was. I gave up the essence of who I was and it took being in the women's movement many years later and working on my own personal issues, along with the healing touch of other women, to nurture the eight-year-old girl who is now a proud woman.

Although I was never traumatized or mistreated while growing up, I was seen as a sex commodity as is every single girl born in the world who is not affirmed in her stages of growth. At age 14 I fulfilled the role that was expected—I wore pretty clothes, let boys win all the games, tried out for cheerleader.

My mother had some problems accepting me because she hadn't dealt with her own pain and issues about being a woman. My brother was her favorite. She lived in a very prescribed way as a housewife, dependent upon her husband even though she was the boss of the family. He was an alcoholic, but as is frequently the case with co-dependents, my mother died before him, at age 53.

I had a lot of healing to do around my 'wounded child.' I was the one who usually wound up outside the family, which is why I now have a support system made up of people working on healthy relationships. My desire for inclusion is why I was drawn to the circular model that allows for everyone to be included. I know how painful exclusion is.

Where is my connection with the girl child? When I was treated differently than my brother, and was not given an opportunity to learn what I wanted to learn. It was expected that he would go to college but I had to use very convincing arguments to win over my parents' biases against girls' higher education. I swam, always upstream. Not until the women's movement, struggling in a traditional marriage I resisted because there was no way I was going to do the expected things—pick up after a husband, or be denied full expression of my work—did I start to become my full self. When I became an advocate for other women, I became an advocate for myself. I didn't want to die at age 53, unfulfilled, as did my mother.

Lucy's Story...

I was the only girl of three children. My father only really noticed me or approved of me when I was doing "boy" things. He had no sense of what women really were, how they operated, what they thought, how women love. He didn't know anything about it. My mother was a shy, gentle woman with a good many fears. She lived under the paternal thumb as did I. I passed through all of my school years as a "nothing." I had little sense of myself as a girl, or as one on the way to womanhood. I was essentially neutral.

Then when I married, I met women in the local Episcopal Church who were—imagine!—feminists! I established some great friendships. That's when I became aware of my own strengths, and that it was all right to speak out. I had never expressed my own opinions because my father led me to believe that girls' thoughts weren't particularly valuable. I spent a lot of time day-dreaming, writing stories and poems, and in the outdoors, hunting and fishing with my brothers. Those were good times but not times for deepening my understanding of myself as a woman.

I went to work for a newspaper and learned to drink black coffee and stay up all night and express my ideas freely. I was the only woman working with a group of men, but they respected me and encouraged my self-expression. I think that helped when I finally met strong women and became a part of their lives. We had a group called the Mary Magdalene Society to assert our independence. We'd meet at the beach where we'd sit around and talk about the most intimate and powerful things. Back at the church, the men would tease us and say, "Oh you're just sitting around criticizing your husbands!" But that was never any part of it. We talked about God, life, what we were committed to, what we wanted for our children, poetry, books, music, nature. It was a kind of informal "salon" but not in the literary sense. These kinds of friendship changed my life and each person here has continued to change it.

Sister Heléna Marie's Story...

When we were little my sister and I used to baptize our cats. We would set up a baptismal font, using a small table and a bowl with water. Then we would lure our two cats into our "church" for eternal salvation. We baptized them many times, enough for each of their nine lives, and then some. We were imitating our father, who was a Lutheran pastor. We wanted to be just like him. But we knew that in real life girls couldn't be pastors.

I grew up knowing that other careers choices, too, were limited to me because I was a girl. My father was an amateur composer, and I inherited his passion for music. I began composing pieces for the piano when I started playing at age five, but gradually ingested society's notion that "girls can't write music." As I began absorbing the heritage of Western classical music, I realized that the only music I ever heard was written by men (dead white men). Although performing was a field somewhat open to women, there was an attitude in my home and church community that women shouldn't try to have such careers but should devote themselves to marriage and the raising of families. Having a career was selfish and egotistical. My own mother gave up a budding career as a pianist for the sake of raising us children.

Now, more than 30 years later, the options have expanded. Women are pastors (although not in every denomination), performers, and even occasionally conductors.

But old attitudes die hard. I recently talked with a high-ranking male church musician, trained in the best music schools in the country. He was incredulous when I suggested that his choir perform a piece by a woman composer, because "everyone knows that women can't compose." This attitude sends a message to the girls and women in his congregation that they are somehow genetically incapable of the inherently male art of musical composition. Never hearing women's music performed reinforces the idea that women can't compose.

It is extremely important that women be seen and heard as role models in new roles. Girls need to see women pastors and women conductors; they need to hear women's music and women's sermons. For this reason the women's office at the Episcopal Church Center is helping to produce a hymnal of women's music, to include contemporary pieces as well as compositions going all the way back to the twelfth century (some *do* exist). We are showing that women CAN compose.

Nancy's Story...

I had a wonderful life as a little girl and I think it was because my father was a lover. He loved my younger sister and me and all women because he had a pronounced feminine side and could relate to our needs and emotions. He was an actor, a musician, a writer, an artist, and he encouraged me to dream and create and give my imagination free range.

My parents adored one another because they had received little love in their childhoods. Daddy was an only child, labeled a "sissy" by his schoolmates. He retreated into the world of books and music. He dreamed his whole life, longing for love, until he found it in my mother.

My mother's girlhood was a time of pain and loneliness. Her

mother died from complications following an abortion. Her father was ill, unemployed, an alcoholic, who couldn't handle caring for his two little girls alone. He sent them to school one morning and upon their return they found he had deserted them. They never saw him again, never got to say good-bye to their "papa" they loved.

After a few months with an aunt, the sisters were put up for adoption. My mother's sister, 18 months younger, was a dimpled, cherubic child with cascading blonde ringlets. Mother was skinny with straight, mouse-colored hair. A family wanted only the "pretty" sister, not Mother. But the little girls had promised each other never to separate. With reluctance, the family adopted them both. All of her life my mother knew she was unwanted.

In their new life they were subject to severe discipline and religious fervor. When her adoptive mother was away, the husband, who had died before I was born, took my mother to bed and "consoled" her by fondling her breasts, calling them his little "pincushions." She was tied to a chair in the attic for lying about a poem that she had actually written but that her parents believed she wasn't clever enough to have composed.

After their father's death, the girls and their adopted mother went to college and graduated together. My parents and my aunt and uncle were married in a double ceremony. They remained close the rest of their lives.

Because of a lack of love in childhood my parents were thoroughly devoted to one another and to their children. As survivors they brought into my life overwhelming love, security, encouragement, and fun. Discipline was never harsh, always fair and deserved. Until they died they always listened to me. My family sat for hours around the dinner table in the evening sharing thoughts, events, and pains. When my own children were growing up they visited their grandparents after school just to talk and laugh with them and to learn from their wisdom and experience.

Do we survive... or what?

In the "Creative Journey," a leadership training program of the Episcopal Church's Office of Women in Mission and Ministry, we write about our maternal family tree. We look for patterns, for success stories of women who have survived girlhood. We are likely not to find a Nobel Prize winner but to find brave women who have lived through physical abuse and the knowledge of being unwanted.

If indeed we are survivors then we know there is always a way out. God is providing a loving relationship someplace for our safety and support. There is good coming out of everything—an indiscourageable Good Will toward all of creation.

This chapter began with a story told by the Rev. Roger Alling in a sermon in 1993. He concludes with these words: "Nothing stands still. Things move on. Jesus joins his cousin, John, in the river of Baptism. They meet and their ministries merge for an instant, only to part again, and behold, a new thing has begun. A new message is sounding forth. Listen for it. It sounds familiar, so familiar that many believe it is the same. 'The Kingdom has come, repent, and believe.'

"The message is rooted in John's message, but it is not the same. It has been turned upside down and inside out. It is no longer 'Repent for the Kingdom is coming.' It is, 'The Kingdom has come, therefore repent and trust and believe.'"

Today we are aware of our responsibility for all girl children. The girls who have been isolated are no longer isolated. All issues are now open issues. There are to be no more "family secrets." We are learning to protect the innocent, to alleviate the destructive forces toward girls and women, without causing more hurt. The secrets are out so the healing can begin.

Girls know they are no longer alone. Girls know there is hope for not being discriminated against because now there is public pressure, magazine articles are being written, voices are being heard—not yet in all countries, of course, but a lifeline is beginning for women and girls all over the world. Any destructive "custom" or "tradition" must elicit a human outcry against it.

Girls are being born by the thousands each day—many poor, abused, neglected, hungry, sick, murdered. Some we know, some we minister to, and some we only read about or hear their horrendous stories told at workshops in forums like those at Huairou.

Together we need to keep them in our minds' eyes, and in our souls' spirits.

We need to bow low at the altars of our hearts in awe of their births. But more, we need to commit our time, knowledge, and resources to relieving the suffering and traumas of those innocent ones.

The futures of my safe and happy grandchildren, and of their children, depend on the safe and happy survival of each one of their little sisters all over the world.

Sources

The Burden of Girlhood, Neera Kuckreja Sohoni, Ph.D.

San Mateo County Times, May 24, 1996.

Convention on the Rights of the Child, United Nations, 1994.

Children of the Night, Vicki Jo Radovsky.

Action Guide for Girls' Education, San Francisco Bay Area Girls' Education Network.

Improving the Quality of Life of Girls, Kathleen M. Kurz and Cynthia J. Prather, AWID.

Facts and Figures 1994-1995, UNICEF.

The Rev. Roger Alling, sermon on Commemoration Day 1993.